Diva Nation

The publisher and the University of California Press Foundation gratefully acknowledge the generous support of the Leslie Scalapino – O Books Fund, established by a major gift from Thomas J. White.

Diva Nation

Female Icons from Japanese Cultural History

EDITED BY

Laura Miller and Rebecca Copeland

UNIVERSITY OF CALIFORNIA PRESS

University of California Press, one of the most
distinguished university presses in the United States,
enriches lives around the world by advancing scholarship
in the humanities, social sciences, and natural sciences. Its
activities are supported by the UC Press Foundation and
by philanthropic contributions from individuals and
institutions. For more information, visit www.ucpress.edu.

University of California Press
Oakland, California

Library of Congress Cataloging-in-Publication Data

Names: Miller, Laura, 1953- editor. | Copeland, Rebecca
L., 1956- editor.
Title: Diva nation : female icons from Japanese cultural
history / edited by Laura Miller and Rebecca
Copeland.
Description: Oakland, California : University of
California Press, [2018] | Includes bibliographical
references and index. |
Identifiers: LCCN 2018000763 (print) |
LCCN 2018004780 (ebook) | ISBN 9780520969971
(Ebook) | ISBN 9780520297722 (cloth : alk. paper) |
ISBN 9780520297739 (pbk. : alk. paper)
Subjects: LCSH: Women in popular culture—Japan.
Classification: LCC HQ1762 (ebook) | LCC HQ1762 .D58
2018 (print) | DDC 305.40952—dc23
LC record available at https://lccn.loc.gov/2018000763

27 26 25 24 23 22 21 20 19 18
10 9 8 7 6 5 4 3 2 1

Contents

Illustrations

Acknowledgments

Ideas for this edited volume stretch back to at least 2012, when a group of us came together at the University of Missouri-St. Louis for a symposium on "Pop Heroines and Female Icons of Japan." The gathering was hosted with support from the Ei'ichi Shibusawa-Seigo Arai Endowed Professorship in Japanese Studies, International Studies Programs, and a grant from the Northeast Asia Council, Association for Asian Studies. Fellow symposium participants who did not ultimately contribute chapters but were still inspirational for the project include Hideko Abe, Hiromi Tsuchiya Dollase, Masayo Kaneko, and Karen Nakamura. The chapters in this volume by Bardsley, Copeland, Yano, and Miller were also presented as papers on the 2013 panel "Diva Nation: Female Icons from Japanese Cultural History" at the Association for Asian Studies Annual Meeting in San Diego. We owe gratitude to discussant Karen Nakamura for her insightful comments and to William Tsutsui for being a gracious chair.

Our editor at the University of California Press was the incomparable Reed Malcolm, who is always willing to help out the bad girls. We thank him for the encouragement and interest in our concept. We also thank our editorial assistant Zuha Khan for her patience and hard work. The art department staff at the press are amazing. We would like to thank the two anonymous readers of the manuscript for their insightful comments.

We were fortunate to receive permission for many fine images of divas. We thank the following people and publishers: Yamamuro Keishiro and

Otsuka Kazuhiko of the Visionary Company Ltd., as well as the artist Ōno Yuriko; the Takumi Promotion Company, Hiromatsu Kozue, and the Kojiki Yaoyorozu Kami Ukiyoe Museum in Hita City and So-hyun Chun; the Rev. Lawrence Koichi Barrish and the Tsubaki Grand Shrine of America; Okubo Masami and Kirino Natsuo; Corinna Barsan and Grove Atlantic; Shimoda-san and Heibonsha; Ando Chieko and Shinoda Seiji of the Permission and Publication Department, and the Idemitsu Bijutsukan; Koizumi Takayoshi and Gakken Kyōiku Shuppan; Yamauchi Hideyuki and the Yamatokōriyama City Tourist Association; the artist Debuchi Ryoichiro; Stephen Herrin and Monash University Library; Baldwin Saho and Hanagiri Madoka of Bungeishunju Ltd. (Bungei Shunjū); and Endo Tetsuya and Kobayashi Jun of the Literature and Non-Fiction Department, Kadokawa Corporation. Mahalo to Dania and Mayumi Oda, and many thanks to Rebecca Jennison for helping us find the perfect cover image.

Many thanks to the sculptor and manga artist Rokudenashiko (Igarashi Megumi). We are thrilled that a reigning diva of the art world added allure to our volume with an adorable Manko-chan manga. We are grateful to Anne Ishii for facilitating her contribution.

We owe gratitude to our respective universities, the University of Missouri-St. Louis and Washington University in St. Louis, for technical and financial support. We are grateful for the brilliance and collegiality of all the contributors to this project. Finally, we received input and comments from friends in various settings, but special mention goes to the Chesterfield Writer's Camp, which was extraordinarily memorable and productive.

Laura Miller and Rebecca Copeland
August 2017

Preface

Transnational and
Time-Travelling Divas

LAURA HEIN

According to my dictionaries, the diva is defined blandly as "a famous female singer," judgmentally as "a self-important person, typically a woman, who is temperamental and difficult to please," and, fundamentally as "a goddess" (Stevenson and Lindberg 2005–2011, Cosgrove 1997). Moreover, as this book demonstrates, divas systematically draw our attention to the performative nature of identity, to gender, and to battles over control of female bodies and female sexuality. A diva is invariably a strong personality who "uses her body to speak when language fails," as Laura Miller and Rebecca Copeland stress in the introduction to this volume. At the same time, "the diva represents dislocation," something that presupposes a stable historical or geographic past and so is an excellent entry point into understanding social and political tensions in a specific time and place. Divas identify dissonance in a generalizable way but they always do so by capturing unexpressed aspects of specific experiences. Moreover, by showing their perspective to rapt audiences, they wittily and theatrically make themselves impossible to ignore. Divas convey the point that their pain was unfairly inflicted; without social injustice, there could be no divas. As Miller and Copeland put it, "divas are not born," but rather, they are "generated" from "the friction produced when female genius meets social stricture."

Every diva has her own story to tell and a single individual can figure in a variety of narratives. Josephine Baker (1906–1975), the African American performer who became globally famous after moving to Paris provides a glamorous example. Not only was she a magnetic and extremely sexy stage performer, she ran her life by her own rules and also used her prestige to desegregate American concert halls and to assist the French Resistance. Like the other divas in this book, she has never really died, most recently reappearing on her 111th birthday as a Google Doodle (Moyer 2017). Baker embodied an irrepressible creativity and self-expression despite enormous obstacles—the heart and soul of the diva's social power. Since gender is baked into the definition of the diva, of course that creativity was inseparable from Baker's female identity and especially her sexuality, offstage as much as when she was center stage. Baker exemplified the 1920s global phenomenon of "the New Woman," who delayed marriage and childbearing, worked for pay, and lived away from her family. She also was an international poster girl for the racier version of the New Woman, the short-skirted, short-haired, sexually active flapper, *moga*, and *la garçonne*, to give only the derisive American, Japanese, and French terms.

But Baker's explosive impact on the twentieth century also derived from the variety of ways she engaged with the specific places where she—or her image—lived and visited. Baker destabilized gender, sexuality, race, and national identity in different ways in her two countries of citizenship. In the United States, where she was born and grew up, Baker represented the struggle of African Americans for full inclusion in an aggressively hostile society, particularly after she refused to play segregated concert halls on a 1951 tour. Meanwhile her effect on interwar French culture was subtly different, as analyzed by Tyler Stovall (2008). Stovall notes that Baker could freely perform topless and choose white lovers in Paris in contrast to New York, where such behavior contravened obscenity and miscegenation laws. Baker's racial alterity as an African American *garçonne* was not enough to explain why the women she portrayed in French films "never got the guy: that is to say, never achieved success as romantic leads." Her cinematic characters actively pursued the men they wanted, and were invariably punished for doing so, much like Izanami in Copeland's Chapter 1.

While French observers were perfectly willing to acknowledge Josephine Baker's transracial allure, unlike American cultural producers, they still could not treat her as worthy of long-term love with a European man. That was because she challenged French anxieties about colonialism, not just about sexuality and race. Baker's adoption of African and Caribbean dramatic story lines and dance steps in her performances—most famously in her banana skirt—associated her with France's imperial possessions even though at that point she had never visited any of them. The French state had only eked out victory in World War I by absorbing colonial labor, both as soldiers on the front and as farmers and factory hands imported into France itself. As Stovall notes (2008:3), "This unprecedented presence of the colonized in the *métropole* both reaffirmed the global greatness of France and called into question some basic assumptions about French identity."

By 1919, convinced of the centrality of the colonies to national survival, but increasingly anxious about the implications of that fact for national identity, French leaders promoted white family settlement in the colonies rather than the older pattern in which single men paired up with native women in marriages of convenience. "In an empire struggling to create a safe space for white domesticity, it made sense to acknowledge the attractions of native women while ultimately demonstrating the impossibility of interracial relationships" (Stovall 2008:6). The "native woman could come to Paris as a spectacle" (Stovall 2008:6), which acknowledged the colonial creativity and (wo)manpower that France so desperately needed, but filmmakers denied to the diva herself, or to the characters she played, fulfillment of their hearts' desires. Josephine Baker thus simultaneously challenged and reinforced "the idea of the New Woman as savage," enacted "celebrations of empire [and] at the same time anticipated its loss," revealed "the gendered nature of French ambivalence about colonialism," and showed that "blackness in Europe is central, not peripheral to the European experience as a whole" (Stovall 2008:7). That is a heavy weight for one pair of shoulders, no matter how shapely.

Many of the Japanese divas gathered here, like Yoko Ono, Misora Hibari, IKKO, and Kanehara Hitomi also wielded influence across national boundaries. Ono was part of the phenomenally influential avant-garde New York art movement that included composer John Cage and video artist Nam June Paik, but never gained equivalent attention for her ideas. In part that was because her international audience saw her as a Japanese woman in ways that made her seem less of an artist, as Carolyn Stevens discusses in this volume (Chapter 6). At the risk of caricature, the ideal Japanese woman is reserved, calm, and exhibits great forbearance while cheerfulness, pep, and optimism—qualities associated with ideal women elsewhere—are the attributes of delightful children rather than adult females. When a Japanese diva commands attention, even when performing her art with "calm," she is already breaking a social norm. By contrast, having a magnetic personality and "believing in oneself" is in itself less transgressive in the United States, masking the radicalism of Ono's art. And while divas everywhere trust their own judgment over that of other people, IKKO seems very Japanese indeed, as Jan Bardsley argues in Chapter 7, when the celebrated beauty expert describes the key to her own personal growth as learning how to stop misinterpreting other peoples' suggestions as bullying and instead "overcome her own stubbornness to learn from others."

Divas also build on each other's performances. It seems highly likely that the much younger Misora Hibari (1937–1989) carefully analyzed Baker's performance style and that her own self-presentation as "spunky orphan," "nascent cosmopolitan" in tails and a top hat, and the embodiment of "grit and determination" owed something to Baker's commanding diva presence. It seems even more likely that, when, according to Christine Yano in Chapter 5, Misora's audiences felt "a certain kind of yearning for premodern sexuality," she was affecting them in much the same way as did Baker her Parisian fans. The persistent rumors that one of Misora's parents was Korean underscores that surmise, and also suggests that, just as Baker did in France, Misora's performances opened up space in postcolonial Japan to wonder if national vitality might have been powered by colonial energy. The refusal of the modern Imperial Household Agency to excavate Himiko's tomb, probably because doing so would reveal artifacts made in Korea or modeled on older Korean objects, raises similar issues.

Moreover, figures such as Izanami, Himiko, Ame no Uzume, and Izumo no Okuni have served as potent sources of imagination in the modern period, as amply illustrated in this volume, because attempts to minimize their power and significance are so obviously encoded in the official record. Himiko was the first Japanese ruler whose name we know from a contemporary written source, suggesting that she was an ancestor of the current emperor. Women today are barred from ascending to the Chrysanthemum Throne and the current government is on record as committed to retaining that restriction, even though nearly all the young members of the imperial family today are female. That context means that invocations of Himiko in the twenty-first century remind people that Japan was ruled—and ruled well—by a woman in the past. As Laura Miller suggests in Chapter 3, Himiko can never just be a focal point for lighthearted tourist activities, particularly after other divas from the ancient mythical record have captured feminist imaginations.

Writing in 2008, Kirino Natsuo focused on the unfairness that Izanagi and Izanami experienced such different fates after begetting a world full of gods and people. In Kirino's retelling of Japan's version of the myth of

Adam and Eve (another wronged diva), the traditions that banished Izanami to the dark underworld of death were nothing but cruel selfishness by cynically powerful people. Similarly, in an example not in *Diva Nation*, contemporary visual artist Tomiyama Taeko began her 2007–2009 series, *Hiruko and the Puppeteers*, with the abandoned "leech-child," the *hiruko*, born after Izanami and Izanagi's first sexual encounter, which they put in a boat and sent out to sea. The leech-child drops out of the mythic record but, like Kirino, Tomiyama wondered what happened to the unwanted and cast-off people in these long-ago stories. She imagined the *hiruko* on a transformative sea journey during which it became the folk god Ebisu and joined other gods and puppets below the waves (Hein and Jennison 2017; Tomiyama and Takahashi 2009).

Tomoko Aoyama (Chapter 2) skillfully invokes another powerful goddess hiding in plain sight in one of Japan's creation myths. When Ame no Uzume lured the Sun Goddess back into the world, she enacted a creative performance that highlighted her sexuality and evoked laughter, which both banished fear and purged the world of evil. Uzume was a "diva of the masses" in this reading, while Uzume's twentieth-century champion, Tsurumi Shunsuke (2001), went even farther, framing her as Japan's first democrat, both because the changes she made benefitted everyone and because she sparked an emotional connection that engaged all the members of her audience, laughing with rather than laughing at her. Moreover, the real kicker was that even the fiercest warriors, like Sarutahiko, enjoyed the fact that Uzume was in charge. So does Tsurumi Shunsuke; he describes Uzume as, among her other virtues, "full of vitality, which brings out the life force in others." These ancient stories—and their modern interpretations—suggest a world in which women unashamedly celebrated their bodies and their creative and comic gifts. The men around them—with the exception of Susa-no-o—respected their productive labor as weavers, diplomats, and wise rulers. Perhaps such a world never existed, but imagining it still feels liberating.

Divas from Japan's more recent past also reveal women who were robbed of respect for their creative endeavors. Not all of them appear in these pages; another individual who would have fit comfortably within this book is Hōjō Masako (1156–1225), one of the key people who established warrior rule in Japan. But, to return to *Diva Nation*, as Barbara Hartley explains in Chapter 4, when Ariyoshi Sawako stopped to think in the 1960s about the origins of kabuki, she soon imagined an entire novel from the implied narrative inherent in the bare facts: one woman whose name we know, Izumo no Okuni, applied her Shinto shrine-dance knowledge to secular themes in 1603 and created a new and instantly wildly popular performance genre. Because she had no access to then existing stage venues, she and the other women she trained had to perform in a dry river bed. More comfortably situated male performers regularly stole her ideas. Nevertheless she persisted. A quarter-century went by, during which the government was codifying and controlling social status to an unprecedented extent; in 1629 women were permanently barred from kabuki, a ban that continues to this day.

Family life was notably inhospitable for these divas, beginning with Izanami, who was fatally wounded by her son and then reviled by her brother/husband. Both the sun goddess Amaterasu and Ame no Uzume were attacked and ritually defiled by Susa-no-o, Amaterasu's brother. Uchida Shungiku, whose father attacked and ritually defiled her by raping her and whose mother then wounded her by withholding protection tells a similar modern story in the chapter by Amanda Seaman (Chapter 8). Uchida's reclaiming of her physical and emotional life after those betrayals matches the imaginative redress performed through Ariyoshi and Kirino's novels but is all the more impressive because she is a real human being coming to terms with literal assaults. Successful divas are debt collectors—their honesty is a claim for reparations but their demands are rarely met with an equally honest response.

Uchida achieves her own measure of redress by reclaiming both her body and a loving family life or, as Seaman puts it, "what sets Uchida apart . . . is the degree to which both sexuality and motherhood define her dramatic persona and performances." Like her sister divas, Uchida is phenomenally talented, creatively mixes prestigious and popular artistic forms, and foregrounds her own sexed body, but she also seems to have found a pathway through her own suffering to nurture her children as well. As David Holloway reveals in Chapter 9, Kanehara Hitomi also now lives happily with her children, although she emigrated from Japan in order to do so. Asada Mao, the subject Masafumi Monden introduces in Chapter 10, retired from competitive ice skating in April 2017, opening up space for a future family life if she desires it.

These women are inventing their own families as best they can. Chapter 7's IKKO does something similar, in a way that draws on Japanese cultural resources, when she adopts an onē-kyarakutā stance as a helpful older sister. The idealized post-World War II Japanese family—the first generation born after the wide dissemination of birth control—was composed of a girl and then a younger boy, so that big sister could help her little brother with tasks that girls were better at than boys, such as arithmetic homework. When IKKO offers to be a "big sister" to Japanese teens, everyone involved knows exactly what that relationship means. Josephine Baker, too, created a family more nurturing than the one she was born into and she went to Japan do so. While Baker met many Japanese individuals in interwar Paris, including painter Fujita Tsuguharu, for whom she modeled, the most meaningful such friendship for Baker herself was with Miki Sawada, whose husband worked in the Paris embassy. The two women met again in New York in 1935, when Baker stayed at Sawada's apartment after being refused service at a hotel that catered only to whites. Their feminist union produced a transnational family in 1954, when Sawada arranged a tour to benefit the Elizabeth Sanders Home for abandoned mixed-race children, which she had founded in 1948. Josephine Baker not only gave thirteen concerts while in Japan, financially supporting Sawada's kids, she also adopted two boys from Sanders and took them to France, after sitting through a newly invented Shinto adoption ceremony invoking Amaterasu, the sun goddess (Ara 2010). Baker went on to adopt ten more children from around the world, bringing to life on a small scale her utopian vision of a postcolonial, postracial global family.

Diva Seductions

An Introduction to Diva Nation

LAURA MILLER AND REBECCA COPELAND

Divas . . . rise above trivialities like nation or law. . . .
—Koestenbaum 1993:132

DIVA INSPIRATIONS

We did not go searching for her, this diva from Japan. She was already there. When we opened standard histories of Japan, we could not forget the brief mention of Himiko, the shaman queen; this, despite the pages upon pages about shoguns and emperors. Did she really rule with sorcery? When we entered the kabuki theatre, drawn initially perhaps by the alluring *onnagata,* it was Okuni who captured our imagination. Who might she have been? And why was the stage taken from her? Brought up on masculine fantasies of Oriental Butterflies, we were caught off guard by a woman as powerful as Yoko Ono. How could a mere woman wreck the Beatles? And, should we hate her for it? The *New York Times Book Review* may have encouraged us to read Murakami Haruki, but we found the fiction of Kanehara Hitomi and Kirino Natsuo stayed with us longer. She lodged herself firmly in our consciousness, this diva of Japan. She seduced us.

For many of us the diva has directed the course of our research, guiding us through our projects, insisting that we give her the attention she is due. Occasionally she thwarts us when we try to pursue her, tricking us with her elaborate costumes and masks. She taunts us until we learn to see through her performances. Or more accurately, perhaps, to *see* her performances for what they are—playfully political portraits of national anxieties and shifting social ground. Certainly, there are thousands of Japanese divas who have not been accorded a chapter in this volume. The cutely illustrated *Bijuaru Nihon no hiroin* (Visual Japanese Heroines) by Rekidama Henshūbu (2013) highlights more than eighty famously admirable women, many of whom could easily be considered a diva. However, our choice of whom to discuss was not determined by any particular measure of importance. The decision was more personal. In this volume are the divas who accrued to us, who came to us indirectly, surprisingly, slipping into our consciousness very nearly of their own accord. In the course of doing research on Japanese beauty queens, for example, Jan Bardsley kept encountering IKKO, the transgender beauty expert extraordinaire. Unexpectedly, Himiko repeatedly made an appearance in Laura Miller's fieldwork on divination services and locally designed tarot cards. And Asada Mao, with her sequined costumes and sequenced discipline, skated her way into fashion scholar Masafumi Monden's research.

Given the diva's magnitude and blatant presence, our goal in *Diva Nation* is not a celebration of notable women, or a quest to uncover the concealed or neglected women of history. We owe gratitude to the scholars who came before us and opened so many doors. But we are now beyond the "find-the-woman phase of feminist research" (Conor 2004:4).[1] These divas are not veiled, unseen, obscure, or hidden. They are all too overt, with their exposed breasts, satin sheaths, and tattooed male drag (Figure 1). Surely there are those who have tried to push the diva back into the shadows, cloak her nudity with modest drapes. The diva is not always an "acceptable" woman. She often refuses to behave, to follow the rules, to act with decorum. "The diva is a stubborn species, fated to survive" (Koestenbaum 1993:119). She will not be covered, or silenced, or tucked away. Take for example, Ame no Uzume. The most conservative, patriarchal defenders of the male imperial line in Japan inevitably must bring in Amaterasu, the Sun Goddess and legitimizing ancestor of all the emperors. It is as if her very presence as a shining role model should be enough to satisfy (and silence) the legions of women who came after her. May they all be like Amaterasu, sunny and distant. But how do we account for the erotic Ame no Uzume, the goddess who lured the Sun Goddess out of her cave? Is it not she, more than the Sun Goddess, who captures our imagination and appeals to our earthly selves? And speaking of mythic divas, in Kirino's *Joshinki* (2008; translated as *The Goddess Chronicle*, 2012), the mythological story of Izanami, the diva-goddess is allowed a voice, a feminist one that forces us to recognize her unrepentant anger. We therefore have no choice but to acknowledge the diva. She is already there, thrusting

1. Ame no Uzume on a seal stamp calligraphy board. From the Tsubaki Grand Shrine of America. Photo by L. Miller.

herself in our faces and troubling us with her stories and provocative representations. The diva does not simply survive, she flourishes. She is ripe for expansion, fantasy, eroticization, and playful reinvention, yet her unavoidability also makes her a special problem. She may be memorialized, celebrated, or demonized, but she will not be ignored.

Our inspiration for *Diva Nation* culminates from curiosity over the insistent presence of unruly women, women who refuse to sit quietly on the sidelines of history but who nevertheless have not been fully admitted into mainstream scholarship or routine knowledge. What does their sequestering tell us about the formation of national myths or the establishment of gender roles? How does the diva disrupt or bolster ideas about nationhood, morality, and aesthetics? Our case studies of these individual divas are less concerned with offering archival portraits or

伊耶那美命

Izanami-no-Mikoto

2. Izanami no Mikoto from a deck of oracle cards, *Nihon no Kamisama kādo: Gods and Goddesses of Japan,* drawn by Ōno Yuriko (Visionary Company 2008).

biographies than with interpreting historically and culturally informed diva imagery and diva lore. Our aim is to consider her a worthy object of analysis rather than simply an obligatory persona. She has become fodder for creative productions and reinterpretations that transcend time and space (Figure 2). Because she will not go away, she reappears in unexpected contexts, disrupting our assumptions and complacency.

Our goal is to track diva eruptions and sightings, and to consider her effects in a spectrum of national and personal realms.

DIVA DIVERSITY

Where do we find the diva? Divas might surface in particularly gendered domains, such as beauty culture or narratives of rape and childbirth (IKKO, Izanami, Uchida Shungiku). Her power might also propel her onto a larger stage, beyond local boundaries and gendered concerns. As Koestenbaum (1993:132) reminds us, "divas . . . rise above trivialities like nation or law. . . ." Undeterred by national boundaries, she travels, she moves, she lives in shadowy underworlds (Yoko Ono, Kanehara Hitomi, Izanami). The diva represents dislocation, she can be anywhere and everywhere. She spans eons and centuries with no regard for time constraints. Today, third-century Himiko appears as a rubber-suited mascot in local town festivals and a cute mascot doll (Figure 3). The impetuousness of Ame no Uzume encourages the twenty-first-century vagina artist Rokudenashiko, and all women who publicly enjoy and expose their sexuality. And Yoko Ono's performance art is restaged in different countries by different kinds of artists. There are divas embedded in core national myths and histories about whom every schoolchild learns (Izanami, Himiko, Izumo no Okuni). Some divas are associated with innate musical or athletic talents that make them irresistible or perhaps notorious in mass media both within and outside Japan (Misora Hibari, Yoko Ono, Asada Mao).[2]

Divas push the boundaries of expression, asking us to question what is natural, what is normal, what is culturally appropriate (Yoko Ono, Kirino Natsuo, Kanehara Hitomi). And even when she presents herself as upholding gendered norms, her performance of femininity is so obvious, so exaggerated, she calls into question the very nature of those norms (Uchida Shungiku, Asada Mao). Despite her efforts to blend in and stick to the rules, her diva-ness shines through.

In his tour of the grand divas of the Italian opera, Wayne Koestenbaum (1993:105) notes that "the ungovernability of a diva's performance contributes to its power." Similarly, the extravagances of a diva, and her corporeal representation in Japan, is unpredictable and beyond anyone's control—a quality that sparks pleasure, obsession, disgust, and other emotions. Audiences were variously thrilled, shocked, and pleased at Misora Hibari's gender-bending and cross-dressing performances. Reportedly, Okuni drew huge crowds of appreciative gawkers

3. Himiko mascot for the city of Sakurai. Photo by L. Miller.

when she took to the stage in a fantastic costume collage complete with a samurai's sword and a priest's crucifix. The diva draws us in. She touches something innate in our own natures as we suffer her triumphs and humiliations vicariously. When Yoko Ono presented her own body in her live art acts, audience members were both mesmerized and cruel, actively engaging in her performance—exposing more of their own sad nature with each snippet of clothing they cut from her body. Even the *kami* (deities) could not look away from the erotic dance Ame no Uzume performed before Amaterasu's darkened cave (Figure 4). We covet the diva because she indulges the desires we are too ashamed to own; she wears the wounds we are too afraid to touch.

Popular divas promote consumption, nationalism, and identity construction. Misora Hibari's songs and films were a balm to postwar Japan's national sense of self, offering entertainment while serving as a symbol of national grit and perseverance. Himiko brand sake asks you to drink ancestrally, imbibing your own national history. Asada Mao allows us to pump our collective fists in the air and celebrate Japan's national strength

4. Amaterasu and Ame no Uzume in the Eight Million Gods set of postcards (Takumi Promotion Company 2016).

without exposing uncouth brawn. Hers is the "cultured" power of a lithe and leggy girl.

The diva serves a purpose for us, she works for us, otherwise her traces would have blown away long ago. Asada is proof to contemporary strivers that discipline and perseverance will bring success. New Age adherents pursue divination practices that put them in touch with their essential shaman abilities, their inner Himiko. Kirino Natsuo allows the readers of her fiction to explore their anger, to own it. Uchida Shungiku and Ame no Uzume restore to women their innate sexual desires.

One function of the diva is to expose efforts to control femininity and the female body.

She offers a productive perspective on restrictive gender norms. IKKO teaches us that even (or perhaps especially) transgender bodies can achieve diva status, and that anyone can become a diva if they follow their dreams. From her we see behind the curtain to view the constructed nature of gender. Kirino, too, offers her own curtain-lifting. She pulls us down into the mythic underworld to expose the patriarchal tyranny of female suppression. Skater Mao allows us to try on new costumes, new national personas as we strut and twirl through life. She and Misora Hibari provide a space for female play. It is not that many women want to emulate her, but that she provides an avenue for vicarious pleasure and admiration. Her display of vitality and fearlessness gives us hope.

GROWING UP DIVA

Divas are not born. They are made. Certainly, a diva must possess a unique talent, a strong heart, and a fierce determination. But her brilliance ignites when her combustible nature brushes up against the barricades society erects to contain her. A diva is generated from the friction produced when female genius meets social stricture. The story of her comet-streak through the heavens of history is a story that illuminates the smaller lives of lesser women. The diva writes large what most women live but cannot speak.

The diva grows up aware of her talents, aware that she is extraordinary, aware too that she can use her genius to her own ends. As a girl, the diva's genius can serve to isolate her from others. The diva is often the girl on the edge of town, the girl others revile. Like the young Yoko Ono she is despised for her privilege or like the adolescent IKKO she is shunned for her difference. She moves from circle to circle, always on the outside, never allowing herself to be absorbed by mediocrity or comfort. Like Kirino Natsuo she cherishes her outsider stance because it allows her to see what others miss. Her intelligence sets her apart from her peers, and she draws strength from her peripheral status.

The diva learns to live within her own sphere of interest. She is aloof, proud, but nonetheless often wounded. She is abused by those she trusted, like Uchida Shungiku; manipulated like Misora Hibari; and like Asada Mao, she is pushed to soar beyond human limits. Her wounds mark her. They register her difference but also her strength. It is from her wounds that her talents emerge—nourished on the blood of her pain and isolation.

The diva crosses borders. She is transgressive. She has to be. Like Asada Mao, her strengths make her manly. Like Okuni, Misora Hibari, and IKKO she learns to cross-dress, to masquerade, in short, to perform (Figure 5). The diva uses her body to speak when language fails. Like Yoko Ono, Okuni, Uchida Shungiku, and Uzume, she exposes her breasts, her lithe limbs, her sweet flesh in a display of sexual power. Her body perplexes, terrifies, refuses to be owned. She indulges her body,

5. Misora Hibari movie poster for *Lonesome Whistle* (Ieki 1949).

gratifies it, and wields her sexuality like a sword that mows down any mere man who thinks he might control her.

THE DISPLAY OF DIVAHOOD

The diva performs. She constructs herself through performance, and her "performance allows a liberating and autonomous force" (Abowitz and Rousmaniere 2004:10–11). She acts like a queen, a bitch, a shaman. Her audience is drawn to her waywardness. She is the hero they are not. She is the whore they profess to hate. The diva is spectacular. But she is also a spectacle, having great "cultural presence" (Conor 2004:2). When Yoko Ono conducted the "Bed-in for Peace" antiwar protest in 1969, televised and photographed wrapped in white newlywed sheets with John Lennon, the press and the public responded with prurient interest and disgusted bewilderment. Yet the event is still remembered in popular culture around the world. More than three decades later, Japanese pop duo Puffy reproduced the famous bed-in scene for the cover of their album *Nice* (Sturmer 2003), with Onuki Ami and Yoshimura Yumi taking the place of Yoko and John. Centuries of woodblock prints, statues, and *manga* (comics) still commemorate the lascivious gyrations of Ame no Uzume and the hybrid Southern Barbarian-samurai ensemble worn by Izumo no Okuni.

A certain theatricality is expected, it is one of the diva's duties. We expect her to be larger than life, talented, and somewhat egotistic. "Narcissism doesn't seem silly when a diva practices it" (Koestenbaum 1993:86). IKKO strutted in front of television cameras in a tight yellow gown, and Asada Mao whirled across the ice in a flamboyant blue outfit covered with Swarovski crystals. The diva's public performances in the media, or in writing about her, might give off an air of fabrication or contrived effort. At times, we wonder if the diva persona is only a façade, or an act. The scripted nature of diva public life calls into question her authenticity and sincerity. We might read it as prescripted effort when IKKO, in the face of homophobic comments, nevertheless shouts out her trademark expression "*Dondake!*" (Osaka dialect for "What the . . . ?"). Aspects of the diva's public life also contain elements of intentional camp. Misora Hibari wearing samurai drag is an obvious appeal to a certain middle-aged female audience. Kanehara Hitomi, with her thigh-high leather boots, mini-skirts, and practiced ennui performs perfectly the pose of disaffected youth—appealing to twenty-somethings and middle-aged men with misplaced lust. It is not unusual for the diva to perform stilted versions of femininity, as if completely capitulating to enforced gender norms. "Yet divas twist the feminine into a commanding source of authority through their performance *as* powerful people" (Abowitz and Rousmaniere 2004:8).

Occasionally she even performs ordinariness. Keen to the communal need for "the girl next door," she conceals her powers and cloaks herself in an assumed mediocrity—her disguise brilliant in its convincingness: Kanehara Hitomi seems so vapid; Asada Mao so feminine; Misora Hibari so "Japanese." Her chameleon nature allows her to be just like us, to earn our sympathy while at the same time she reminds us—with

6. Ame no Uzume as she is represented in the Noh play Uzume. On the votive plaque (*ema*) from Tsubaki Grand Shrine of America. Photo by L. Miller.

her brilliance—just how very dull we are. We can take comfort in our dullness, knowing the diva is there to stockpile our desires, our subversive dreams, our secrets. We cannot contain her. We cannot really name her. She twists from our grasp. And in her slippery formlessness she terrifies a patriarchal system that demands order and knowability.

DIVA NATION

The diva's visibility depends on the type of texts and technologies that go into her public construction. Her iconicity needs the TV camera, the venerated history, the movie poster to immortalize her. Stories by and about her expand her fame and are read back into her image. A diva never really dies. She may exit the stage. Like Greta Garbo she may draw behind the shadows of anonymity. But her absence only enhances her diva lore. Her divahood endures, finding new chapters, living new lives (Figure 6). Charting the waxing and waning of the diva story helps illuminate national narratives and national memory and assists us in understanding the ways the nation is imbricated with notions of gender, nostalgia, and identity politics.

NOTES

1. *Diva Nation* is built on scholarship on women in Japan, including landmark books about famous foremothers by Sievers (1983), Bernstein (1991), Mackie (2003), and Mulhern (1991).

2. Japanese names in the text are given in the Japanese style, with surname first followed by given name. The exception is when the Japanese author publishes in English or is a well-known artist or musician such as Yoko Ono.

CHAPTER I

Kirino Natsuo Meets Izanami

Angry Divas Talking Back

REBECCA COPELAND

This tale may be spun from my words but I speak for
the goddess, the one who governs the Realm of the
Dead. My words may be dyed red with anger; they may
tremble in yearning after the living; but they are all, each
and every one, spoken to express the sentiments of the
goddess. . . .

—Kirino 2012:3

But Izanami's anger did not abate. . . .

—Kirino 2012:136

Japanese goddess Izanami has every reason to be angry, at least from a
twenty-first-century perspective. Betrayed by her erstwhile partner,
Izanagi, and shamed by his judgmental regard of her body, she is locked
for all eternity into the dark world of death. Meanwhile, Izanagi is free
to roam both the heavens and the earth, giving birth of his own accord
to one celestial deity after another. And what did the primal goddess
do to deserve such treatment? She suffered a mortal wound in childbirth
and as a result was designated the embodiment of death and its attendant impurity. It wasn't fair. And while all eyes were trained on her prolific ex and his shining progeny, she was forgotten, save for the occasional celebration of conjugal union that brought her forward as a
paragon of wifely chastity. The irony must surely have been infuriating.
But other than one momentary expression of wrath, Izanami is denied

access to even a residual anger in traditional sources. Rather she is treated—if she is treated at all—as the vessel of modest silence.

The Izanami-Izanagi sequence is an integral part of the Japanese foundation myth as related in the eighth-century *Kojiki* (Record of Ancient Matters). The primal pair are the first of the myriad gods to take human form. And from their sexed bodies they produce a multitude of offspring representing natural matter in the Japanese archipelago. All is well until Izanami is fatally burned while giving birth to fire. She slips off into Yomi, a separate realm, once she has died. But her consort, Izanagi, longs for her. He chases after her and discovers her in a darkened chamber. She forbids him to look upon her but he cannot contain his curiosity. He lights a torch and finds her fetid body. Repulsed, he flees. She gives pursuit and is close to overtaking him when he hurls a giant boulder into the passageway to Yomi, sealing her permanently in her realm of death. At their parting, she pledges to kill 1,000 lives a day in Izanagi's world. In turn, he pledges to build 1,500 birthing huts. He goes on to lustrate in a nearby river, purifying his body of the taint of death. And Izanami retreats into a dark silence, never mentioned again.

How would the silent Izanami have reacted if she were a twenty-first-century woman, aware of the inequities in the system and unrepentant in her anger? Might she have given voice to her fury, lashing out at Izanagi and the system that saw her marginalized and barricaded from her former power? Perhaps she would have taken on the mantel of Lauren Berlant's (1997) "Diva Citizen" and allowed her anger to flash up like a glorious flame. Author Kirino Natsuo, herself something of a diva citizen, imagines just such an outcome. In *Joshinki* (The Goddess Chronicle, Kirino 2008), her creative retelling of the Izanami-Izanagi myth sequence, Kirino picks up where the *Kojiki* leaves off, inventing an angry afterlife for the female goddess Izanami.[1] In doing so she forces readers to wonder why only the female is consigned to the realm of death, while her male consort produces the deities who will shape the imperial line. And she questions how the positioning of the female deity predicts the status of real-world women. In the process Kirino invents not only a sequel to the *Kojiki,* but a parallel story that unfolds in the mortal realm, suggesting a human counterpoint to the fancifulness of myth. In this chapter, I discuss the way Kirino defies earlier gendered expectation and stereotypes by reconstituting Izanami with a diva-esque interiority. After briefly introducing the author Kirino and the concept of diva citizen, I explore the way she activates Izanami's angry voice in resistance to the mythic imperative that would see her anchored with both the precarity and potency of national symbol.

KIRINO NATSUO: ANGRY DIVA WRITER

Kirino Natsuo (b. 1951) is a writer diva. In many ways, she is larger than life, her image frequently projected on bookstore posters and featured prominently on her book jackets. She is a striking woman.

In one of her iconic, black-and-white book jacket photos she stares pensively off to the side as she lifts the edge of her dark turtleneck collar over the corner of her well-formed lips (Figure 7). Her fingers are perfectly manicured. Her posture projects poise, sophistication, and intelligence. Although she does not appear to brandish a particularly difficult ego—part and parcel of the stereotypical diva image—she is a performer of celebrity status. Thus, she fits the definition Jeffrey Jung (1999:4–5) notes of fin-de-siècle actresses in the West: she is "one whose power and influence within her profession allow her to dictate the terms of her performances, asserting control over her peers and putative directors. . . . She cultivates a personality that befits such attention: a magisterial and confident pose, elegant diction, graceful movements, and a studied indifference to the mundane and tedious elements of daily life." Kirino has perfected her performance of aestheticized smartness. But it is a performance that is all the more provocative because it suggests defiance. With her carefully tousled shoulder-length hair, her porcelain-smooth skin, and her penchant for clothes that accentuate her figure, she is intensely feminine and exudes a magnetic sexuality. Even so, the uninformed often assume that she is male, based on the intentional ambiguity of her chosen pen name, Natsuo. A popular writer, she has nevertheless earned the accolades typically awarded more highbrow authors. In many ways, then, her diva status is all the more potent because it derives from these moments of transgression. She is difficult to define, or name, or own because she defies easy categorization. And in refusing to be pigeonholed, she both exerts her control while she simultaneously removes herself to the margins where she is excluded from normal channels of power.

Kathleen Abowitz and Kate Rousmaniere (2004), drawing on the work of Lauren Berlant, identify the elements that characterize the "diva citizen." I list these elements here because they apply equally to Kirino Natsuo and her goddess diva, Izanami. In the first place, the diva citizen, though marginalized from both knowledge and power, gains strength through marginalization by being disruptive. She twists her differences in ways that draw attention to the limitations and falsehoods implicit in the structures of power that would marginalize her. Her disruptiveness

7. Kirino Natsuo. Book jacket publicity photo by Watanabe Makoto, 2003.

is often derived from her ability to use "humor, irony, and bombast" (Abowitz and Rousmaniere 2004: 11). Diva citizens have strong, dynamic personalities that sometimes discomfort. In discomforting, they work to improve the lot of others who toil on the margins. Of this last point Lauren Berlant states that the "diva citizen" does not change the world. Even so, her acts of resistance not only force a reconsideration of the status quo but by "flashing up and startling the public," she is able to take control of the dominant narrative and retell it "as one that the abjected people have once lived sotto voce, but no more." The diva citizen "challenges her audience to identify with the enormity of the suffering she has narrated and the courage she has had to produce, calling on people to change the social and institutional practices of citizenship to which they currently consent" (Berlant 1997:222–23).

Often heralded as a pioneer of feminist noir (Davis 2010:222), Kirino Natsuo has made a career out of putting "the dominant story into suspended animation." Since her earliest works Kirino has explored the social constructions of gender, class, and ethnicity, critiquing contemporary Japanese society, picking uncomfortably at our assumptions, and digging beneath the surface of polite lies.[2] Her stories feature immigrant workers, transvestites, homosexuals, older women, and others who have been chased to the fringes of society. She has been recognized as the voice of "new proletarianism" (Gregus 2014:12), or as "Fighting Kirino" for the way she champions the so-called "yellow trash" (as opposed to America's "white trash") of society (Iwata-Weickgenannt 2012:20).[3] But whereas Kirino *does* fight social injustice in her novels, she is also just as apt to fight the labels used to promote her works. Her novels struggle against the boundaries of genre expectations. They are layered with different narrative approaches: diaries, letters, reportage, and frequently, unreliable narrators and quixotic endings, confounding readers. *The Goddess Chronicle* is no exception as it is at once fairy tale, myth, science fiction, and modern horror tale.

If Kirino has been consistent in anything over the course of her career it is her anger at the unrealistic and unequal expectations women have been made to endure. Her novels bristle with rage and her female characters invariably are two-faced, dangerous, and socially aberrant. Not only do they defy stereotypical images of Japanese womanhood, they defy readers' expectations of feminist rebellion. Her heroines frequently let us down. They don't stand and fight, not for the downtrodden and sometimes not even for themselves. But by presenting their unhappy stories, Kirino stages her own protest. She will not adhere to seamless narratives of success or cater to expectation. In order "to change the social and institutional practices of citizenship" that Berlant (1997:222–23) describes, Kirino must dismantle it wholesale, and often with the finesse of a sledgehammer. Frequently she presents readers with competing narratives—none of them trustworthy—and each of them vulnerable to extinction in the end. From the shards, between the gaps, we piece our way back to a new understanding.

Kirino enjoys lifting the masks Japanese women have been expected to wear, uncovering the dark visages that lurk beneath. In her 1997 bestseller *OUT* (AUTO, in Japanese), for example, she explores the murderous rage that simmers within the breasts of those women who have been exiled to the darkness of the home—the middle-aged housewife. The novel draws together four unlikely women who bond over their experiences working part time on a factory assembly line. When one of them snaps and kills her philandering husband, the other three rise to her defense. With assembly-line precision they dismember and discard the body. Before long they find themselves caught up in the body disposal business. All but forgotten by the media, the workforce, and in many cases their own families, these invisible women launch a lethal rebellion. In an interview with journalist Howard French (2003), shortly after *OUT* debuted in Stephen Snyder's English translation (Kirino 2003a), Kirino noted that she was less concerned with writing about the particulars of a crime, the police procedural, or the reinstitution of order that inevitably concludes a crime novel. Her interests lay with the way crimes expose the psychology of the criminal and the callousness of society. "A crime is like a crack in reality, and it is the author's role to explore those cracks. As a writer, I like to see how they impinge on people," Kirino explained in the interview. Society is ever vigilant to maintain the polite façade of order and normalcy. But a crime challenges this order and allows an opening, a way to peer beneath the myth of civility. Many of Kirino's works, appropriately, employ an archeological motif as she scrapes away the surface, digs into the cracks, and peers down into the darkness below.

Grotesque (Gurotesuku, Kirino 2003b), for example, refers to Cambrian fossils, to a prehistoric life beneath the sea, to a subterranean survival of the fittest. Based on a sensational crime in which the murder of a prostitute uncovers her secret double life as a successful career woman, Kirino's 2003 "re-narration" reveals not so much the hidden identity of the protagonist as the seedy double life of society itself. The crime that inspired the novel offers Kirino the crack that she needs to expose the perverted sense of justice in contemporary society and the utter invalidation of former value systems. The female protagonists in this novel drill deeper and deeper into the depths of degradation, chasing dark desires into self-destruction and nihilistic extinction. It is not surprising, then, that in her *Kojiki* retelling, Kirino (2008, 2012) pulls us down into the cavernous underground world of death. "Huge stone pillars towered above the cold rock floor, each set an equal distance from the next. . . . They extended as far as the eye could see, the distant ones melting into the darkness. They were massive, so wide that three people could join hands around one and still not encircle the girth, and so tall the tops disappeared into the darkness above" (Kirino 2012:98). Here we accompany Izanami on her daily task of taking one thousand lives. We open into a story that the *Kojiki* had closed.

INTRODUCING "THE WOMAN WHO INVITES"

The first Japanese god to have taken female form, the *iza* in Izanami's name means to beckon or to invite while the phoneme *mi* identifies the female. Thus, Izanami is "the woman who invites." Or as given in the translation below, "She Who Beckoned." Having assumed a bodily form, she and her consort, Izanagi, descend from the heavens to the island beneath and build a palace there. Having done so, Izanagi turns to his partner and asks:

"How is your body formed?"

She replied, saying:
"My body is empty in one place."

And so the mighty one He Who Beckoned proclaimed:
"My body sticks out in one place. I would like to thrust the part of my body that sticks out into the part of your body that is empty and fill it up to birth lands. How does birthing them in this way sound to you?"

The mighty one She Who Beckoned replied, saying:
"That sounds good."

And so the mighty one He Who Beckoned proclaimed:
"Well then, let us walk around this mighty pillar of heaven and then join in bed."

So they pledged thus, and then straightaway he proclaimed:
"You circle from the right to meet me, I will circle from the left to meet you."
So they pledged thus and then circled around it.

The mighty one She Who Beckoned spoke first, saying:
"What a fine boy!"

The mighty one He Who Beckoned spoke after her, saying:
"What a fine girl!" (Ō no Yasumaro 2014:9)

As the myth unfolds in the *Kojiki,* Izanagi betrays Izanami, usurping her power, on several occasions. First, following the encounter described above, their initial offspring are flawed—one is a "leech child" unable to stand. The other is too small to be considered worthy, and both are cast out to sea. Concerned by their failure to produce excellent children, they consult with the heavenly beings and are told to redo their greeting. And so they circle the pillar again and this time the male speaks first—appropriating the female's language. When they again unite, they produce the varied islands of Japan and the various natural elements. The worthiness of these offspring underscores the silencing of female initiative and the advancement of male privilege. Aggressive, confident women are doomed to produce failure.

In a second betrayal, Izanagi ignores Izanami's request. Following her death, she retreats to the underworld. After Izanagi comes in pursuit of her, she beseeches him not to look on her but he refuses her request and

8. Izanami in a state of decay (Shintō no Kokoro o Tsutaeru 2016).

lights up her chamber where he beholds her putrefying corpse covered in maggots (Figure 8). Gazing upon her body without her consent, in fact, in a direct violation of her request, demonstrates another of Izanagi's attempts to enact control. Sight leads to knowledge, knowledge to power. And the power he wields over Izanami keeps her locked in her state of dark shame.

But perhaps it is what follows that results in the final humiliation. Once Izanagi leaves—having sealed Izanami in her tomb—he bathes in a rushing river and produces from his now purified body the Moon God, Tsukiyomi, the Wind God, Susa-no-o, and the Sun Goddess, Amaterasu. These three gods, produced singularly from the body of the purified male, will become the most important deities in the Shinto pantheon. While Izanagi is thus linked to the wholesome power of harvest, fecundity, and life. Izanami—the mother of the Japanese archipelago—becomes the embodiment of death. She is, in one body, both life and death. In many ways Izanami becomes the container of the nation—the source of its mythic power and the site of its vulnerability as well. She represents the danger of contamination and the need to enforce rigid borders. Jennifer Coates (2014), in writing of the diva persona in Japanese cinema, describes the often abjected, dangerously unbounded female body on screen in terms that apply equally to Izanami as mythic mother: "The reflexive image of the female body as nation and nation as female body is. . . self-perpetuating, in that the ideology of nationhood is figuratively housed within the female body; the female body then comes to symbolize aspects of the nation, particularly those gendered 'feminine' (Coates 2014:30). Those "feminine" qualities reside precisely in the acute accessibility of her body, a body that is known for its precariously permeable boundaries.

Read as a symbol of a "diva nation," Izanami stands for both the sanctity of origin and the threat of incursion. In one body she houses the power of national identity as well as the fear of its abjected, leaky border. As such, she has features in common with primal female goddesses and deities the world over. Like Kali in India or Persephone in Greek myth, Izanami represents both life and death—the terrible mother. Unlike Eve, however, in the biblical traditions, she is not inscribed with sin or evil. Her desire and her bodily decay are represented as natural processes—natural but nevertheless untoward. They need to be recognized, controlled, and quarantined. And as with other myths featuring powerful females from around the world, the traits that identify Izanami (fertility, defilement, and containment) become inscribed on later generations of women. Or perhaps more accurately we might conclude that the treatment of women that existed when these myths were evolving, was written back into the story, thus serving to legitimate contemporary attitudes toward women.

FEMINIST READINGS OF THE *KOJIKI*

Furukawa Noriko (2011:54–56) in her exploration of Izanami focuses on the importance of fire in the myth sequence. Fire is associated, symbolically, with the birth of civilization—with the advent of pottery and more importantly iron products. Kirino (2012:120) makes the association explicit in *The Goddess Chronicle*: "Fire and the sword have an inseparable connection, do they not? The sword is borne from fire, and the right to fire is controlled by the sword." In Izanami's case, fire springs from the body of the earth mother. And it is by fire that she dies. It is also through her association with the fires of the underworld—the ingestion of the products of those fires—that she is bound to her role as death. The suggestion is that to develop into the brilliance of civilization, the earth mother—with her raw sensuality and unlettered wisdom—must be isolated and controlled. Izanami must be sealed into the realm of death and silenced where she—and by extension all subsequent women—are associated with impurity in the Japanese psyche—an association which Alan Grapard (1991:7) refers to as the "bio-degraded" female condition. Women, by their own physiology, are perforce contaminated. And they are controlled by the threat of the sword—this most potent of phallic symbols that could not exist without the earth mother's life-giving fire.

Other *Kojiki* scholars note the way these creation myths have been used for centuries to retroactively enforce gender roles by rendering women inactive, fixed in place. In a sense, Izanami had been the original *nampa*—or "pickup artist," inviting, desiring, naming man, as Nakayama Chinatsu (1994:16–28) playfully notes in her feminist study of Izanami and other goddesses. Whereas her male counterpart was allowed to wander, indulging his desire at whim, she, like other women after her, was forced into grottos—the unnatural state of silence and stasis constructed for her by a system eager to control reproduction. It is her fixed position—the original womb located within a womblike enclosure—that renders her an image of female chasteness, and thereby, a heroine of model behavior. In the seventeenth-century handbook for women, *Onna chōhōki* (A lady's treasury), for example, author Namura Jōhaku (1989) holds Izanami up as an example of purity. Seemingly eliding Izanami's fate as impurity personified, Namura revises the myth to fit his message and views Japan's primordial mother as pristine, uncorrupted, and genuine. He places stress on her procreative role and assigns to her "a vision of female lifestyle crafted on purposeful fertility . . . and, importantly, epitomizing a woman's larger sense of moral clarity in offering her body and mind in obedience to the needs of her husband and in-law's household" (Lindsey 2005:47).

In contrast to the stasis of these female deities, the male deity is free to roam and stake his claims, replicating over and over the female deity's saucy *nampa* (seduction). Izanagi travels to Izanami's cave of his own volition. Later he is allowed to exact order and rule—as a consequence of his ability to travel to the river in Himuka where he purifies his body.[4] The six *kami* (deities) that are born from his purified body become culturally and politically the most important *kami* in the Shinto pantheon—undergirding the tripartite functions of the politico-religious, agricultural, and military realms. Or as Grapard (1991:11) notes: "Culture, i.e., social partition, organization, and management is a male prerogative that required the death of a woman . . . as well as a distancing from nature through the performance of a symbolic act of violation and its corollary, purification." Without a placeholder for all that is abject, unknowable, and untoward, there can be no pure; no sacred without the profane. Izanami becomes that placeholder in Japanese myth—allowing the near "immaculate" conception of the Japanese state. Kirino exposes the constructed nature of this social partition—

particularly of gender roles and our assumptions about their presumed *natural* state—by inventing not just an afterlife for Izanami, but juxtaposing it alongside that of a mortal society.

THE GODDESS CHRONICLE: BRIEF PLOT SYNOPSIS

Kirino's alternative story is set in the human realm—on a beautiful teardrop-shaped island known as Umihebi, or "The Isle of Sea Snakes." Namima, a young priestess on the island, becomes the linchpin who bridges the mortal world with Izanami's realm of death. Upon her premature death, Namima finds herself in Izanami's dark underworld court. She speaks for the goddess. And she weaves her own sad story into her narration of Izanami. Namima had enjoyed an idyllic childhood, frolicking near-naked along the seashore with her elder sister Kamikuu until one summer she learns that she is destined to serve the island as the priestess of darkness, entrusted with tending to the dead. Her sister, on the other hand, inherits the role of priestess of light, charged with praying for the seafaring menfolk and serving as a model of fecundity. Their separate roles' are determined by their birth order and an elaborate yin-and-yang ordering system, as Namima explains:

> And so it came to pass that sisters who had been the best of friends were forced to follow separate paths. "Separate" is not quite the right word. Our paths were more distinctly different, as if she were to follow the day and I the night; or she the inner road and I the outer; she to traverse the heavens and I the earth. This was the "law" of the island—this was our "destiny" (Kirino 2012:19).

The importance of these binaristic positions is emphasized on the island by the presence of a large stone that blocks the passage to the sacred precincts where the pure sister performs her prayers. The stone physically draws a line between the sacred and the profane. Known in Japanese as the *oshirushi,* or more literally "the mark, the sign," the island stone echoes the enormous boulder that Izanagi uses to seal Izanami in her realm of death. The placement of the stone suggests an end but also a beginning. It marks the beginning of our recognition of life/death; pure/impure—in a word, the beginning of our ability to discriminate, to see the world as a system of dualities. The stone creates the original slash (/) mark. Like the *oshirushi* on the island, it marks, literally, the point of difference and warns of the outcome to any disruption of the order it imposes.

Although the ritualistic aspects of the island's culture suggest that Namima's position as the fallen is destined by the gods, readers are soon made aware of just how capricious this "destiny" really is. With a clever use of seduction and murder, the islanders easily defy destiny. Purity/impurity, though represented as divinely determined, are nothing more than a human mechanism for social control. When Namima gives birth to a daughter, by all rights she should be counted among the "pure." But due to the sinister machinations of Namima's erstwhile lover, the daughter's identity is obscured, and she is presented as the next "priestess of darkness," tender of death and other impurities. By digging down into the foundational myths of Japan, the myths that buttress the platform upon which the patrilineal emperor system is built, Kirino reveals the origins as no more than corrupt manipulations, the lie of power. The corruption in Kirino's parallel world leaks over into the world of the *Kojiki* myths. If it is easy for mortals to manipulate sacred functions, then why not manipulate the accounts of the gods themselves? The scapegoating of Izanami as the vessel of impurity and death is as much a fabrication as we would find in any account of the victor's justice. With one pillar of the foundational myths thus undercut, it does not take much to topple the sacredness of the emperor system itself. The nation is bogus. And gender roles—heretofore represented as *natural*—are constructions of convenience.[5]

It is not surprising that in her excavation of patriarchal myths Kirino would lead us into Izanami's womb of darkness. In effect, it represents another "crack in reality," a kind of crime that lays the blame on Izanami, one that requires excavation in order for justice to be done. Mother of Japan, mother of female corruption, Kirino's Izanami represents the mythic source of female desire and female failing—undone by her own body. She disintegrates into maggots and filth while her consort ascends to a position of purity. Namima, as her human counterpart, also dies after giving birth to the child that liberates her lover from his position as social pariah. Childbirth links the two women, tied as they are to their fallen state by their own female biology. Both are equally connected to experiences of betrayal at the hands of the men they had trusted—a betrayal that fixes them in positions of defilement. As Namima says, "The trials she has borne are the trials all women must bear" (Kirino 2012:309).

Izanami is not only trapped in her role as the dark mother by the giant boulder that imprisons her in her place, she is also locked in by language. Kirino uses language to mark Izanami's capture visibly and aurally. We see this most emphatically in Kirino's second chapter, where she introduces the creation narrative. Izanami tells Namima how she came to be, her voice taking on a new solemnity:

> Perhaps you are wondering what it was like at the time? Indeed, the earth floated upon the seas as formless as oil, bobbing through the waves like a jellyfish. And so here as well two gods came into being. The first was the god Umashi-ashi-kabi-hikoji, the Esteemed Deity of the Reed Shoots, who gave life to things by blowing upon them with a vital force. The other was Ame-no-toko-tachi, the Heavenly Eternal Standing Deity, who guards the heavens for all eternity. These gods protected the permanence of the heavens, and spurred the development of the earth below—their very existence points to the value of both. Neither Umashi-ashi-kabi-hikoji nor Ame-no-toko-tachi took a physical form. And so the five gods that I have just now introduced, having neither body nor sex, are known as the Five Separate Heavenly Deities (Kirino 2012:107).

Izanami's recitation of the creation myth goes on for pages. Prior to this section, the narrative had been melodious and magical, as befits myth, but the radical departure at this juncture marks a telling point in Izanami's access to language and in her ability to narrate her, and the nation's, story. Some of the critics of the English version of *The Goddess Chronicle* censured Kirino (and by extension her translator) for the way this lovely language comes to a screeching halt. For example, a reviewer for *The Independent* writes, "there is a second strand which seems weighed down by the author's reverence for the source material; an almost biblical retelling of the intricacies of the legend that slows the story unnecessarily" (Epstein 2013). As the translator, I do not think this mode of telling is unnecessary: I think the heavy ponderousness of the narrative *is* the point. Here we see the power of a masculinist logos. The section in question details the creation of the Japanese archipelago, the origin of binaristic logic, and the naming of the original deities—the founders of the Japanese race and the source of its patriarchal triumph. It is this proud lineage, this history of creation that surrounds Izanami, locks her in her dark cave, and refuses her self-fulfillment. It is the same narrative that releases Izanagi from a similar fate, allows his purification, and sees him as the single source of the Imperial line—untainted by female interference. It is also a language that Izanami cannot bear to speak. Midway through her recitation of the creation myth, when she comes to the occasion of her death, she halts abruptly and another denizen of the underworld takes over.

DIVA BODIES AND NATIONAL ANXIETIES

Kirino Natsuo's foray into mythic retelling was occasioned by an invitation from Canongate, a press in the United Kingdom, that challenged authors from around the globe to retell one of their country's or culture's myths "in a contemporary and memorable way."[6] Kirino's decision to write about the Izanami-Izanagi sequence from the *Kojiki* allowed her to take her customary exploration of male privilege and female bitterness to a foundational level. As Susan Sellers (2001:22) has suggested of the act of rewriting myth, it "is not only a matter of weaving in new images and situations but also involves the task of excavation, sifting through the layerings of adverse patriarchal renderings from which women were excluded, marginalized or depicted negatively to salvage and reinterpret as well as discard." In *The Goddess Chronicle*, by imagining Izanami voicing her own narrative, Kirino uses the opportunity to delve beneath the surfaces of Japan's foundational myths, sifting through the loamy legends of Japanese nationhood to find there the origins of male primacy and female subjugation.

In Coates's (2014:24) exploration of screen divas she suggests that their images are "invested with particular affects that reflected and mediated national issues." Whereas the issues Coates discusses are keyed to the aftermath of Japan's defeat in World War II and the resulting occupation, we can see similar affects at work in the image of Izanami—the body of precontinental, pre-logos Japan. Hers is a powerful body that is unbounded and porous, vulnerable to invasion and susceptible to form-altering subjugation. Lacking the rigid dependability of her male counterpart, the female body threatens to live beyond its borders, to ooze, and to defy, thus calling forth, as Coates (2014:30) suggests of the film star Yamaguchi Yoshiko, an abjected figure that challenges the certainty of national boundaries. Referring to the boom in monster movies of the late 1950s, Coates (2014:34–35) notes: "We can understand this motif as a process of abjecting threatening bodies; seemingly non-threatening bodies are made to assume the appearance of threat in order to provide a body upon which to practice the boundary-affirming process of abjecting. In this way, the female body unmasked as formless provides a suitable target for abjecting." Izanami, the first deity to be given female form, is unmasked and in her malleable formlessness, made to assume the guise of all that terrifies and threatens—death, taint, impurity, invasion. By making the female body the site of fear, masculinist discourse is able to contain her, entomb her, and thus erect borders around her that not only keep her in her place but solidify the boundaries of the known, the ordered, the nation.

In Kirino's imaginative retelling of the *Kojiki* story, Izanami and the other denizens of her Yomi world are wraithlike—hardly corporeal. They drift in an abject, uncertain world of death. The goddess herself, though purportedly with a regal bearing, has a body that shimmers with light when she angers, and her face offers no reassurance. "Her eyebrows were drawn tightly together in a deep frown. At one moment she seemed ready to rage and at the next as though she might cry. I had never met anyone with such an unreadable face" (Kirino 2012: 91). Hers is a body that cannot be understood. It inspires both awe and fear. And the space that it inhabits—as limitless as it may appear to the others around her—is nevertheless limned by the presence of the boulder. Izanami can never escape.

The politics of national borders is invoked in yet another way in Kirino's tale. The parallel world that she offers in juxtaposition to the realm of death features a "real" world of mortality, but it is no less mythic. The Isle of Sea Snakes is modeled after Kudaka-jima in the Ryūkyūan archipelago that includes Okinawa, a highly contested region of Japan that in its own right gives rise to uncertainties about national identity and porous borders.[7] Okinawa and other Ryūkyūan islands have long been imagined by scholars as the originator or the repository of indigenous Japanese culture. What was eventually lost on the main islands—due to the imbrications of modern (Western) customs—has been preserved in the more "backwards" and provincial Okinawa.[8] But the colonialist fantasies about Okinawa, rather than recognizing the former Ryūkyūan Kingdom on its own terms, circumscribes the space into a mythic grotto. The imaginary Isle of Sea Snakes, Okinawa, and Izanami are equally marginalized—forced to carry the freight of the noble primitive. Their irrational anger and messy emotions—in refusing to be checked—threaten to disrupt the tidy narratives that would see them silent, accessible to interpretation, and exploitable.

ENTERING THE MATRIXIAL BORDERSPACE

In her retelling, Kirino eviscerates the mythic stereotypes that continue to assign women and ethnic others such as Ryūkyūans the negative pole in binary constructions that deny their freedom of movement and rob them of their creative genius. Kirino takes the tropes that had earlier been used to shore up male authority and pushes them to extremes, in the process depriving those tropes of their power. Most prevalent in *The Goddess Chronicle* is the trope of binarism and the assignment of the negative to the female or the female-identified half of the binary. The two realms that Kirino portrays are both dominated by the female principle yet defined by male-policed borders. The Yomi underworld is clearly ruled by Izanami. It is her space. But it was a space that was invented by male belligerence. Had Izanagi not sought to "know" that space—to define it—it might have continued in its indefiniteness. It is also a profoundly female space. The characters who inhabit the space are female (Izanami, Namima, and Hieda no Are). The only male presences admitted are deprived of the ability to act or to assert male privilege. They are blinded, confused, and unable to legitimize their claims to knowledge or selfhood. While the Yomi underworld would appear on the surface to be frightful and sterile, it is surprisingly also full of positive potential. And we sense this in the relationships between the women who come together in their adversity and find common ground, even comfort, in their shared anger.

The characters in the Yomi underworld, having relinquished their physical forms, continue on as the memory of an embedded female essence. They draw together in what becomes a sort of sanctuary, an interior womb-like haven beyond the exterior world of trauma and binaristic difference. Here we have what we might call, using Bracha Ettinger's (2006) term, a "matrixial borderspace." This space points to the prebirth experience shared by all humans in which the developing consciousness enjoys simultaneously the pleasure and pain of sharing and separating and sensing the inchoate. It is a space pregnant with a powerful sense of immanence, or of potential becoming that is prior to the imposition of logos and knowing. It is, as Ettinger (2006: 90) describes, a "borderspace" in which plurality and partiality are conjoined. "In that open space where presence-absence conjoin . . . where a beat of pulse acts against the stability of visual space and the coherence of visual form. . . . In this space of plurality-*and*-partiality, it raises the enigma of the shareability of trauma and phantasy and the possibility of *co-response-ability with/for* the unknown Other" (Ettinger 2006:90).

The matrixial borderspace thus moves us beyond the either/or binarisms in which any reappropriation of male-authorized myth merely inverts the power hierarchy and introduces a realm where, as Ettinger (2006:90) explains: "In the phallus, we confront the impossibility of sharing trauma and phantasy, whereas in the matrix, to a certain extent, *there is an impossibility of not sharing* them."

The female-centered world in the parallel realm of the Isle of Sea Snakes is far from a woman's paradise, and much of the tension and drama in Kirino's work resides in the way the women's sacral roles are co-opted for personal gain by others, particularly by men. Kirino's underworld realm seeks to restore this power by offering an alternative that in its deviance is hardly desirable. There is in Kirino's text a mobius structure where woman is the beginning and the end. She is the victim and the victimizer—the source of her own undoing. Kirino does not offer spiritual redemption or even a political accusation. The goddess is herself cruel—her vindictiveness exacting a high price. But in her underworld of death Kirino calls out the problematic aspects of the foundational myths, criticizing the institutionalization of the emperor and the inevitability of corruption. She foments a powerful counternarrative that while celebrating the power of subversiveness, also hints at its own limits and potential for abuse.

A DIVA IS NOT A DAMSEL IN DISTRESS

Readers of *The Goddess Chronicle,* frequently female, tend to report a near visceral reaction to the novel. Regardless of their nationality, they see the myth as speaking to their national origins and to their contemporary social situation (Figure 9). For example, one British reader posted: "This book put me under a spell. I loved it so much it hurts, seriously. . . . In a way it was the perfect book for the person I am right now—while the book is about many things, what stood out most for me was how it captured what it means—and meant—to be a woman, the pain, the expectations, what happens if women refuse to fulfill the role 'society' (read: men) want them to fulfil" (Sophie 2016). Whereas another reader had this to say about exactly the same point: "But, really, this book made me angrier and angrier with every page I turned. The unfairness of basically every female character in this book, made my head boil. . . . I think the sad part of it all is that it's so close to the truth, the world is changing to a better place (hopefully) but it's a slow process . . . " (Zombiehero 2013).

At its core, Kirino's novel is about anger, about the power of anger to seep through the fissures of barricading boulders, to resonate across borders of time and space, between the pages of myth and reality, and to activate recognition and identification. As the novel nears its conclusion Izanami confronts her erstwhile lover. who returns to her cave to seek forgiveness and to implore her to relinquish her anger. Izamami is

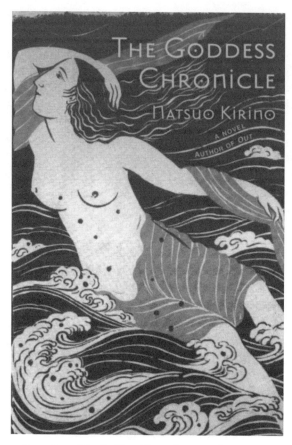

9. Cover from *The Goddess Chronicle* copyright © 2012 by
Natsuo Kirino. Used by permission of Grove Atlantic, Inc.

allowed a choice. She can work to establish good in the world of the
living and help comfort those who fall into her realm. Or she can go on
with her deadly ways. Izanami rebuffs Izanagi's effort to redeem her:

> My defilement bothers me not in the least, and I have no interest in saving
> anyone! All who end up here will stay here forever, doomed to drift, direc-
> tionless. . . . It is my lot, my *choice* to accept all of the world's defilement.
> And should one delve deeper and deeper still into the heart of this defile-
> ment, one might discover there something entirely unexpected. But, Izanaki,
> that has nothing to do with you (Kirino 2012:306).

Izanami refuses to play by Izanagi's rules. After all, he never had to
play by hers. He broke her injunction, he pushed his way into her sanc-

tuary, and he violated her with his sight. As the story ends, she deprives him of his own. She asserts her power by choosing her own destiny and acting on her own will. But her choice is unsettling. It goes against the grain of our readerly expectations. She stays behind in her world of death, stewing in her anger. A blogger who reviewed the translation calls the ending "strangely anticlimactic and unsatisfactory. There were no resolutions whatsoever" (Azad 2013). In fact, there are resolutions, just not the ones we wish for or expect. Trained as we are on "happy ever after" fairy tales . . . on Cinderella leaving with her Prince or Sleeping Beauty awakening to hers, we anticipate that Izanami will just be a good girl, agree to leave her dark surroundings, step out into the sun, and smile. When she asserts her divine privilege to choose the unthinkable, we are nonplussed. But should we be? Might we consider that perhaps Kirino has in fact created a character who steps outside the system of representation by choosing that which cannot be represented, choosing instead the diva nation?

To rephrase the choice using fairy tale tropes, Izanami refuses to be a rescued "damsel in distress." She will not be defined by a restoration of her purity or a rescinding of her power. As a rescued damsel she would be expected to submit meekly to her fate so that her rescuer might be seen as heroic. But Izanami will not be a mere conduit to Izanagi and his tale of suffering or his quest for happiness. After all, what lies beneath the surface of the rescued damsel story is always the story of the male hero's weakness or guilt over his inability to perform his socially prescribed patriarchal duty to protect family (Sarkeesian 2013). Izanami will not accept a position of victimhood or a loss of power to advance Izanagi's story. He has entered her realm, her story for the last time.

In a way Izanami refuses to allow, as Sara Ahmed (2010: 20) describes in *The Promise of Happiness*, "the happy ending" to beguile her back into socially appropriate behavior. "To kill joy . . . is to open a life, to make room for possibility, for chance." Hayashi Kumiko (2012:6) suggests that Kirino offers us a new beginning, with her story's ending. She celebrates Izanami's will to survive on her own terms. Izanami refuses to be overcome by hope. Instead, she stands proud as the Goddess of Yomi. She wraps her anger around her like a regal garment. Hers is an anger only she as a diva goddess can manage; the other spirits who surround her cower in her presence, dismayed and confused. And yet, her anger speaks for them, too. Her anger invigorates the stories they refuse to speak. Or, as Namima states: "She was the goddess who invited our desire and also our defilement; she bore the weight of the past and lived on into the future forever. . . . Izanami is without doubt a woman among women. The trials that she has borne are the trials all women must face" (Kirino 2012:308–9.)

Through the vector of Izanami's unbridled anger, Kirino Natsuo challenges her readers, as Berlant (1997:223) suggests, "to change the social and institutional practices of citizenship to which they currently consent." To quote Jennifer Waelti-Walters (1982:82), "Any woman, then, who speaks out, who thus has control over her situation . . . who makes choices and carries them out with authority, who recognizes and fulfills her own desires, is almost certain to be found inconvenient by the men around her, and runs a great risk of being labeled eccentric or mad by them, as they attempt to diminish her sphere of influence, undermine her strength and confidence and prevent her speech from being heard." Kirino invents an angry diva, whose inconvenient speech refuses to go unheard.

NOTES

I am grateful to the many friends who read early drafts of this paper, including Jan Bardsley, Nancy Berg, and most particularly Laura Miller. In fact, Laura lit the initial spark in the spring of 2012 by hosting a day-long symposium, "Pop Heroines and Female Icons of Japan," where I first had the opportunity to present a version of this paper. From there I took the work on the road, reading different renditions on a number of campuses in the United States and Japan. For this I am indebted to Seth Jacobowitz, Elizabeth Oyler, Giorgio Amitrano, and their students and colleagues who offered helpful feedback. I also appreciate the opportunity to share the paper with the Midwest Japan Seminar.

1. *Joshinki* was published in 2008 by Kadokawa Shoten (Kirino 2008). The translation was released in 2012 by Canongate. In the novel, Kirino refers to the male deity as Izanaki. Premodern references to the *Kojiki* preferred to use the spelling *ki;* the *gi* became more commonplace in modern reference. Whether spelled *ki* or *gi*, the phoneme identifies the male principle, whereas the *mi* of Izanami refers to the female. In both names, the *iza* means to invite. In this essay, I will follow Kirino's "Izanaki" when citing from her novel.

2. Kirino Natsuo is the pen name of Hashioka Mariko (b. 1951). She spent her childhood in Sendai, until her architect father moved the family to Tokyo when she was fourteen. After graduating with a degree from Seikei University, Kirino worked in various occupations, including magazine editing. She married at twenty-four, and it wasn't until she was thirty, when she had had her first child, that she began to write professionally. Her early works conformed to romance fiction. She began writing mystery fiction ten years later and it was then she started to receive critical recognition. Since that time, she has written over twenty novels and her interests have turned from mystery fiction to crime fiction to psychological noir. She claims as her influences writers "as diverse as Flannery O'Connor, Anne Tyler, Hayashi Fumiko, and Reinaldo Arenas" (Davis

2010:10). Her works have won numerous awards, including the Edogawa Rampo Award and the Naoki Prize. *Goddess Chronicles* won the Murasaki Shikibu Literary Award. For more on Kirino's biography, see Davis 2010.

3. Gregus (2014:120) refers to the studies of Lisette Gepphart (2010).

4. Susa-no-o, inheriting his father's mobility, blows willfully through Amaterasu's palace, motivating her temporary removal to a cave. (For more on this episode, see Tomoko Aoyama's Chapter 2 in this volume.) And even after he is banished from Heaven, he is free to roam about Izumo slaying dragons and rescuing maidens.

5. As Hara Takeshi (2008) notes, it is surely no coincidence that Kirino's novel appeared shortly after the controversy over the gender of the emperor's successor erupted in 2005 when government officials began to discuss publicly solutions to the "heir crisis." On September 6, 2006, Princess Akishino delivered a baby boy, which largely diverted the crisis. But discussions of allowing women to succeed to the throne (once again) are ongoing—drawing into question binaries of male/female and pure/impure.

6. Authors in the Canongate series include Margaret Atwood, Karen Armstrong, A S Byatt, David Grossman, Milton Hatoum, Natsuo Kirino, Alexander McCall Smith, Tomás Eloy Martínez, Victor Pelevin, Ali Smith, Su Tong, Dubravka Ugresic, Salley Vickers, and Jeanette Winterson. Website at http://www.themyths.co.uk/ [accessed 12 July 2016].

7. Kirino based her descriptions of the fictional Umihebi, or "The Isle of Sea Snakes," and its sacred matrilineal functions on Kudaka Island in Okinawa and its Izaiho rites. Kudaka is a sacred island a thirty-minute ferry ride from Chinen in southern Okinawa. Known as "the island of the gods," it is believed that the original goddess and creator of Okinawa, Amamikiyo, descended upon this island. During the era of the Ryūkyū Kingdom, men were prohibited from entering certain sites on this island, which were kept sacred for the performance of important ceremonies. One of the most important ceremonies was the Izaiho, in which women between the ages of thirty and forty-one made the symbolic transition from young females into celestial beings. The ceremony was performed every twelve years for over 600 years. But the last occurrence was in 1978. It has ceased to be performed because apparently there are no more participants. See Hara (2008:261–62).

8. Okinawa historian Ifa Fuyū and folklore scholar Yanagida Kunio claim that the Okinawan shamanic religion—with women at its center—was the forerunner to Japan's Shinto. See Barske (2013:76).

CHAPTER 2

Ame no Uzume Crosses Boundaries

TOMOKO AOYAMA

Ame no Uzume no Mikoto, "the mighty one Wreathed Woman of Heaven" (Heldt 2014:76), is widely regarded as Japan's first comic erotic diva. She is, as Kōno Nobuko (1995:127) characterizes her, "the most shamanistic goddess," whose appearance is always accompanied by "theatrical devices." Ame no Uzume appears in two important scenes in the *Kojiki* (Record of ancient matters, completed in 712 CE), and *Nihon shoki* (Chronicles of Japan, also known as *Nihongi*, 720 CE). In both episodes Uzume uses her body and performance effectively to establish communication and overcome actual and potential crises. In this chapter, I first outline the portrayal of this goddess and some of the issues surrounding her, in particular, her ability to cross various boundaries and find ways to communicate even in the most dangerous and challenging situations and with potential opponents. I argue that the mythological diva Ame no Uzume presents a valid and effective model that transcends time, space, culture, and language. To discuss the aspect of border-crossing further, I introduce Tsurumi Shunsuke's study of Ame no Uzume. The final section of the chapter examines the significance and validity of the Uzume model of comic subversion and revitalization by applying Tsurumi's theory to one example drawn from current society, namely the "vagina artist" Rokudenashiko, to show how our diva, Uzume, continues to use her body in an exemplary fashion to stave off crises in our present-day misogynistic society.

THE DANCING DIVA RESCUES THE WORLD
WITH LAUGHTER

Ame no Uzume first appears in a climactic scene of one of the most celebrated episodes of Japanese mythology. The Sun Goddess Amaterasu is devastated when her wild younger brother, Susa-no-o, commits a series of sacrilegious and destructive acts. At first his sister tries to defend him: "What looks like excrement must be vomit . . . spewed out in a drunken stupor," she claims, and "his ruining the paddy ridges and burying their ditches" must be "because he thought good land was going to waste" (Heldt 2014: 74). However, his transgressions escalate: he makes a hole in the roof of Amaterasu's sacred weaving house and drops through the hole the pelt of a piebald horse that has been skinned backwards, violating multiple taboos. "Startled by the sight, Weaver Woman of Heaven slammed her weaving shuttle into her privates and died" (Heldt 2014:74).[1] In Miura Sukeyuki's (2002:43) modern Japanese translation of the *Kojiki*, the horse's skin falls onto one of the weaver women. The horrified woman falls back from the loom and the shuttle she has dropped pierces her private parts, fatally injuring her. As Miura and other scholars have noted, one of the variations on this episode in the *Nihon shoki* narrates this as something that happens to Amaterasu herself. The horse, the shuttle, and the damaging of the roof of the sacred weaving house all suggest sexual violation, which, if interpreted as being committed by Susa-no-o against Amaterasu, involves the violation of three major taboos, as Ōtsuka Hikari (2011:41) points out:

1. incest between siblings born of the same mother
2. sex between a sister dressed as a man[2] and a brother
3. rape of an older sister by a younger brother, inflicting injury and death

In the *Kojiki*, immediately after the death of the weaving woman, Amaterasu conceals herself inside Heaven's Boulder Cavern. Without the Sun Goddess the world becomes dark and beset by calamities. As Miura, Ōtsuka, and many others note, it is possible to interpret the act of seclusion in the cave as a metaphor for Amaterasu's death, which in turn can be associated with the universally acknowledged seasonal end of the productive cycle and arrival of winter, that is, the winter solstice (Nakanishi 2013:73–76). The dark cave reminds us of Yomi, the realm of the dead, where the goddess of creation Izanami goes after her death (see Rebecca Copeland's Chapter 1 in this volume). It can also be interpreted, as it is by Ōtsuka (2011:51–54) as an act of severe depression on the part of Amaterasu, who is the victim of sexual and other violations, and something similar to the contemporary social issue of *hikikomori* (acute social withdrawal).

Ame no Uzume plays a key role in resolving this crisis by enticing Amaterasu out of the cave. She does this not on her own but in close collaboration with Omoikane and other deities (*kami*) and with carefully prepared props, costume, and setting, all of which enhance Uzume's performance:

> Overturning a bucket before the entrance to Heaven's Boulder Cavern, she stamped loudly on it and became possessed, showing her breasts and pushing the girdle of her skirt down past her privates (Heldt 2014:76).

Uzume's comic, erotic, and shamanistic dance creates resounding laughter among the eight million *kami*. It is so loud that it reaches Amaterasu inside the cave, prompting her to ask:

> "Because I had concealed myself, the high plains of heaven grew dark and the central realm of reed plains was cast in utter gloom, or so I thought. Why, then, does Wreathed Woman of Heaven [i.e., Ame no Uzume] sing and dance, and all the many spirits [*kami*] in their multitudes laugh out loud?" (Heldt 2014:77).

In response, Uzume tells Amaterasu that it is because they have found a *kami* who is "even more magnificent" than Amaterasu. Two other deities hold out a large mirror so that Amaterasu can see her own image through the small mouth of the cave, and when she tries to see better by coming a little closer, the Strong-Armed Man of Heaven, who has been hiding by the door, grabs her hand and pulls her all the way out of the cave, and another *kami* draws forth a sacred boundary rope to prevent her from returning to the cave. Thus, light, order, and life are restored to the world.

Ame no Uzume's performance in this episode involves not merely her physical dancing and chanting in a "possessed" state but also careful preparation and well-coordinated collaboration with other *kami*. Like other divas, however smooth, natural, and spontaneous Uzume may look in her powerful performance, she is playing a role to attract the audience's attention at center stage after elaborate planning and rehearsal, and with the support of staff *kami*. She has two different audiences: firstly, her fellow *kami* outside the cave, who also contribute

10. Ame no Uzume performs in front of the cave. By the artist Kōno Fumiyo, in *Bōrupen Kojiki*, Vol. 1:101 (Tokyo: Heibonsha 2012).

to the performance by laughing; and secondly Amaterasu, for whom the entire play is produced, though not to entertain her but to invite her out of the cave (Figure 10). Uzume's performance consists of dance, chanting, and verbal communication. The dance includes the imitation of erotic sexual movements, while her words and the mirror serve to trick the supposedly most powerful *kami*, Amaterasu.

The nudity and sexual elements in Uzume's dance have a number of interpretations. Anthropologist Yamaguchi Masao (1990:14–15) explains them in terms of grotesque humor. Laughter helps to overcome the fear of internal and external monsters and evil spirits. Examples of this kind of laughter that purges fear or resolves a problem can be found in a wide range of cultures. The Greek goddess of the harvest, Demeter, is often compared to Amaterasu in more than one respect. When her brother Poseidon, who, like Susa-no-o, reigns over the seas, tries to seduce Demeter, she disguises herself in the form of a mare, but he still finds and rapes her. Deeply upset, Demeter hides in a cave, causing famine throughout the world (Ōtsuka 2011:40–41). In another version, Demeter refuses to eat when the god of the dead, Hades, abducts her daughter, Persephone. A woman called Baubo then lifts her dress and reveals her genitalia, which makes Demeter laugh and begin to eat again. Another similar example Ōtsuka cites, based on studies by anthropologist Claude Lévi-Strauss, is from Egyptian mythology. The sun god, Ra, is displeased, and lies down, refusing to join a discussion of who should be his successor. When his daughter, Hathor, who is regarded as the goddess of joy, love, and dance, displays her private parts, he laughs and rises to return to the discussion (Ōtsuka 2011:65). Referring to Mikhail Bakhtin's study of carnival (1984a and 1984b), Kawamura Kunimitsu (2005:202–3) writes that "divine possession, laughter, and sex (or exposure of sexual organs) may seem to be three different entities but they all have the power to bring change to the world, and are all related to each other." When all three are combined, as in the example of Ame no Uzume's performance, the power multiplies, "filling the earth with abundant spiritual power and natural energy, revitalizing the human soul, and fertilizing animals and plants" (Kawamura 2005:203–4). The laughing deities are, as Ogasawara Kyōko (1978:93) notes, "not [the passive] audience of a drama but participants in a ritual who perform the act of laughing that purges the evil."

In relation to Uzume's exposure of her private parts, Nagafuji Yasushi compares the scene with other references to female private parts in the *Kojiki* and *Nihon shoki,* including Izanami's death when giving birth to the fire god and Amaterasu's weaver woman's death. It is clear that "female genitals are an ambivalent sign of the boundary of life and death" (Nagafuji 2004:23). Nagafuji creates a neat binary table contrasting Uzume and Amaterasu: while the former represents life, outside, the caller/inviter, genitals, exposure, laughter/opening, and fertility, the latter inside the cave represents the opposite—namely, death, inside, the called/invited, the cave, hiding, closure, and sterility (2004:26–27). This binary approach helps to explain the significance of Uzume's dance as an opening and calling (back) to life.

In his annotated modern Japanese translation, Miura (2002:45–46) uses two key verbs, *asobu* and *eraku*, to translate the dialogue between Amaterasu and Uzume, noting the different meaning of the former from its modern usage and the need to use these verbs in his translation even though the latter is not generally part of the modern Japanese vocabulary. *Asobu* in ancient Japanese signified the act of welcoming a god or a spirit and the enjoyment of being together, hence "to sing and dance." Both Donald Philippi (1968:85) and Heldt (2014:77) translate Amaterasu's question about why Uzume "makes *asobi*" as "sing[s] and dance[s]." According to Orikuchi Shinobu (1966:394–95), there is a difference between *asobi* (the noun form of *asobu*) and *mai*: while they both mean "dance," *mai* signifies stamping [the ground] and calming [the spirit], whereas *asobi* also involves music, and, more importantly, the calling back and shaking of the spirit (*tama*) through various actions (i.e., the act of *tamafuri*). Thus, *asobi* invites the external spirit to attach to or come inside the dancer's human body. This *asobi*, or to be more precise, *kami asobi*, is the origin of *kagura*, the sacred Shinto music and dance. The term *eraku*, on the other hand, signifies the expression of pleasure through voiced laughter. It is different from the more familiar verbs *warau* (laugh) and *emu* (smile). Of these three verbs *warau* alone contains a derisive or insulting element; it is unilateral laughing at a specific target. Conventionally, the Chinese character 咲, which in modern Japanese is used for flowers to "bloom" (*saku*), has been read in *Kojiki* studies as *warau*. It is indeed possible to interpret the laughter of the eight million *kami* as a signal to Amaterasu of their (acted) derision of the weak and inferior leader who is hiding away in the rock cave. However, while accepting the reading of this character as *warau* for other examples in the *Kojiki*, Miura (1993:16–19) questions that interpretation in this particular scene and proposes *eraku* as an alternative reading, noting that there are many other examples of the same character having more than one reading in the text.

> If the reading is *eraku*, then it means that captivated by Uzume's comic and lewd performance, the eight million *kami* are in an ecstatic trance, as if they were drunk. Hence Uzume, who is performing an indecent act, and the laughing (*eraku*) *kami* find affinity and all the deities in Takamagahara except for Amaterasu, who is hiding inside the cave, become one. Just as *emai* (smile) [invites the other to smile too], their *eraki* draws Amaterasu out of the cave (Miura 1993:18).

It seems convincing that the laughter is joyful, inclusive, and inviting rather than derisive. The joyous mood is captured in the portrait of Uzume by Kosugi Hōan (1881–1964), with the sun already out (Figure 11).

11. Ame no Uzume no Mikoto, painting by Kosugi Hōan (1951). Used with permission of the Idemitsu Museum of Arts, Tokyo.

THE GLARING DIVA CROSSES
THE HEAVEN/EARTH BOUNDARY

After the celebrated and intriguing dance scene, Ame no Uzume disappears from the text until much later in Book One of the *Kojiki*. Although not as famous as the cave scene, the next episode concerns yet another major crisis of heaven and earth. After a series of failed attempts to rule the earth, "the central realm of plentiful reed plains," Amaterasu finally decides to send her grandson, Ho no Ninigi, to earth. When Ninigi is about to descend, a fearsome giant stands at a crossroad. This stranger emits powerful, glaring lights that even reach heaven. Amaterasu calls upon Ame no Uzume and says:

> "Although you are a weak-limbed woman, you are a spirit [*kami*] who has the power to confront others and stare them down. Therefore, go by yourself to question this spirit thus:
>
> 'Who is it who stands on this road that will take our mighty heir down from heaven?'" (Heldt 2014:115)

In the *Kojiki*, when Ame no Uzume asks this question, the stranger immediately replies by clarifying his identity: he is a local *kami* called Sarutahiko (or Sarutabiko, "Monkey Guard Lad," Figure 12). There is no real confrontation; Sarutahiko readily pledges allegiance to the new ruler. As Miura (2002:99n7) remarks, it seems anticlimactic that the fierce indigenous deity is so ready and willing to serve an external *kami*

12. Ame no Uzume and Sarutahiko. By the artist Kōno Fumiyo, in *Bōrupen Kojiki,* Vol. 3:11 (Tokyo: Heibonsha 2013).

and to ensure his safety. However, Miura explains that this is because of the immense power of Uzume's visage and gaze, before which even the glaring Sarutahiko pales. Thus, Uzume resolves the problem single-handedly, or rather, single-facedly. She is not just an erotic dancing diva who attracts everyone's gaze but a fearless and invincible glaring diva.

Once the potential enemy has been transformed into a loyal servant, Amaterasu's grandson, Ninigi, descends from heaven, with the three sacred treasures: Amaterasu's "long strands of many curved pendants, the mirror used to lure her out of Heaven's Boulder Cavern, and the sword Grass Scyther" (Heldt 2014:115). Accompanying him are five deities, including Uzume. Each of the five is assigned to oversee a sacred profession, in Uzume's case the performance of sacred rituals. Uzume is also told to accompany Sarutahiko to his land, Ise, and bear his name.[3] Hence, she becomes the founder of the clan known as Sarume no kimi. Heldt (2014:118) translates Sarume as "the Mummer Women," which may suit the often earthy and even obscene comic performance seen in various forms of ritual music and dance called *dengaku* and *kagura.* Nevertheless, these are, as in the case of Uzume's performance outside the cave, sacred Shinto rituals for and with the *kami* and the imperial court as their supposed direct descendants. One theory, supported by Orikuchi Shinobu (1966:379) and others (Heldt 2014:25–26), claims that Hieda no Are, whose recitation of the mythological narrative was recorded and compiled by Ō no Yasumaro to form the *Kojiki,* was a woman of this clan, Sarume no kimi. Thus, the performing diva not only settles in on earth but continues to perform important roles for generations through her descendants.

VARIATIONS AND TRANSFORMATIONS OF UZUME

There are some notable differences in the descriptions of these two scenes concerning Ame no Uzume in the *Kojiki* and the *Nihon shoki.* In *Nihon shoki,* for instance, Uzume's performance outside the cave does not involve any striptease-like act; even though details of the elaborate props and costume are given, Uzume's performance itself is described simply as "skillful" (Borgen and Ury 1990:79; Ōtsuka 2011:59). In the second scene with Sarutahiko, however, the descriptions are more detailed than those in the *Kojiki.* Sarutahiko is described as having an extremely long nose and a very red mouth and bottom, reminding us of the monkey, as well as of the *tengu,* the legendary figure with an extraordinarily long nose, which is regarded as a sign of arrogance and often associated with the phallus in popular culture. In this version, Uzume bares her breasts and pulls her skirt string down to reveal her private parts, just as she does in the cave scene in the *Kojiki.* However, it is Uzume herself who laughs loudly; Sarutahiko is completely taken aback by this unexpected and extraordinary act. As Miura (1993:20) remarks, "Uzume has successfully invalidated Sarutabiko's power by revealing her private parts and with her loud laughter." In this version of the episode, Uzume is not the object or cause of laughter but the enactor of laughter.

In addition to the differences between the texts and their variants, we may note that there are changes within the same text and the same characters. As Saitō Hideki (e.g. 2006, 2010) elaborates, deities and other elements in the mythological narratives are not fixed but continue to grow and transform both within and outside the texts. These transformations often signify historical and political changes. In his discussion of the many transformations of Amaterasu, Saitō (2010:161) writes:

> Amaterasu as an armed female shaman is defeated by Susa-no-o and dies by hiding in the cave. When she emerges to re-vive and re-reign, she has grown into a higher-rank goddess who issues commands unilaterally.

Maral Andassova (2013:142) points out that the reappearance of Amaterasu from the cave not only indicates the restoration of order on the high plains of heaven (Takamagahara) but also the strengthening of their influence over the central realm of reed plains (Ashihara no naka-tsukuni), which suggests a change in the ancient politics among the clans. There are changes and differences within the character of Ame no Uzume, too. She is depicted as a member of the Takamagahara deities and an agent of Amaterasu's authority. However, with Ninigi's descent, she becomes the founder of the Sarume clan who functions as a mediator between heaven and earth. Whether she is merely a minion of the authorities is debatable. In a subsequent minor episode, Uzume gathers all of the fish together and asks whether they will serve the mighty child of heaven's spirits. All except the sea slug affirm that they will, and Uzume cuts the sea slug with a knife, saying, "This mouth is a mouth with no answer!" (Heldt 2014:119) This is the type of tale that explains the origin of things, and may well derive from a separate source that was originally unrelated to Uzume (Miura 2002:103n31). Despite these indications that Uzume was on the side of the authorities, however, there are subversive and ambiguous aspects to her character, very much like the carnival king/fool. And this makes her one of the most interesting figures in the *Kojiki* and *Nihon shoki.*

TSURUMI SHUNSUKE'S STUDY OF AME NO UZUME

To understand this intriguing mythological diva better, the most helpful source is Tsurumi Shunsuke's *Ame no Uzume den* (originally published in 1991, included in Tsurumi 2001:3–121). It is a comprehensive and original study of the significance of Ame no Uzume—not just within the mythological, literary, and performing arts traditions but in all sorts of other areas and across time and space. Although Tsurumi uses the term *den,* which would, in such a context, normally mean "biography," "legend," or "The Life of," his interest is not limited to the study of mythology or hermeneutics; instead he offers a free and profound discussion of what Uzume, as an archetype, represents and signifies and of how we can find her in many different forms in various historical times and cultures. It is, in a sense, similar to the ubiquity and vast variations of Himiko, as Laura Miller's Chapter 3 in this volume explores. However, Tsurumi's discussion includes examples that are unrelated to Uzume but can be regarded as sharing some characteristics. Tsurumi's writing is erudite and full of highly original observations. At the same time, it is written in accessible language and includes a wide range of surprising and at times hilarious examples—very much in the spirit of Uzume.

Tsurumi identifies the following characteristics not only in the "original" Ame no Uzume but in those who may be nicknamed, or compared to, Ame no Uzume:[4]

1. They are not beautiful but are charming.

2. They do not care about their appearance. They move without inhibition and are not concerned about respectability.

3. They invite and encourage people to enjoy the party/company.

4. They are full of vitality, which brings out the life force in others.

5. They make people laugh and relieve anxiety. They will even tell a lie to reassure others.

6. They do not shy away from obscenity. They play a role that goes beyond sexual repression.

7. They do not mind if an outsider joins the company; they are open-minded and do not find it necessary to guard themselves closely (Tsurumi 2001:20).

In addition to these characteristics, Tsurumi (2001:21) cites another: the ability to create illusion through the act of exposing their private parts: "The combined expressions of the face and the private parts form a creative power." This amalgamates the two scenes and the two different versions of Uzume's act in confronting Sarutahiko, as even when one of the two, the face or the private parts, is in focus, the importance of the other is clear. However, Tsurumi's consideration is wider and more profound than this. Referring to Susanne Langer's (1957) *Problems of Art*, he emphasizes that dance as expression is not the movement of the body itself but the illusion that the movement leaves behind. In Ame no Uzume's case, "it is not the sexual organ itself but the illusion that it creates in combination with her face," "the illusion that there is another face." Uzume can create such illusions both within a group (as in the cave scene) and with an individual (such as Sarutahiko).

One of the key points in Tsurumi's theory is that Uzume is regarded as someone who has the potential to create a democratic opening in a closed, discursive system or establishment through subversive laughter. The scene she creates may appear to be chaotic, but it can usher in a new democratic phase. He also points out that Ame no Uzume is not a single person/goddess but can be regarded as "already reincarnated many a time within the history of the Heavenly Plain" (Tsurumi 2001:17); in other words, there were multiple Uzumes in the mythology, and the multiplicity and mobility she represents are also found in those who are nicknamed, or likened to, Uzume millennia later. This corresponds with the notion of ever-growing, ever-changing deities and mythologies that Saitō Hideki, Maral Andassova, and others emphasize.

UZUME AS DIVA OF FREEDOM AND DEMOCRACY

To add to the richness of Tsurumi's study, there is a particular historical and biographical significance, in particular, concerning the "democratic" aspect of Uzume. As he explains at the beginning of the book, the germination of a fresh way to look at Japanese mythology took place in Adelaide, South Australia, in 1937. Tsurumi's father, Yūsuke (1885–1973), a member of the Japanese Diet (House of Representatives), spent around three months touring various Australian capital cities as a delegate to the New Education Fellowship Conference. Accompanying Yūsuke was Shunsuke's elder sister, Kazuko (1918–2006), nineteen. Kazuko, who was later to study at Vassar, Columbia and Princeton, and become an internationally acclaimed sociologist, was already recognized as an exceptionally articulate and accomplished young woman, studying English literature at Tsuda College, traditional Japanese dance with Hanayagi Tokutarō (1878–1963), and *tanka* poetry with Sasaki Nobutsuna (1872–1963). Shunsuke (1922–2015), fifteen, was also in Australia at the same time but instead of accompanying his sister and their father, he was with his father's secretarial assistant, who also served as his tutor. In stark contrast to Kazuko, the young Shunsuke was a "bad boy," according to his own accounts: he regularly skipped school and shoplifted, and after a series of poor marks and report cards, stopped attending secondary school altogether. He was sexually precocious; from an early age he was conscious of his strong sexual drive and was ashamed and embarrassed about it. This may be at least partly related to his difficult relationship with his mother, Aiko (the daughter of Count Gotō Shinpei, 1857–1929), who bullied and abused Shunsuke physically and psychologically from his early childhood—not because she did not love her son but because she did love him and wanted him to meet her high moral standards. Another important factor is that the young Shunsuke's individuality and intelligence were not compatible with the rigid Japanese school system that espoused totalitarian nationalism. He failed his exams not because he was scholastically weak but because the academic level was not challenging enough and he refused to conform. By 1937 Shunsuke had attempted suicide a few times, by cutting his wrists, by trying to jump off a cliff (although he did not actually go ahead with this), by an overdose of sleeping pills, and by eating cigarettes. Aiko had him committed to a mental hospital three times (Shindō 1994: esp. 56–58; see also Tsurumi and Kurokawa 2009:81–142). It is rather tempting to compare the bright and magnificent Kazuko to Amaterasu and the "bad boy" Shunsuke to Susa-no-o, although Shunsuke was never violent toward anyone but himself. The self-harming, depressed boy suffering in isolation has an element of Amaterasu in the cave as well.

None of this biographical background has any direct connection to the content of Tsurumi's engaging study of Ame no Uzume. And yet it does help us to understand the emphasis placed on freedom, democracy, and open-mindedness in his book. The key incident that relates to his *Ame no Uzume den* is mentioned on the opening page of the book (Tsurumi 2001:4). In early September 1937 Shunsuke was invited to a meeting of a group of people in Adelaide who had an interest in Japanese language and culture. At the time there were no Japanese living in the South Australian capital but the members of what we can identify as the Japanese Language Club (Shimazu 2004: 188) taught themselves Japanese using books and a radio program that was broadcast from Melbourne by a Japanese language instructor, Inagaki Mōshi (Shimazu 2012:19). At the meeting they welcomed the *real* Japanese visitor(s)[5] and handed out printed materials that described a democratic gathering of eight million deities, including a (mythical) god of typewriters and a god of striptease (Tsurumi 2001:4). The young Shunsuke was amazed at this "free" translation of Japanese mythology, which was completely different from the version then being taught in schools in Japan. This stunningly liberal interpretation, as Tsurumi recollects, continued to take shape inside him for half a century.

Following the introduction of the eight-point analysis of Uzume's characteristics outlined above, Tsurumi discusses a number of wide-ranging examples of those who may be regarded as Ame no Uzume in one way or another. These include charismatic and shamanistic dancers such as the founder of kabuki, Izumo no Okuni (1572–?; see Barbara Hartley's Chapter 4 in this volume), the founder of the Tenshō Kōtai Jingūkyō (Religion of the Shrine of the Heavenly Goddess, a.k.a. Dancing Religion), Kitamura Sayo (1900–1968), and the legendary striptease dancer, Ichijō Sayuri (1929–1997), who was arrested nine times during her twenty-year dancing career for alleged "obscenity." Tsurumi also discusses some modern women writers: poet Nagase Kiyoko (1906–1995), writer of children's literature Okkotsu Yoshiko (1929–1980), novelist/ nun Setouchi Harumi/Jakuchō (b. 1922), and novelist/essayist Tanabe Seiko (b. 1928), as latter-day Ame no Uzumes. Tanabe and her protagonists are, as Tsurumi names his chapter on them, "Katei ni haitta Ame no Uzume" (Ame no Uzume in the household). This "household" is not the oppressive and repressive *ie;* it has room for pleasure (singing, dancing, drinking, eating, chatting, and joking, among other things), as well as for domestic and professional work. The threshold does not enclose this space, as it "expands towards the outside" (Tsurumi 2001:95). Tsurumi's examples are not limited to Japanese women; he also discusses Shakers (The United Society of Believers in Christ's Second Appearing) and the Native American tribe Oneida, whose social and ceremonial dancing is well known. Referring to Orikuchi Shinobu (1966), Inoue Mitsusada (1964), Mikhail Bakhtin (1984b), and many other scholars and thinkers across multiple disciplines, Tsurumi (2001:34) argues that "numerous Ame no Uzumes have been active in the world," and that to think in this way, without limiting her in terms of time, space, culture, etc., would also suit her liberal personality. Thus, Mohandas Gandhi, Kimura Keigo's (1942) comic operetta film *Utau tanuki goten* (The palace of the singing raccoon dogs), and even inanimate objects such as animistic "phallus" and "vagina" stones are discussed in Tsurumi's 2001 book as incarnations of Uzume. The example of Gandhi may be more surprising than the others. Tsurumi (2001:62) recognizes Gandhi's repressive behavior toward his own wife, children, and other young people under his watch. "Despite these differences, Gandhi resembles Ame no Uzume in his attitude of revealing his naked body to an unknown opponent." Tsurumi then quotes a long passage from George Orwell's (1949) "Reflections on Gandhi," and identifies the points of similarity and difference between Uzume and Gandhi:

> Deep inside Gandhi was jealousy, which made him a narrowly focused and resilient political activist. Ame no Uzume's humanity is liberated from such repressed revulsion for sex, and it helped to bring forth change out of the darkness that was caused by Amaterasu's hiding away, and became the force to change racial/ethnic conflicts into peace. There are many things we can learn from the allegorical meaning of having a striptease dancer as one of our ancient political leaders (Tsurumi 2001:64).

AME NO UZUME CONTINUES TO MULTIPLY

We have seen Ame no Uzume as a subversive comic diva who plays important roles in two crucial scenes in the Japanese myth. As a mythological figure, her characteristics vary. The multiplicity and transformations of Uzume can be partly explained by the nature of mythology. However, as Tsurumi has identified, various features of Uzume can be understood as representing a prototype found across time and space. He himself is an Ame no Uzume who does not place one gender, culture, ethnic group, age group, language, genre, style, or field above others, but moves freely between them and brings out the life force through his critical and creative performance. Like Ame no Uzume's performance, Tsurumi's writing creates an opening, a free and democratic turning point, through surprise and laughter, and through the illusion of the upper face/head and the lower, usually concealed and dismissed, corporeal and sexual body merging into one. And the seed for this discovery was planted back in 1937 in South Australia. In a sense, Shunsuke found a light that allowed him to transform himself from a depressed "bad boy" into an Ame no Uzume: he discovered that Uzume's flexibility and communicative ability remove our fear and prejudice and revitalize our world.

Tsurumi passed away in 2015. However, Ame no Uzume continues to grow and multiply. It is even more important to recognize these incarnations and aspire to be one in contemporary society, where we find many signs of violence and oppression that remind us of the 1930s and early 1940s. Tsurumi's work shows how easy it is to find contemporary examples of Uzume around us. Were Tsurumi writing his book today or revising it with updated examples, he would undoubtedly include the "vagina artist" Rokudenashiko as a contemporary Uzume. (Her artist name translates literally as "Good For Nothing Girl"; her given name is Igarashi Megumi. See the Afterword to this volume.) Rokudenashiko has created a kayak and many other objects based on a 3-D image of her own vagina. Amazingly, in a country where sexually explicit two- and three-dimensional objects have been abundant for millennia, she was arrested in July and December 2014 for obscenity. The striptease dancer Ichijō Sayuri, discussed in Tsurumi (2001:56–59), spent seven months in prison for showing her private parts as a final special present to her fans in her retirement show in 1972. Unlike Ichijō, Rokudenashiko "exhibited" her art rather than her body. She was released the day after her July arrest, but in December she was held in custody for more than three weeks. She insists that neither her vagina nor the common term *manko* is obscene (McCurry 2015).

Instead of crying out in rage, Rokudenashiko continues to fight back with humor, articulating with her manga, installations, and other art and words how ridiculous and biased the accusation against her is. The cover of her book *Waisetsu tte nan desu ka?* (What is obscenity? Rokudenashiko 2015) shows the artist with the usual big smile on her face, and a small pink *manko* art figure in her hand. The speech bubble coming from the pink figure says, "I, who was called 'the self-proclaimed artist,'" in reference to her disparaging treatment in the media. Thus, Rokudenashiko practices Tsurumi's eighth point: "the combined expressions of the face and the private parts form a creative power." Almost uncannily like Ame no Uzume, and happily, this contemporary vagina diva found her supportive "Sarutahiko" in the musician and lead singer of The Waterboys, Mike Scott, and they were married on October 22, 2016. On her homepage she posts, together with some photographs of their wedding and a parody of Yoko and Lennon's "Bed-in," her four-cell manga depicting the police making a speech at their wedding as their "matchmaker."

Rokudenashiko also conforms with Tsurumi's descriptions of Ame no Uzume as outlined above, as well as in the following concluding paragraph of his book:

> Standing at the parting of Heaven and Earth, and before the odd-looking stranger, Ame no Uzume sought equality rather than exclusivity. This is precisely the sort of attitude we should seek today. She presents a model for interceding between Japan and foreign lands, and Heaven and Earth. She disrupts the pursuit of rigid ideologies to which the authorities aspire. On second thought, perhaps it is better to follow the example of Sarutahiko and be ready to deal with an Ame no Uzume when she comes from the outside (Tsurumi 2001:120).

So we can be an Ame no Uzume, or discover numerous Uzume-type divas around us and appreciate them as the eight million *kami*, Amaterasu, and Sarutahiko all did.

NOTES

1. In Borgen and Ury, the subject of this sentence is translated as the plural "women weaving heavenly garments" (1990:70).

2. When Susa-no-o visits Amaterasu to bid her farewell, the latter is so alarmed that she dresses like a male warrior, armed with thousands of arrows and with her parted hair in two looped locks (Miura 2002:36–37; Heldt 2014:69).

3. Interpretations vary, as the text does not name the two deities that are assigned to look after what is now Ise Shrine. Miura follows Saigō Nobutsuna's interpretation that they are Ame no Uzume and Sarutahiko (Miura 2002:100n10),

whereas Heldt (2014:116) interprets them to be Omoikane and Ninigi. Philippi (1968:140n12) suggests that they may be the mirror and Omoikane.

4. An earlier version of this summary of Tsurumi's book was included in my paper presented at the 2011 AJLS conference (Aoyama 2012:213–15).

5. Presumably Shunsuke was with his father and sister or with his tutor, but this is not specified. It is also unclear to what extent he spoke and read English in 1937. In his recollection Shunsuke writes that he did not understand English at the time (Tsurumi 2015:229). There are a number of Australian newspaper articles published in 1937 that report on the activities of Yūsuke and Kazuko, but none mentions Shunsuke.

CHAPTER 3

Searching for Charisma
Queen Himiko

LAURA MILLER

AN ANCIENT DIVA

I sat in a rustic and cozy restaurant named Shinobuan Café, eating an unusual dish. The handmade pottery bowl contained a fragrant mix called *Himiko meshi* (Himiko cooked rice). It was a special type of *ankake* (thick sauce poured over ingredients), and the server assured me that the broth was handcrafted. The rice was covered with tiny tapioca pearls and dense brown consommé, with green onions and dried seaweed sprinkled on top. I saw another woman order it, and asked the master if it was a popular item. Yes, she said, many women order it when they come in for a special meal with friends. I asked about the name—Why Himiko? It's Himiko style, she said, because the rich broth brings up associations of earthy ancientness, it's easy to eat, and women like it. Her explanation had a weird logic that would only make sense in the larger context of cultural assumptions and local promotional campaigns. I was on a quest to discover why a hipster restaurant in a small town was naming things after a legendary female ruler from the third century. I also wanted to find out why so many other businesses, services, and events also claimed such a linkage.

   Himiko was the paramount chief of the earliest Japanese polity, described only briefly by Chinese historians in records like the *Wei zhi* (Record of Wei, compiled 233–297 CE).[1] In that account she is described as the supreme ruler of 100 chiefdoms, unmarried, and adept at magical

13. Himiko the shaman queen (Ohishi and Himekawa 2012:81).
Used with permission of Gakken Kyōiku Shuppan.

arts. She is the first Japanese person whose name was recorded in any historical record. Himiko claimed her place in history with religious authority, political acumen, and groundbreaking diplomacy. She was an "astute fringe neighbor" of the Chinese Wei court (Kidder 2007:53). Even so, her modern incarnations range from regally wise to insipidly cute. In contemporary media she is cast as an elder priestess or a beautiful shaman (Figure 13). At other times she plays the role of a lascivious sorceress. Historical *manga* (comics) are often kind to her, and feminists generally celebrate her as an effective ruler (Yoshie 2005, 2013), or as one of the heroines of Japan (Rekidama Henshūbu 2013). She morphs from ancient dictator to ditzy gal in video games and anime (Miller 2014a). Representations of Himiko fluctuate according to the historical era and the aims of her image makers. Some twenty-first-century culture producers, such as film, anime, and manga creators, see in Himiko an aberrant and unwise attribution of political authority to women. But in other settings, including the Shinobuan Café, she's a mighty girl who inspires positive admiration.

This chapter explores these many reinventions of Himiko in order to track how her varied iconography encodes assumptions about identity, gender, and history. My aim is to survey a few contemporary uses of Himiko as a diva and icon. She is not only used as an intriguing personality or character in media narratives, she is also a symbol representing ancient history, authenticity, and mystical power. Using ethnographic and cultural studies methods (collection and analysis of artifacts, texts, and representations), I investigate how Himiko is fashioned in popular sites such as restaurants, souvenir shops, divination services, and more. Ethnographic observations and informal conversations and interviews in the Kansai region (located in the southcentral part of the island of Honshū) allowed me to see on the ground how Himiko's image is used to promote local interests. In Nara Prefecture, I frequented Sakurai city and the town of Yamatokōriyama in order to talk to people in those communities and to see firsthand how Himiko is deployed. I also visited the Hashihaka Kofun (Chopsticks Tomb) in Sakurai, where many scholars believe Himiko was entombed. I spent time in the small town of Moriyama in Shiga Prefecture, where a competing theory places Himiko's headquarters. In addition, I mined texts, media, and Himiko representations in other parts of Japan that speak to audiences in search of pristine food culture or forms of female energy and spirituality. What makes her appealing to public audiences today? Is it that she was reportedly a shaman, a female ruler, or for some other trait? Which aspects of Himiko's hazy legend are modified or amplified in order to make her effective for contemporary promotional efforts or as a modern-day diva?

In the course of my quest, I discovered that Himiko provides rich fodder for contemporary regional boosterism as city mascot, beauty contest theme, and touristic motif. Several cities claim her as their very own emblem of local identity and historical authenticity. I found that she also gives foodies and health proponents a method to reintroduce ostensibly healthy food practices from the past. Finally, Himiko imagery is popular in New Age and occult domains, where she serves as a metaphor for female agency and innate magical abilities. What we know about Himiko is so provocative and blurry there is much room for creative intervention. Building on research on the creation and production of local community "tradition" (Robertson 1991), the pilgrimage industry and how it symbolizes cultural heritage (Reader 2005), and gender representation (Miller and Bardsley 2005), I draw on popular activities, public texts, and imagery in order to trace how the obscure yet tantalizing aspects of Himiko's ancient story contribute to the creation of contemporary Himiko personas and Himikoland places. In Himiko, we find a diva from the Japanese past colorfully alive in the present, her larger than life stature and magical allure lending new meanings eagerly adopted by a range of individuals and institutions.

PUTTING A DIVA TO WORK

According to the Chinese historians, Himiko unified a collection of small chiefdoms into a state confederation known as the country of Wa when she was a young woman, around 190 CE. She ruled until her death in 248 from her seat of power known as Yamatai. But where was her province of Yamatai located? Over the centuries competing theories have placed Yamatai in either north Kyūshū or the Kinki region. The debate over the location of her realm provides an opening for several cities to use her to buttress tourism and advance local pride. Two cities in present-day Nara Prefecture, Sakurai and Yamatokōriyama, have a long history of naming Himiko as their own diva queen. Another recent candidate in the Kinki region is the city of Moriyama in Shiga Prefecture, based on the so-called "Ōmi Theory" that locates Himiko's palace there (Sawai 2010; Gotō 2010). The strongest contender in this field is the site of the Hashihaka Kofun in Sakurai. It is officially identified as the burial of a shaman known as Yamato-totohi-momoso-hime-no-mikoto, the aunt of an emperor (Suijin). Although the consensus is that Himiko is interred here, one story connected to this royal princess is suppressed and does not become part of Himiko imagery in any local promotional drives. According to the Japanese chronicles, she wed a *kami* (deity) named Ōmononushi-nushi. On his nocturnal visits she could not clearly discern his appearance, so asked if she could view him in daylight. He warned her not to display shock if he did allow her to view him. He indicated that he would be found in her cosmetic case, and when, at daybreak, she opened it and saw a tiny snake, she let out a cry of astonishment. The *kami* transformed back into a human shape, explained that she had caused him great shame, then fled to Mt. Miwa. The princess was overcome with contrition, and committed suicide by stabbing herself in the genitals with a chopstick. When she was buried, her tomb became known locally as the Chopsticks Tomb or Hashihaka Kofun.

Himiko semiotics and promotional ecology is significant because she offers a contrast to the more commonly found male historical figures. For example, in Kyoto the dashing figure of an Edo-period samurai named Sakamoto Ryōma (1836–1867), who was involved in a plot to overthrow the Tokugawa Shogunate, became an enormous touristic magnet after a deluge of romanticized TV dramas, books, manga, and films about his life. Similarly, the Heian-era wizard Abe no Seimei (921–1005) was popularized in manga, novels, and film, bringing fresh troops of fans to his shrine in Kyoto in the early 2000s (Miller 2008c). We find other male personages such as the Buddhist saint Kōbō Daishi (774–835) used to promote the pilgrimage industry in Shikoku (Reader 2005), and the twentieth-century film character Tora-san, used to bring tourists to a museum and shops featuring him in Shibamata near Tokyo. Himiko, never deified as a *kami*, nevertheless became a diva representing all women in a field dense with famous men.

The first stop on my journey to find Himiko was Sakurai city, which is where Himiko is presented as the official city mascot. It is located in a mainly rural area with a population of less than 65,000, south of Nara but still within Nara Prefecture. Sakurai is one end point of perhaps the oldest walking trail in Japan, the Yamanobe Road. The trail rings the foothills of the Nara basin, wending through small farming hamlets while skirting ancient burial mounds and medieval temples and shrines. While walking around the commercial district near Sakurai station, I appreciated the long, light pink banners streaming from the fronts of various businesses, flapping in the wind. Each banner announced that the shop was a "premium business," and was decorated with the cute figure of Himiko-chan, the city mascot. Mascots such as this are often called *kyara* (characters). According to her profile, she is a twelve-year-old girl who likes sweets and games. She likes doing things at her own pace, and can be a tad lazy. She wears a white robe with a red sash, a large blue-beaded necklace, and a red headband with a pink flower.[2]

Seeing the pastel banners and adorable image of Himiko-chan in Sakurai reminds us of her status as a unique figure for interrogating and understanding how urban policy actors, local residents, and tourists mobilize different and perhaps conflicting visions of a selected mascot.

Civic leaders in Sakurai began vigorously promoting Himiko as their town mascot following news reports and scholarship indicating that Hashihaka Kofun is most likely her burial place.[3] *Kyara,* or amateur mascot characters, began to proliferate in the 2000s, most often taking the form of humanoid animals or objects. These *kyara* were different from professional commercial characters such as Hello Kitty. The *kyara* were created to represent a range of places or institutions, including parks, museums, landmarks, ski resorts, castles, airports, and police stations. The Tokyo Metropolitan Police Department even created their own mascot named Pipo-kun (he appears in the manga by the artist Rokudenashiko in this volume). Mascots that represent cities and towns (called *yuru kyara* or *gotōchi kyara*) were produced to boost tourism, local identity, and economic development (Occhi 2014). Supposedly, promoters went overboard, so there were threats of "mascot extermination" because of overpopulation (Ito 2015).

It is unlikely that Sakurai city will eliminate its beloved mascot, Himiko-chan. She greets tourists on maps and in shop displays. Signs around town exclaim "Welcome to Himiko country!" with the mascot's image. City officials promote Himiko-chan on the official town website, and sponsor a Himiko-chan Twitter account. The city's website features three short anime films, easy to click on and view.[4] In her various appearances on posters, maps, and elsewhere Himiko assumes one of her five official poses: basic, welcome, dancing, walking, and divination. Her menu of poses is variously deployed in promotions, animating her profile. There's also an older Auntie version of Himiko in the YouTube anime and on a few goods, such as cellphone straps. The city is happy to loan out their Himiko-chan *kigurumi,* a padded costume that turns the person wearing it into a massive plushy toy, to local civic groups for promotional events. Around the websphere there are many photographs of someone dressed up as a stuffed Himiko at picnics, festivals, and grand openings. Himiko-chan graces city bus schedules, contest flyers, and city posters and banners. At one Kintetsu bus stop, the information board says, "The bus for Himiko's village." Himiko's diva magic communicates Sakurai as a unique place, important in Japanese history, yet welcoming to visitors who want a sweet and simple version of Yamato, the name originally used for this area, and later by extension, for the ancient kingdom as a whole.

The Himiko mascot is an interesting case for a number of reasons. Her undeniable popularity in the Sakurai area highlights the mascot wars going on in other parts of Nara. Himiko is the only mascot in Sakurai, but within Nara Prefecture there have been more than sixty mascots in the pantheon. A few were failures that never caught on, such as Sento-kun described below; others are part of a continuing image battle among city factions. In addition, the fact that she is one of the few female mascots in Nara Prefecture marks her as unique. There is a strong identity in Sakurai as a place predating the establishment of Nara city (the old capital of Heijō). Having their own mascot that symbolizes this history makes sense, and new archeological work lends support to the Sakurai area as the location of Himiko's palace. Himiko frames Sakurai as the birthplace of the Yamatai province (and by extension, the Japanese state).

The rivalry among mascots within Nara city heated up after the creation of a mascot named Sento-kun. Nara created this particular mascot in 2010 to commemorate the 1300th anniversary of the ancient capital of Heijō. Sento-kun was greeted with derision, and many young women described him as *guro kawaii* (grotesque cute). The Buddhist monk-child with antlers sprouting from his head was unpopular, and different groups responded with their own Nara city mascots. There were several, but notable are Namu-kun, created by a Buddhist group who didn't like the freaky and blasphemous Sento-kun; Shikamaru-kun, a cute deer; and Manto-kun, a sort of blob. Outside Nara city are many other local mascots. The official mascot for the town of Kashihara is Sarara-chan, a vaguely creepy winged female celestial nymph (*tennyo*) with purple hair. She is part of a region-wide interest in the Tenpyō era (729~749 CE). However, at the Kashihara Archeological Institute Museum they made their own mascot. The museum has a fine collection of pottery figures called *haniwa*, which were used to decorate ancient tumuli (*kofun*). The mascot they created is named Iwamin, based on a *haniwa* excavated in Iwami. As fellow mascots from the ancient world, Himiko and Iwamin both establish the Nara region as the origin place for Japan's earliest civilization.

When I first exited the Sakurai station, after taking the Manyō-Mahoroba line of the JR (Japan Rail) system, I found Himiko right away. Walking out of the north exit, I encountered a sign with a painting of Himiko and the words "Himiko's Village" engraved in the wood. Across the street facing the station was a small shop named Mahoroba no Sato Himiko (Figure 14). *Mahoroba* is an old Yamato word meaning "surrounded by mountains," and later meant an idyllic location. It is used in the shop name to mean "Himiko's splendid old village." Three middle-aged women greeted me on my first visit to the shop, full of excitement that a foreigner was so interested in Himiko. They said they

14. Mahoroba no Sato Himiko, a small shop in Sakurai. Photo by L. Miller.

were volunteers from the Women's Auxiliary of the Sakurai City Chamber of Commerce, and were responsible for the operation and running of the shop. The Women's Auxiliary had solicited investment for a new corporation, Himiko Co. Ltd., which opened the shop in 2010. They sell local packaged goods and souvenirs, as well as ice cream, iced coffee, and freshly-made specialties such as skewers of small grilled rice dumplings (*mitarashi dango*) and grilled rice cakes skewered like popsicles (*gohei mochi*). Using Himiko and her "old village" of Yamatai creates a civic space that is different from the nearly exhausted *furusato* (old hometown) motif that characterized the Japanese media landscape for more than forty years. As Robertson (1988:37) noted in her study of civic reinvention and promotion, the concept of *furusato* had great potential to imbue localities with authenticity and sentimental old-timeyness. *Furusato* became a keyword in domestic tourism campaigns and in the construction of national nostalgia, and habitually appeared in commercials, advertisements, songs, films, and other media. But this concept does not capture the same sense of early Japanese origin myths and history as well as an icon like Himiko. Himiko is revered as a symbol of the misty past that predates the farm villages where ancestors once lived. She is both ancient and mysterious, not simply a form of nostalgia for the rural prewar past.

On the shelves of the Himiko shop were many souvenirs for sale, some of them adorned with the Sakurai city Himiko-chan mascot, such as barley and sweet potato liquor (*shōchū*), and thin wheat noodles (*sōmen*). The shop also sold steamed confectionery red bean paste buns stamped with an image of Himiko, Himiko-chan mascot dolls in three sizes, and Himiko-chan cellphone straps.[5] One unusual object was a small garish clay replica of Hashihaka Kofun with Himiko hovering over it. The ladies gave me extra Himiko-chan souvenir wrapping paper and a free cup of green tea. They also insisted on taking my photo outside where I placed my head in the life-sized *kaohame* standing cutout Himiko figure. They agreed with me about the cuteness and appropriateness of Himiko-chan as a representation of the birthplace of Yamato, and praised me for making the effort to visit Hashihaka Kofun.

Himiko also figures in the festivals (*matsuri*) and other events that are created to commemorate and celebrate local history, famous products, and artistic performances. These forms of visible culture are important components of the narratives people tell themselves about who they are as a community. Although beauty pageants often serve as affirmations of nationalism (Bardsley 2013), they may also be part of the configuration of unique local identities. For example, in California a Miss Gilroy Garlic Festival Queen is selected each year, partly based on her speech in praise of garlic, a major crop in the fields around the town of Gilroy. There are many local contests in Japan as well, and among them at least three communities host a Himiko contest as one method for formulating a distinctive profile.[6] These are not beauty pageants in the usual sense because their purpose is not for display of idealized female bodies, and most often a young woman who embodies wholesome girl-next-door femininity rather than beauty is selected to represent the community as the Queen Himiko. An important criterion is that the winner is willing to do extensive promotional work in the local area, and the entrance forms and interviews stress this requirement.

To see such a contest, I ventured to another location within Nara Prefecture. The town of Yamatokōriyama is located just south of Nara city, with a population of less than 100,000. It is a modern city with industrial plants for Panasonic and Sharp. Tourism is also an important industry, so there is promotion of goldfish cultivation, a trade originating there in

1724, with contests and festivals. The town is also the site of Koriyama Castle, built in the sixteenth century, traditional indigo dyeing workshops, and many Edo-period shrines and temples. Additionally, it hosts a Queen Himiko contest. In 1982, Yamatokōriyama established the contest based on an author's contention that this is the site of Yamatai (Torigoe 1975). There are other Himiko contests in Japan (including one in Moriyama, discussed below), but the one in Yamatokōriyama is the oldest.

From 1982 until 2014, the Himiko contest was a public event held in October. The promotional posters were beautifully artistic, featuring a profile of a young woman with long unbound hair wearing a headband. When I visited in 2015, I learned that the city would no longer hold the contest as a public event. They would solicit applications from young women interested in serving as Queen Himiko, and interviews and selection of the queen would be done in private meetings. I asked city workers about this change, but they were unable to give me an adequate reason. Apparently, the flooding of news about Hashihaka Kofun in Sakurai as the most likely candidate for Himiko's grave has usurped Yamatokōriyama's claim. The poster advertising the revamped semi-secret contest also offers a clue to how city planners wanted to recast the event (Figure 15). It features an image of Himiko dressed in post-Kofun era clothing with her hair in a bun characteristic of the Tenpyō era. After Kyoto set the stage with its enormously successful tourism effort that allows anyone to dress up as an apprentice geisha for the day (Bardsley 2011), Nara came up with its own version of historical costume play. A shop in Nara's tourist center has been doing a thriving business selling Tenpyō era dress-up gear to tourists. There are several options on the menu, a choice of Tenpyō hair styles (either a decorated bun or two little ponytails) and make-up. Another type of dress up involves donning the type of clothing that might have been worn in Himiko's time, the late Yayoi and early Kofun eras. But since there are different reconstructions of what these styles may have looked like, the imagination takes center stage in most Himiko reenactments.

Next I ventured on to the town of Moriyama in Shiga Prefecture, because it also has a claim to Himiko. It is a smallish city (population less than 80,000) on the east side of Lake Biwa, around twenty minutes northeast of Kyoto. It was once part of the historic Ōmi Province and was a lodging stop on one of the major routes during the Edo period, the Nakasendō. One of the town's main shopping areas has the feel of a 1960s district, with many Mom and Pop stores interspersed with newer bakeries and restaurants that line both sides of the street. Moriyama also

15. Queen Himiko contest poster. Used with permission of the Yamatokōriyama City Tourist Association.

sponsors a Miss Queen Himiko contest, fondly nicknamed "Himikon." The name is a clipped form of Himiko and *kontesuto* (contest). Himikon explicitly promotes the Ōmi theory that establishes ancient Yamatai in present-day Moriyama.

Himikon was revamped in 2015 after being held as a more traditional contest. When the contest was inaugurated in 2011, the male city planners invested great energy in commissioning the Himiko costume to be worn by the winner. There were many news releases showing a group of men ringed around a gauzy, disembodied Himiko dress. The discussions and troubles regarding the execution of the dress design, created by a Moriyama designer named Mama Riina, occasionally appeared in social media and other commentary. The designer's goal of using authentic textiles and colors, such as a shawl the color of red sludge, apparently clashed with the male city workers' dream costume. After a few years of having the selected Himiko wear the official outfit, the contest was changed to something of a performative "cosplay fashion show." In promotional materials the organizers state that they are "looking for a charming, lively and lovely modern Himiko." Each contestant creates her own homemade costume, and sponsors as well as the participants now see it as a fun dress-up event that takes place during the town's annual Summer Festival. This shift reduces the retro aspect of old-style beauty contests. The amateur results are entertaining, although occasionally reflecting anachronism, with contestants wearing kimono or Nara-period garb. Because Himiko lived during a transitional time between two named historical eras that covers roughly 600 years, the clothing and hairstyles associated with her can vary greatly in media representations as well as in the public imagination. Contestants, sponsors, and audience are aware that most likely Himiko resided in Sakurai, but the Ōmi theory is an angle that allows for a pleasant civic ritual that features an activity enjoyed by many young women. Historical accuracy seems to be less relevant than creating a fun atmosphere. A waitress and other young women told me that the contest, held in the area in front of the Moriyama train station, is entertaining and enjoyable, with lots of joking and irreverence. The promotional flyers and application forms make it clear that the contest is designed to promote Moriyama. Winners are expected to do emotional labor for the community, described as the "village where Himiko sleeps." The official website urges Himiko participants to "use your smiling face to make Moriyama lively."[7]

INGESTING ANTIQUITY AND EATING LIKE A DIVA

In the course of my hunt for Himiko, I found that she is also associated with food, and that this is another aspect of her contemporary diva-hood. The history of Japanese food is often retold through the nation-alistic lens of *washoku* (Japanese cuisine), a reified and modern view of "traditional" food. Early Japanese people borrowed the Chinese con-cept of the "Five Grains," a grouping of staple crops that varied over time and often included beans. The Five Grains appeared in the *Kojiki* (Record of ancient matters, completed in 712 CE). In one story, the brother of the Sun Goddess Amaterasu, Susa-no-o, demanded food from another goddess named Ōgetsuhime, a deity of food. Various edi-ble things spewed forth from her body, which offended him so much he killed her. Grains and other items were then discharged from her corpse: rice came out of her eyes, millet from her ears, red beans from her nose, barley and wheat from her genitals, and soybeans from her anus. The story tells us that many types of grains were valued in the ancient period. Yet, over the centuries white rice took center stage.

Most people in Japan grew up with the idea that short grain white rice has always been at the core of the Japanese diet. In recent decades, heath experts became aware of archaeological evidence that during Himiko's time people ate *akamai* (red rice, also called *akagome*) or *zak-kokumai* (multigrain rice, red rice mixed with other grains). Other important grains that were eaten together with or in place of rice were *hie* (barnyard millet), *kibi* (broomcorn, egg millet, or proso millet), *awa* (foxtail millet), *mugi* (barley), and *soba* (buckwheat).[8] Red rice was originally used in Shinto ritual events, but over time it was replaced with white rice steamed together with azuki beans, giving it a similar mauve color. Called *sekihan* (red rice), this type of white rice dish is eaten at holiday celebrations and birthdays. White rice also has a long history of symbolic meanings of national identity, affluence, and purity (Ohnuki-Tierney 1994).

Health writers are recommending that people switch to nonwhite varieties of rice or other grains in order to access better nutrients. Yet eating nonwhite rice varieties, as well as millet and barley, has associa-tions of wartime deprivation. White rice had long been the preferred type, associated with urban life and higher social class. Indeed, during the Meiji era (1868–1912) the military promised new conscripts daily rations of white rice as an enticement. Before that, people in rural areas or from non-samurai backgrounds ate a diet in which rice was perhaps half the starch consumed, the other half made up of millet, barley, wheat, and sweet potatoes (Cwiertka 2006:66). As Rath (2015) notes, mixed grains and rustic foods were disdained as lowbrow and unpalatable. Himiko is therefore a productive hook for shifting the old associated meanings of nonwhite rice grains to positive images of Japaneseness and historical legitimacy. Her ancient food will serve as a link to new connotations of sustainable agriculture, organic farming, better health, and ancient Japan. Convincing people to think beyond white rice therefore involves manipulation of the discourse surrounding Japanese food, and entails more than simply touting its healthful properties from a scientific stance.

In attempts to transform narratives about national food, writers and advocates look to archeological and historical studies of prehistoric and early eras for inspiration and guidance. One result is a Japanese version of the Paleo Diet. Popular in the United States, the food regimen is founded on the premise that humans evolved with a diet rich in meat, seafood, and vegetables, and that we should therefore return to a preagricultural nutritional pattern and eliminate grains, dairy, and all the other foods of civilization. In Japan, the Himiko Super Longevity Diet (*Himiko supā chōju shoku*) does not reject agricultural foods, but it similarly works on the principle that modern people should eat the same foods as did people in the ancient past. The Himiko Diet has been described in several places, and stock photos of a bucolic food display often accompany the author's presentation. Ancient food needs a little aesthetic positioning in order to be appealing. In a book on the cultural history of food, Nagayama Hisao (2010:20–21) includes a gorgeous full-page photo of Himiko's feast, beautifully staged in rustic, earth-colored pottery bowls and artfully arranged on a reed mat. In his article on Yayoi era food, Matsugi Takehiko (2013) also includes the same photo.

On Himiko's menu we find walnuts, mountain potatoes, steamed burdock root, grilled sweetfish, salt, red rice mixed with millet, *wakame* seaweed with a condiment called *hishio* (or *mamebishio*), soybeans, wild rocambole (garlic), tiny purple vine potatoes called *mukago*, and clam soup. The people of Himiko's time also ate other types of soups, many boiled vegetables, raw side dishes, sardines, and other seafood. In his survey of early eating habits in Japan, Hirono (2012) lists the many plentiful vegetables, grains, seafood, meat, and fruits that made up the everyday diets from the Jōmon to the Heian eras. Hirono's book, *What Did Himiko Eat?* promotes the philosophy *ishoku dōgen*, which means something like "eat well to be well." Hirono admonishes readers to "resurrect the ancient dining table now!" He is joined by other authors with the same message (Kanaseki 1999, Nagayama 1997); there's even one for schoolchildren (Sumita 1996).

Similar to the Paleo Diet, the Himiko Diet is a form of displacement of modern food worries onto an imagined period when humans ate natural food perfectly suitable to their innate conditions. Food concepts such as the Paleo Diet promote ideas perceived as missing in contemporary life (Knight 2011:706). Such diets can be modernized as a celebration of ethnic identity and nationhood. In his cultural history of food, Nagayama (2010) juxtaposes the admirable Himiko Diet against Western ways of eating, which purportedly do not include things such as raw foods and vegetable soups. He writes, "Even Queen Himiko is thought to have eaten uncooked food and vegetable soup. Therefore, people who have become accustomed to a Western diet should assimilate to ancient Japanese eating style and its benefits" (Nagayama 2010:9). The Himiko Diet is as much a theory of what it is to be Japanese as advice for better food choices. It also reflects anxiety about modern food, spurred on by Japan's food poisoning scandals and radiation fears.[9]

Some agricultural associations and organic farmers in and beyond the Kansai region have used Himiko to imprint their artisanal rice products as organic, GMO free, and ancestrally significant. In place of white rice, the Himiko Diet features varieties of red rice and other nonwhite varieties, so it is not surprising that *kodaimai* (ancient rice) is experiencing something of a revival (Itoh 2013).[10] For example, the Lake Otsu Agricultural Cooperative has a few dedicated webpages devoted to Himiko foods, such as Himiko's fermented soybean soup and Himiko's ginger.[11] Organic farmers often use Himiko in their advertising and product development campaigns. A rice dealer in Nagasaki Prefecture hosts the Himiko Cafe online store. They sell rice, *amazake* (sweet rice wine), and other products named Himiko that are made with rice, including shampoo and rice bran soap.[12] Maeda Beikokuten in Kumamoto sells a rice cake made of black rice that is named Himiko, describing it as the taste of ancient rice and full of nutrition.[13] The Aso Design Farm in Kumamoto Prefecture sells nonwhite rice packs that they link to Himiko in an unusual manner. They claim to be exclusive in using a soil mineral named limonite that purportedly Himiko gave to the Chinese Wei court as tribute.[14] The Archaeological Museum at Yamaguchi University periodically holds red rice sowing events at which participants and staff, wearing Yayoi clothing, scatter the rice seeds over a dedicated plot. In autumn the rice is harvested with Yayoi period tools, and cooked in clay pots based on an ancient design.

Himiko's imprint is also used to boost Japan's flagging sake industry. Because the Chinese historians noted that Himiko's people "are fond of sake" (Kidder 2007:15), many purveyors of alcohol use Himiko in their product names. An example is Tanzan Himiko Ancient Rice Sake, made from red rice or ancient rice (*kodaimai*).[15] Ikinokura Distillery in Nagasaki makes Himiko's Dream (Himiko no Yume), and the Hinatayama Jōzō distillery in Kagoshima makes Himiko Fantasia, both distilled liquors (*shōchū*). The distillery advertises that "In the name, which harkens back to Himiko, queen of Yamataikoku in ancient Japan, one can feel the pride in this shochu as Japan's national liquor."[16]

Himiko is one of a range of attributes in the Kansai area that are available for promotional exploitation, but few can match the value of ancientness she represents. She is used as an endorsement for many food products in order to mark them as tied to a specific locale that is claiming identity as Yamatai, her domain. In Nara city there is a souvenir shop named Ezuya, which sells character goods and merchandise featuring popular Nara mascots, including Sento-kun, Iwamin, and Himiko-chan. The shop holds a Most Popular Souvenir contest each week, and ranks the best-selling items in a special section of the store. In one week during October 2015 the number-five item was Himiko Love Sōmen, a single serving of the thread-like white wheat noodles. The package was adorned with Himiko-chan holding a purification wand (her official divination pose), with white zigzagging paper streamers. *Sōmen* noodles have been produced for more than 1,200 years in the town of Miwa, a spot approximately one hundred meters from the Hashihaka Kofun. Another popular item is Himiko Five Color Sōmen (Figure 16). The thin wheat strands are pigmented with flavorings from purple yam, egg, green tea, and plum in addition to the plain version. On the manufacturer's website they claim that "Freshly five-colored hand-pulled *sōmen,* born at the foot of Mount Miwa, the land of Himiko, allows you to experience beauty and ancient times," and that the noodles are "based on the idea of Himiko being the embodiment of Yin-Yang and the five elements."[17] It isn't simply noodles, however, that are linked to Himiko.

The city leaders of Moriyama in Shiga came up with the idea of asking local shops to create an original Himiko-themed dish or other item in order to "spread the romance of Moriyama's history" and to "support the Ōmi Theory of Yamataikoku" that asserts that Himiko reigned

16. Himiko Five Color Sōmen with the Himiko-chan mascot on packaging. Photo by L. Miller.

in present-day Shiga Prefecture (Gotō 2010, Sawai 2010). The result was the Moriyama Himiko map, a guide to the businesses that participated in the campaign (Figure 17). There are numerous cafes and restaurants that support this Himiko scheme by featuring named or themed items on their menus, such as a Himiko hot pot, Himiko *dorayaki* (a red-bean pancake), and Himiko parfait. I set out to visit each of the twenty restaurants and bars on the Himiko map that offer Himiko-themed items.[18]

In Moriyama I ate the Himiko omelet rice at Café Ponte. When I asked Erika, my waitress, why it's Himiko style, she said it's because it's cute. At the Mon Reve bakery I learned that they only make the Himiko *magatama* (curved bead) cookies in summer or made to order.[19] The Tanaka *dorayaki* shop also told me they only make Himiko-themed items during the summer festival. The Aoigatsu cafe couldn't make the Himiko parfait because they were out of strawberries. However, the bars

17. Moriyama Himiko map, a guide to businesses with Himiko-themed offerings.

in the area cheerfully made Himiko cocktails, which did not have anything in common other than the fact that they contained alcohol. Interestingly, it was at the two female-run establishments, Shinobuan Café (the place where I ate Himiko cooked rice), and Café Ponte, that the staffs were still eagerly engaged with Himiko PR. In most cases, the Himiko food item had little or no link to the historical Himiko or the food she might have eaten. Moriyama and Sakurai both eschewed the great effort that would be required if they tried to produce heritage food commodities such as ancient fermented soybeans or red rice (an exception might be Miwa *sōmen*). Instead, they used Himiko's name and image to spice up existing commodities. The Himiko food map with its cute *magatama* cookies and Himiko parfaits and cocktails also avoids some of the pitfalls that other local revitalization efforts have encountered, including a potential for "cloying sentimentality" (Kelly 1986:614). Uses of Himiko in these food and drink offerings are humorous and saucy. She lends an air of playfulness and a lack of pretension. Himiko did not eat *magatama*-shaped cookies or drink cocktails, so the invented nature of this campaign is available in advance, allowing customers to enjoy the obvious fakeness and fabrication.

These efforts at ancestral connoisseurship create ingestible links to history and to the charm of Himiko and her time. In addition to her status as a link to discourse about ancient or local cuisine, Himiko has become a resource for feminists and New Age spiritualists as the reigning diva of magical power and female rulership. She props up interest in women's history and the occult in girl's culture.

THE NEW AGE HIMIKO

Himiko was relatively unknown to the public before 1945, yet by 2007, 99 percent of schoolchildren recognized her name (Yoshie 2013:6). Prior to the end of the war, the fascist government only allowed the teaching of the native mythological histories that contained no mention of Himiko (*Kojiki* and *Nihon shoki*). The earlier Chinese sources, which the compilers of these mytho-histories themselves consulted, were banned from the classroom. After the war the Chinese accounts of early Japan became part of the history curriculum. The story of Himiko offered a tantalizing vision of a powerful woman with a spectacular life. Thereafter Himiko became a popular character in girl's manga from at least the 1970s, and she made an appearance in other media such as film and writing as well. For example, a sweet representation is found in a girl's monthly magazine, in a story about a contemporary girl who is able to channel the historic Himiko, and learns that the ancient queen had to forsake true love out of duty as a ruler (Kaze 1974). Himiko continues to be something of a problem for Japanese nationalists, not only because she is not mentioned in the *Kojiki* or the *Nihon shoki,* but also because she disrupts the myth of an unbroken male line of rulers. However, young women not worried about debates about the imperial line are happy to claim Himiko as their own symbol. She is a "charisma queen" (Rekishi no Shinsō Kenkyūkai 2012:302), an emblem of female power and supernatural skill. The English word "charisma" was borrowed into Japanese and used in a new manner to refer to someone, usually a woman, who is an expert in a particular role. In this case, "charisma queen" boosts the idea that Himiko was an exceptional ruler and an alluring diva.

Continuing on my mission to find Himiko, I returned to the Sakurai area in order to again visit the Hashihaka Kofun. Once you exist the Makimuku station and are on the street an enormous green mound can be seen rising beyond the nearby houses. It is a lush tree-covered tumulus in the shape of a keyhole, 280 meters long and rising up 30 meters high. The tomb is in the Makimuku ruins, one of the earliest of the tumuli that characterize the area. It is designated as the burial place of the royal princess Yamato-totohi-momoso-hime-no-mikoto, whose story of marriage to the snake deity was told above. Tombs named as containing remains of emperors or their family members came under the jurisdiction of the Imperial Household in 1871, which has since forbidden all forms of excavation.[20] But some of the nearby nonroyal tombs have been entered, and there is a good sense of what the tomb might contain. Typical artifacts include Chinese bronze mirrors, swords, ritual implements, and *magatama* beads. *Magatama* is the name for curved beads found in many ancient archeological sites, especially those associated with the Yayoi and Kofun periods.

Joining scholars in their fascination with these early tombs are members of the general public. A blues singer who adopted the nom de plume Marikofun claims to have visited more than a thousand ancient tombs throughout Japan. Marikofun and other culture producers use Himiko and her era to suit their own projects. According to her origin story Marikofun became fascinated by the tombs after visiting the *kofun* of Emperor Nintoku in Sakai, the largest keyhole-shaped tumulus in Japan. Standing next to it she felt frustrated that she had no real sense of its shape or size. Since then she has published three guides, all cutely decorated with charming drawings and handwritten script, that are a combination of reverence, information, and intentional kitsch (Marikofun 2015, 2014a, 2014b). There are photographs of each *kofun* with Marikofun posing next to it, wearing her version of Himiko-wear. She also released a music album and video, runs an interesting blog, and gives performances at local festivals where she belts out impressive soul.[21]

Marikofun founded a group called Kofun ni Kōfun Kyokai (Association for Excitement about Tombs), using the near homonyms for "tomb" and "excitement." Her blog tells readers about the latest archeological news, museum exhibits, and where to buy goods such as *kofun*-shaped cakes and cushions. Marikofun designs and wears dramatic outfits over her commanding physique. One ensemble consists of a flowing, diaphanous forest green robe layered over a light beige under-robe, and tied with a large white bow in the front. Descending from the bow is a long white sash with the image of a *kofun* decorating the bottom edge. She wears a headdress with little cutout shapes of *kofun* and *magatama* that dangle over her forehead. Marikofun wrote about Hashihaka Kofun in her book devoted to the tumuli of Nara, and as with all the *kofun*, she provides basic statistics about size, height, and location. She does not discuss the story about the name of the tomb, however. One of her recommendations when visiting is to eat Miwa *sōmen* (Miwa noodles). In her notes she writes: "The idol of the *kofun* world! It has both the perfect body and the keyhole shape. It's really beautiful and cute no matter which side you view it from. How cool would it be if it does turn out to be Himiko's tomb" (Marikofun 2015:40).

It is a charming tomb, with a small pond on one side, a small garden and rice field located at another end, and a line of houses along the road that runs next to it. As I trudged through the overgrown brush and fallen branches on one side of the Hashihaka Kofun, I encountered slithering snakes who ran across my path more than once. They were small and quick, and I couldn't help but recall the tale about the snake deity who was the consort of the entombed woman. There is a house on the other side that has been transformed into a Himiko-themed business. It is named Jade Garden Himiko's Garden and is a cafe, shop, and garden space in the lower level of a regular house found in the row that rings the tomb. The main business is selling newly manufactured *magatama* stones and *magatama* jewelry, which are often romanticized as a symbol of Himiko and her magical powers. At Jade Garden, Himiko's Garden the *magatama* are made of Itoigawa jade from Niigata. (During Himiko's time *magatama* were made of jadite and other materials; it was not until the late Kofun era that jade became common.) The woman running the shop is named Masako, and she is fervent about creating beauty and peaceful spaces. Her narrow shop is a dainty and bright New Age space with the beautiful small garden overlooking the pond that edges one side of the tomb. There is a Himiko's Garden calligraphy art piece on one wall, small Bodhisattva Kannon altars, plants, and *magatama* jewelry displays along the white walls. Masako doesn't see herself as a salesperson but rather an advocate for the magical and spiritual qualities of the jade *magatama*, because, she added "jade is a mysterious stone." Indeed, her space and the atmosphere she created is markedly serene. I ordered an iced coffee to sip while sitting in the small single-table area just outside the shop door, facing Hashihaka Kofun. Masako invited me to stroll in the jade garden, a space she created with huge boulders placed along the rim of the tomb's pond. She said the garden of Himiko is jade, but the tomb itself is the main garden.

Masako's modern *magatama* business is not that unusual. Both Himiko and *magatama* are common themes found in the booming divination industry that is dominated by women and girls (Miller 2014b). The curved bead is popular in girl culture, sold in DIY shops and specialty stores, and featured in the divination industry. *Magatama* are the topic of feature stories in divination magazines produced by and for women. Advertisements for *magatama* most often refer to Himiko or link the power of the stone to her story.[22] Since around 2000 *magatama* began appearing on charms sold at Shinto shrines, and in Kansai area tourist shops.

The *Wei zhi* makes it clear that Himiko was not only a political leader, but a shaman specialist with ritual skills. This aspect of her profile is of great interest to women and girls attracted to the occult and the divination arts. Once I met a divination specialist in Shibuya who offered past life readings and other types of spiritual services. She explained that she was simply continuing the craft that is associated with the celebrated Queen Himiko. Some divination providers go one step further and say they are a reincarnation of Himiko. Hieda On Mayura, author of numerous divination books and articles, maintains that Himiko was reborn in her body.[23]

Extending from her use as an icon for divination service providers, Himiko makes a stunning appearance as a core figure in Japan-made Tarot cards (Miller 2011, Miller 2017). Artists substitute Himiko for the High Priestess (the Papess or female Pope), a card prototype meant to symbolize female religious authority. Occasionally, Himiko is cast in a humorous light, or as a bad girl icon to be emulated for her boldness. For example, in one playful divination book entitled *Akujō uranai* (Poison woman divination, Fumiko and Noguchi 2011), the authors present several famous women from history as model types. One is Villainess Type Himiko, who is described as a divination maniac and self-centered narcissist. In addition to her presence in New Age and divination contexts, Himiko surfaces in many other popular culture domains. The aggressive, fearless side of Himiko is emphasized in many cultural products loved by women. She has been used as a Takenokozoko dance troupe name in the 1970s, and a lesbian bar event. Himiko is the name of the legendary unifier of the Pony-tails, an all-girl biker gang in the cult film and novel *Kamikaze Girls*.[24]

There is a dark, hidden side to Himiko lore that is exploited in manga, novels, anime, and other media, where she is depicted in highly eroticized ways and tied to murky occult practices (Miller 2014a). But civic planners, community product marketers, contest organizers, and others are reluctant to explicitly acknowledge or exploit aspects of her legend that are associated with dangerous sorcery, control over others, and unsupervised sexuality. The story of the suicide of the Yamato prin-cess is not mentioned, and no shop exploits her in order to sell chop-sticks. Similar to the diva of the world of opera, the diva Himiko is only used to support selected operations. As Koestenbaum (1993:102) writes of the operatic version, "Divas, like gay people, fall under the sign of the sick, the maimed, the deranged. The diva is associated with disease and with injuries that prevent adequate voice production. . . . The diva supports cosmologies, and she shatters them." Himiko, like Izanami (discussed by Rebecca Copeland in Chapter 3), is contaminated by her connection to damage to the genitals. Nevertheless, her corporeal link to the body, to food, and her command of the physical world through her shaman skills continue to surface in female-oriented cultural prod-ucts and services.

Himiko is a modern folk celebrity and powerful diva from the ancient world. She drives the creation of other divas. Marikofun, Mama Riina, New Age Masako, and others are divas too, pulling mojo and inspira-tion from their Himiko imaginaries. They create versions of Himiko that city fathers do not necessarily want, and that are not what nation-alistic historians like. They and others are taking history away from the academy and using Himiko's legend for their own fantasies and artistic visions. Himiko attracts creative souls, those who have unbounded dreams and visions not contained by normative notions about women and their proper roles and concerns. Himiko can be as irreverent, dan-gerous, and uncontrollable as one wants her to be. Himiko's nebulous prehistoric domain allows a type of diva agency rarely accomplished by other icons or divas. We find Himiko in a spectrum of cultural products where her presence is expanded through forms of "diva prose," writ-ings penned by fans (Koestenbaum 1993).

Himiko has become an ingestible link to both health and history. She is commodified and objectified in small towns as a touchstone for promotion of commerce and community character.

Her cultural presence in New Age and occult domains joins more pragmatic uses of her persona in civic boosterism and food and diet promotional efforts. Even museums and scholars will use her image to highlight their collections of ancient artifacts and novel theories about them. At the Kyoto National Museum, a replica of a Chinese bronze mirror was dubbed "Himiko's magic mirror" and promoted in an experiment using its reflection to support the claim that it is a special type of reflecting mirror (*Kyodo News* 2014). Her appearance in everyday venues such as tourist kiosks, museums, restaurants and cafes, as well as more unique locales such as divination services and New Age shops, attests to the great malleability afforded by her beguiling diva image.

NOTES

Over the years many hosts invited me to speak about Himiko on their campuses, including Laura Hein at Northwestern University and Jennifer Robertson at the University of Michigan. For this version of Himiko research I am most grateful for the comments from Jan Bardsley and Rebecca Copeland. I also owe sincere thanks to the Japan Foundation for a 2015 Short-Term Research Fellowship for the project Himiko Boosterism in the Kansai Region.

1. It has not been determined what the proto-Japanese language of Himiko's people sounded like, so the pronunciation of her name might have been different.

2. Asakura in Kyushu also has a Himiko mascot named Himiko-chan. In their version, she is an adult who wears red and white robes, pink *magatama* (curved bead) necklace, and a white headband over a double-looped hairstyle (one normally worn by men, called *mizura*).

3. For more on the archaeology of Yamatai, see Watanabe (2008) and Kidder (2007).

4. Sakurai City official webpage online at http://www.city.sakurai.lg.jp/himiko /index.html [accessed 20 May 2016].

5. A line of similar Himiko character goods are sold at the Yoshinogari ruins in Kyushu. They include a Hello Kitty Himiko cellphone strap, crackers, and liquor.

6. Another Himiko contest takes place in the town of Asakura in Kyūshū as part of their Yamataikoku Festival of Flowers.

7. Moriyama Himiko Contest online at http://moriyama-himiko.jp/himikon .html [accessed 20 May 2016].

8. Among the Jōmon people there is evidence of some plant domestication and resource management of burdock, walnuts, shiso, leek, barnyard grass, adzuki beans, and soybeans (Hirono 2012). It is not clear how much of that food culture was adopted by the Yayoi people.

9. There have been a series of food safety scandals in Japan in recent decades. These included a Snow Brand milk poisoning case in 2000, contaminated imported dumplings in 2008, and fears of radiation-tainted food from Fukushima following the 2011 tsunami and nuclear reactor disaster.

10. Gyōdo city in Saitama Prefecture (famous for rice paddy art) began a campaign to promote both the *kofun* in the area and the varieties of rice offered by local growers. Their Sakitama Kofun Park contains nine large *kofun* and a museum (*magatama*-making is one of the experiential activities offered at the museum). In 2012, they introduced Saitama Tomb Gyōda Ancient Rice Curry, in which fourteen local restaurants and one food truck made versions of curry rice, shaping the rice to look like a keyhole shape tomb. The rice was promoted as ancient rice, and consisted of black rice, red rice, or a mixture of nonwhite rice.

11. The Lake Otsu Agricultural Cooperative (Rēku Otsu Nōgyō Kyōdō Kumiai) online at http://lakeootu.jp/index.html [accessed 20 May 2016].

12. Himiko Cafe online at http://himikocafe18.net/ [accessed 20 May 2016].

13. Maeda Beikokuten online at http://www.maedanokomeya.jp/products /himiko.php [accessed 20 May 2016].

14. Aso Design Farm online at http://www.kyushu-brand.co.jp/SHOP/38334 /46792/list.html [accessed 20 May 2016].

15. Tanzan Himiko Ancient Rice Sake online at http://www3.kcn.ne.jp /~noyori/cgi-bin/item.cgi?item_id = nara75&ctg_id = nara&page = 1 [accessed 20 May 2016].

16. Himiko's Dream liquor is sold through the Wonder 500 Project, a government Cool Japan initiative to promote regional products to foreigners. Online at https://thewonder500.com/product/himiko-no-yume-shochu-a-distilled-sake-from-the-iki-region/?lang = en [accessed 20 May 2016].

17. Miwa Sōmen Yamamoto online at http://www.miwa-somen.jp/item/626 .html [accessed 20 May 2016].

18. Two of the shops sell goods rather than food or drink. At the Maeda shop I purchased a Himiko t-shirt, and the owners excitedly gave me another copy of the Himiko map and telephoned other shops to see who was open.

19. Other towns are using Kofun era imagery such as tombs, *magatama* (curved bead), and Himiko, to sell a variety of goods. The Petit Marche bakery in Nara also sells *magatama* cookies, available in three flavors: brown rice, green tea, and purple sweet potato. The bakery also makes a *kofun* cake. Another shop, Ichigo in Niigata, sells *magatama* cookies. Instructions for making *magatama* molds for candy and cookies are easy to find online.

20. It is claimed that the tombs are sacred because they contain the spirits of imperial ancestors. Scholars assume that the ban is partly because many of the tombs have been randomly attributed to mythological emperors, and verification is not desired. In addition, the archeology strongly indicates that early Yamato royalty were linked to a dynasty on the Korean peninsula.

21. Her CD is entitled "Excited About Kofun" (*Kofun de kōfun*, Marikofun 2014c). Her blog is *Kofun shingā Marikofun no tsūkai kofun ni kōfun nikki* (Diary of *kofun* singer Marikofun's thrilling excitement about *kofun*). Online at http://marikofun.cocolog-nifty.com/blog/ [accessed 20 May 2016].

22. In girl culture texts, there is rarely mention of the status of a *magatama* as one of the Three Sacred Treasures (Sanshu no Jingi), which according to legend were brought to earth by the grandson of the Sun Goddess Amaterasu.

23. Hieda On Mayura, Genzai no Himiko (The current Himiko). It is interesting that for her middle name she uses the Sanskrit symbol for "om." Online at http://mayura.pocke.bz/index.php?uid=NULLGWDOCOMO&mmmsid =mayura&actype=page&page_id=sys_top [accessed 27 Dec 2017].

24. The novel by Takemoto Nobara (2008), *Shimotsuma monogatari,* was renamed *Kamikaze Girls* when adapted for the screen and released as a film outside Japan.

CHAPTER 4

Izumo no Okuni Queers the Stage

BARBARA HARTLEY

Izumo no Okuni (1572–?) was a cross-dressing woman whose sensational dance performances took the sophisticated audiences of early 1600s Kyoto by storm. Said to have been a *miko* (shrine attendant) from the Grand Shrine of Izumo sent with a dance troupe to the capital to raise alms, Okuni was first known for her performance of the *nenbutsu odori*, a dance based on the prayer for entry to the Buddhist Pure Land. This chapter profiles the representation of the diva, Okuni, given in Ariyoshi Sawako's (1969) historical novel, *Izumo no Okuni*, which imaginatively narrates Okuni's life from the time of her arrival in Kyoto, with flashbacks to her childhood years. Arioshi's work was translated into English by prominent kabuki scholar James R. Brandon, and titled *Kabuki Dancer* (Ariyoshi 1994). Appropriating the religious *nenbutsu odori* as secular entertainment and replacing the lyrics annually with the words of a "current hit" song is merely one of many fictional creative initiatives attributed by Ariyoshi to this gifted artistic innovator and entrepreneur (Ariyoshi 1994:194). Named in the novel as "the best in the world" (Ariyoshi 1994:204), Ariyoshi's Okuni performed, like her real-life model, for audiences of all social ranks in sites around Kyoto such as the dry river bed, or *kawara,* of the Kamo River.

Historical data on Okuni is scant. Ruth Shaver (1966:35) notes that since most available information is based on legend, it is difficult to know "accurately where fiction ends and truth begins." While Shaver makes a number of dismissive statements about this dancing diva, novelist Ariyoshi—herself one of postwar Japan's great divas—is strongly attracted by the allure of the Okuni legend. A meticulous researcher who trawled archives for information on her fictional representations, in her speculative account of Okuni's life Ariyoshi also surely sought to understand elements of her own experience as a widely feted writer throughout the 1960s and 1970s. The lack of a reliable historical record opens Okuni's narrative to multiple interpretations. Nevertheless, as the onetime editorial assistant for the magazine *Engeki kai* (Theatre world) and personal assistant to Azuma Tokuho (1909–1998), leader of the all-women Azuma Kabuki troupe, Ariyoshi was particularly qualified to write about the kabuki diva Okuni. After serialization in *Fujin kōron* (Women's review), Ariyoshi's narrative was published in book form in 1969. All citations below come from Brandon's 1994 English translation of Ariyoshi's novel.

In Ariyoshi's account, one of Okuni's most famous performance strategies was to "queer" her routines by appearing in exotic male dress. In the second half of this discussion, I probe Okuni's diva desire to choreograph roles for herself as a dandy about town decked in the extravagant "Southern Barbarian" attire inspired by the rich brocades and velvets favored by Europeans who visited Japan at the time. In discussing this "queering" of premodern dance forms, I draw on notions such as utopia and performance as presented by queer theorist José Esteban Muñoz (1999, 2009). As is the case with many divas, Okuni's star eventually crashed to earth and burned itself out. I draw on Muñoz's ideas also to examine the significance of this diva's "failure." Given Okuni's stunning performances as a man, it is deeply ironic that officialdom eventually banned women from the kabuki stage, with their complete disappearance by 1629 (Nishiyama 1983:6).

BACKGROUND TO THE OKUNI LEGEND

Ariyoshi's Okuni arrives in the capital just at the time that the brutally eccentric warlord Toyotomi Hideyoshi (1536–1598) is imposing social order in the final years of the Warring States era (1467–1603). While Shaver (1966:34) argues that this order gave the public time for entertainment and an appetite for new trends, Mitsuru Kamachi (2004) points out that the relative peace that allowed time for entertainers such as Okuni to flourish was, in fact, a function of Hideyoshi's cruelty. The strictly hierarchal social order imposed by Hideyoshi (later entrenched under the Tokugawa regime) deprived many of improving their lot in life. It was in reaction to this, Kamachi (2004:24) argues, that perform-ance became a form of resistance among young people who had been "crushed" by the establishment.

Ariyoshi locates her account of Okuni squarely in the contradictory social milieu of the raucous festive atmosphere that celebrates liberation from over a century of war and unease at the menace of a harshly enforced regime of "peace." The Okuni that Ariyoshi creates, moreover, is a performer of the people who, in championing commoner audiences, repeatedly defies the demands of the elites who exercise control. Nishi-yama Matsunosuke (1983:1) argues that it was townspeople who took the greatest pleasure in Okuni's performances. Accordingly, Ariyoshi's Okuni takes her greatest pleasure in performing for ordinary people. Sankurō is one of a number of fictional characters who appear in Ariy-oshi's text. A Noh musician, he is initially the decision-maker in Okuni's troupe. To Sankurō, spectators from lower social orders are "worthless" or even "scum" (Ariyoshi 1994:45, 137). Okuni, on the other hand, is "carried away" (Ariyoshi 1994:46) when dancing for commoners and has no desire to dance for elites. Dragooned to perform for Hideyoshi, Okuni is repulsed by the "tiny man" with the "sunken eyes" (Ariyoshi 1994:107) and cannot understand Sankurō's obsessive desire to perform before this egomaniac who has cherry trees in full bloom ripped from provincial gardens and brought to Osaka for his own flower-viewing pleasure (Ariyoshi 1994:144). In the final routine she devises before returning, ill and exhausted, to her home village, Okuni stuns her ador-ing audiences with the tale of a love-sick potter pining for a candy-seller girl. In creating this narrative of a "common working woman" (Ariyoshi 1994:308–9) Okuni confirms without doubt that she is a diva of the masses.

While emphasizing Okuni's preference for commoner audiences, Ariyoshi also profiles the physical immediacy and sexual charge gener-ated by Okuni's devotion to these audiences and their response to her routine. In her rather puritanical 1960s account of Okuni, Shaver (1966: 37) accuses both audience and diva of "suggestions of obscen-ity" and of failing to transcend a "level of mediocrity." Ignoring this critic's judgment of Okuni's performance style as "debased" (Shaver 1966:35), Ariyoshi enthusiastically proclaims the value of the diva's "earthiness" with reference to kimono that "casually [open] to expose naked flesh" (Ariyoshi 1994:15). The elation that Okuni feels when performing for field workers recalls the ecstasy she once experienced at plunging into an "erotically swirling" festival crowd (Ariyoshi 1994:46).

In spite of her wild popularity, the novel closes with Okuni bereft and abandoned. Shaver (1966:37) notes the "confusing" nature of "historical records" regarding the real Okuni's "last years." Ariyoshi, nonetheless, gives the kabuki diva a solitary death after performing for iron miners in the mountains behind Izumo where her own father once worked. In terms of divadom, this cannot but recall the demise of the great Maria Callas (1923–1977), who, no longer able to perform, passed away alone in her Paris apartment. Recalling the return of the goddess to the cave, these solitary deaths arguably enhance the aura of splendor and mystique that envelops the diva.

THE DIVA

Before turning to Ariyoshi's narrative, I examine the notion of diva, a Latin/Italian term meaning "female deity" or "goddess." Patrick Dillon (2013:18) notes the association of the term with operatic performances, including the "quintessential diva role" of Puccini's *Tosca*. Eric Myers (2011:27) argues that the diva-goddess generates an electric flow and "plays by her own rules" in a way that inevitably benefits her fans. Referring to African American soprano Leontyne Price, Phillip Kennicott (2014:29) argues that the diva performance style is both "thrilling and disorientating," resulting in a veritable transformation of the ensemble members who support her (2014:30). And as the title of Jason D. Haugen's (2003) discussion of female gangsta rapper divas affirms, divas can be very "unladylike." Like Okuni, the women discussed by Haugen (2003:434–40) reappropriate maleness in a process that, through "flouting" hegemonic norms, paradoxically creates new standards.

As a woman who "plays by her own rules" for the benefit of her fans and who "thrills and disorientates" as she transforms those around her, Okuni most definitely fulfills the listed diva criteria. Perhaps her most diva-like attribute, however, is her ability to innovate and re-create herself continuously in the face of both professional and personal adversity. Okuni takes her troupe to "the best in the world" and Ariyoshi makes clear that this determination to triumph in public operates also in her intimate life. Thus, although conscious of the "cruelty" (Ariyoshi 1994:93–95) of her lover, Sankurō, Okuni makes every effort to triumph over Oan, the woman to whom Sankurō is married. In addition to her ability to innovate and re-invent herself professionally, this strength of will in personal matters confirms Okuni's diva status.

OKUNI'S STORY

Like many divas, Ariyoshi's Okuni is a woman who achieves success in a man's world. The early pages of the novel are set in Osaka immediately after Hideyoshi assumes power as regent to the Emperor and Lord of the Realm. The text opens with Okuni and several Izumo girls dancing under the instruction of farmer-bucolic Sanaemon in order to raise alms for their Izumo village, which is buckling under Hideyoshi's harsh policies. As the twenty-five years or so of the *Kabuki Dancer* narrative unfold, readers witness Hideyoshi's manic exercise of power—including the absurd invasion of the Asian mainland that presages events of the twentieth century—and the seizure of authority by the less flamboyant but equally calculating Tokugawa Ieyasu (1543–1616).

While not impervious to the political situation, it is Okuni's desire to perform and connect with an audience that fundamentally drives this diva's actions. Her brilliant dance skills capture the attention of Ōmura Yūko Hōgen Baien, chief personal attendant to the Lord of the Realm. Upon first watching Okuni perform, Baien detects the sexual frisson that Okuni generates in the "utterly alluring" and "fragrant voluptuousness" of her "fiercely sensuous movements" (Ariyoshi 1994:15). After falling from Hideyoshi's favor, however, Baien callously disowns the troupe outright, depriving them of elite support. This commences a pattern of the group being courted by the rich and/or powerful, only to lose favor through some pique of fate, or through Okuni's refusal to compromise her art. These vicissitudes follow the group as they move from place to place, eventually relocating to Ieyasu's Edo. Nonaristocratic audiences, too, are demandingly fickle, driving the endless imperative to innovate. Diva Okuni, however, repeatedly rises above these challenges and remains unbowed by any adversity.

THEMES

Ariyoshi's novel opens with the volatile notion of the "lie" that reveals the fragility of truth in times of political upheaval. We learn that the Machiavellian Baien has retimed a local Osaka festival in order to trump a similar event in Kyoto. This festival permits worshipping revelers to exchange lies for truth. There are many occasions in the narrative, moreover, when either misunderstanding or outright deceit results in one or another character having a less than reliable grasp of the facts. There is also the inference that the truth of authority is a lie for those oppressed by authority. Baian is highly skilled in this respect and unhesitatingly invents traditions, such as the need for peasants to donate swords to be melted down allegedly for Buddhist statue construction, as a ploy to impose order (Ariyoshi 1994:28–29).

The notion of the lie is closely connected to the theme of sexuality that pulses throughout Ariyoshi's novel. The "truth-to-lie" festival involves a disorderly sea of people crowding into the grounds of a temple and clutching lasciviously through kimono sleeves at each other's bare flesh. Although Okuni is sexually experienced, her first encounter with Kyūzō, the man to whom she was betrothed in Izumo, was "distasteful" and "aroused no feeling in her at all" (Ariyoshi 1994:19). During the truth-to-lie festival, however, Okuni gives herself up to the crowd and to the hands "that grope inside her kimono." These hands search "inside her clothes" to "touch every part of her body," even "brushing her breasts" (Ariyoshi 1994:19). Given the disappointment of her early Izumo encounter, Okuni is surprised to find that this experience gives her pleasure. In fact, "her whole body seemed intoxicated by the spirit of the crowd" (Ariyoshi 1994:19). This scene, which occurs early in the novel, establishes the diva's desire to assert her sexual identity, while her longing for contact with the festival crowd obliquely augurs Okuni's need for the adoration of her audience.

OKUNI'S MEN AND *KABUKIMONO*

Although the centerpiece character of Ariyoshi's narrative is, of course, Okuni herself, she is supported in her endeavors by a number of men. These include her first good-looking but arrogant lover Sankurō, who hides the fact that he is married. Having abandoned the Kanze school of Noh performers, whom he despised for losing political favor during the Hideyoshi era, Sankurō becomes increasingly embittered when Tokugawa patronage enables Kanze to become the most powerful Noh troupe in the land. In Ariyoshi's telling of Okuni's tale it is Sankurō who brings the discipline of formal training to Okuni's natural performance talents. This, in fact, is a narrative strategy designed to showcase the power of diva resistance. Aware that the gendered beat of Sankurō's drum pulls her "soaring spirit down to earth" (Ariyoshi 1994:34), Okuni refuses to accord with her lover's demands. Instead, she creates her own dance style characterized by the vitality of upward movement. Ariyoshi also has Sankurō introduce the on-stage costume change or *hayagawari,* one of the great spectacles of modern-day kabuki. This is a theatrical device which the diva mistresses to perfection and which stuns the private audience for whom it is first performed (Ariyoshi 1994:50–51).

When Sankurō abandons Okuni for a younger woman in the troupe, the diva takes up with Sanza, who is based on the historical figure of a flute-playing samurai, Nagoya Sanzaburō or Sanzaemon (?–1603). In addition to being a key figure in terms of his relationship with Okuni, Sanza is the exemplar *kabukimono*, one of the discontented youth who resist their increasingly oppressive social environment by dressing "in a strange, exotic fashion and behaving in a rebellious manner" (Kamachi 2004:24).

The expression *kabukimono*, which appears quite early in Ariyoshi's account of Okuni's life, is made of two elements, *kabuki* and *mono*. While *mono* means "thing," *kabuki* derives from the verb *kabuku*, meaning "to slant" or "deviate from the normal path" (Kamachi 2004:24). Alarmed at the pleasure she experienced at the touch of the crowd's hands during the truth-to-lie festival, Okuni recalls her grandmother's warning to avoid becoming *kabuki*, a word "used in Izumo to mean strange, indecent, improper" (Ariyoshi 1994:19). Initially alarmed that she might be so labelled when her affair with Sankurō becomes known, Okuni is challenged to return to Kyūzō, the loathsome man to whom she was promised. Ultimately, however, she defiantly declares that, as long as she can be with the man she loves, she would happily be labeled *kabuki* (Ariyoshi 1994:56). This is a turning point in Okuni's life which sees her, in the manner of all divas, prioritize her own aspirations and desires over those of society. And although ultimately betrayed by the heartlessly egotistical Sankurō, committing herself to that relationship on her own terms is an early expression of Okuni's willful diva power.

While *kabuki* or *kabukimono* may have had negative connotations in Izumo, in Kyoto the term denoted a splendid sartorial style based on European influences:

> Young men were called *kabuki* if they dressed extravagantly in Southern Barbarian clothes. . . . A foreign accessory, like a Portuguese white scarf worn over one's collar, was very *kabuki*. . . . While in the past *kabuki* had meant someone who was eccentric . . . it now indicated a trend setter in foreign fashion. In Kyoto, if one wasn't *kabuki*, one was behind the times (Ariyoshi 1994:132).

It is a testimony to Okuni's capacity to read the desires of her audiences that she embraces this style and integrates it effortlessly into her dance

18. Izumo no Okuni, image provided with permission of the artist Debuchi Ryoichiro.

routine. The Christian iconography that featured in European fashion of the time saw Okuni decorate herself with items such as rosaries or a crucifix necklace. Ariyoshi was not the only contemporary artist to be inspired by Okuni's legend, with growing numbers of manga and anime representations of the medieval diva. These, too, often reference her exotic appearance (Figure 18).

If Kamachi regarded *kabukimono* men as engaging in political resistance, Okuni's affiliation with this idea expresses her desire to contest sexual norms. For Okuni, being *kabuki* was to have a sexual identity—an act that was both public and personal. This was in spite of the fact that common knowledge of her love life compounded the pain and humiliation that she endured before all when a relationship failed. We might argue, in fact, that is it the tension generated by Okuni's determination to be "slanted" or "deviant" in terms of what was expected of women's sexual behavior that drives her artistic innovation. The following passage, which explains how Okuni devised the dance forms that made her famous, demonstrates the inexorable connection between diva innovation and diva sexuality.

> As she practiced, she found she was trying to join the two styles of dance together; the leaping steps, *odori*, . . . that fit naturally to [popular music], and the graceful gesture of the Noh dance, *mai*, that Sankurō's singing and drumbeats drew from her hands. Sankurō did not know what was going on in Okuni's mind and so he resisted, using the drumbeats to bring her body under his control. She was in a contest with Sankurō that she was determined to win, but meanwhile she felt proud that her body could answer Sankurō's drum so well. I will never leave him, she thought. She was happy struggling against Sankurō's drum, searching for a way to meld Noh *mai* and popular *odori* into a new kind of dance. She felt close to Sankurō when she danced. There was no room then, as there was at night when Sankurō embraced her, for the terrible fear that he might reject her. As he had [his wife] Oan (Ariyoshi 1994:111).

With its insights into processes of artistic creation, this passage is striking for its articulation of the connection between the diva's private passion and her public performance. The passage also reveals the depth of diva pain.

Following Sankurō's betrayal, Okuni is consoled for a half a year by the aestheticism and youthful physique of the *bishōnen* (beautiful young man) Sanza. Sanza, however, is ultimately unwilling to be the partner of a woman who generates such audience adulation. Secretly departing to fulfill his masculinist dream of building a castle, he ruefully laments that "a woman [like Okuni] who's best in the world doesn't need a castle" (Ariyoshi 1994:232). In accord with the historical record, Sanza eventually dies in an altercation with another samurai before his dream is realized.

While these two men have pivotal roles, the key male in the text is Densuke, the comic dancer and sometime female impersonator whose unrequited love for Okuni brings ongoing agony to this gifted and compassionate man. Densuke's quiet resilience balances Okuni's more mercurial temperament and helps her survive and thrive against the odds thrown up by a society which, while idolizing the diva, would also destroy a woman with talent. Both Okuni and Densuke demonstrate the eccentricity of artistic genius, with Okuni remarking how they make a fine *kabuki,* or deviant, performing pair (Ariyoshi 1994:137). The exchange suggests that, in addition to the meanings discussed above, the term *kabuki* also surely suggests uncompromising creativity or even genius.

The villain of the piece, discounting Sankurō's multiple infidelities and heartless treatment of both Okuni and women before and after her, is Kyūzō. Kyūzō believes that, as the first man to have clumsy sexual relations with Okuni in Izumo, he has proprietorial rights over the future diva. Okuni has different ideas, however, and leaves her home village principally to escape Kyūzō's clutches. Fate takes Kyūzō to Kyoto where he finds Okuni and seeks to assert ownership. Rejected outright, he resolves to destroy the diva through a campaign of "deliberate, malicious revenge" (Ariyoshi 1994:260). Building himself a career as personal assistant to a well-to-do brothel owner, Kyūzō slyly networks with Kyoto powerbrokers whose aid he eventually enlists to crush the woman he would once have had for his wife.

OKUNI AS A QUEER TEXT

Okuni's cross-dressing invites the use of a queer lens to read Ariyoshi's work. This, however, is not the sole justification for such an approach. Equally important is the presence in the text of the notions of utopia and performance, both profiled in the work of queer theorist Jose Esteban Muñoz. To Muñoz (2009:1), utopia is a "mode of desiring that allows us to see and feel beyond the quagmire of the present" and, by invoking the "aesthetic," to "imagine the future." Not limited to the outdated call of high art, the aesthetic functions perfectly well at either the "decorative" or the more everyday "quotidian" levels (Muñoz 2009:1). Queerness, moreover, is "a performative" (Muñoz 2009:1) which, while associated with performance in the theatrical sense, also insists on action and the refusal to be passive in the face of social injustice. This action can create the "concrete utopia" that is the desired outcome of "historically situated struggles" (Muñoz 2009:3).

While there is tragedy in the text, Ariyoshi's Okuni narrative is largely utopic and I am struck by the manner in which a number of Muñoz's elements, such as "imagining a future," the decorative and/or everyday "aesthetic," the "performative," and the desire for a "concrete utopia" arising from "historically situated struggles," assists us to understand the challenges faced by Okuni as a woman from the margins contesting the conventions of the center through her dance. Since dance has been discussed at some length above, I focus below on utopia, in particular its association with historically situated struggle and the aesthetic. In addressing the latter, I will refer to the exotic and to the power of cross-dressing, matters that feature both in Okuni's narrative and in Muñoz's work. Finally, I consider Muñoz's (2009:173) ideas on failure, particularly as this relates to the fundamental diva quality of virtuosity.

UTOPIA AND SITUATED STRUGGLE

Okuni's utopic vision is expressed through her desire to dance not for elites, but for the socially dispossessed and those without power. *Kabuki Dancer,* however, is no hagiographic account of some ideal woman. Like all divas, Okuni has a will of iron and we are treated to displays of her volatile temper and her sometimes downright bad behavior. Through all this, nevertheless, her search for performance inclusivity never falters and she is unwavering in her desire to challenge parameters set by elites. This challenge is often expressed by the tension between Noh dance and the *kabuki* performance style that she creates.

Okuni despises Noh performers. This is not because of their art per se, but because through their art Noh players defer to the irrational demands of political authority. Okuni's own personal "historically situated struggle" and her search for "concrete utopia" is evident in her refusal to be cowed by officialdom as much as it is in her demand for creative freedom. For Okuni, artistic control and political control are two sides of the same coin. This is because deference to either inevitably results in social normativity. In this respect, Noh is particularly culpable. While Noh dance draws the body down in an artificially generated posture of deference, Okuni explains that her body must "be up to be free" (Ariyoshi 1994:196). Of her resistance to Sankurō's demand for compliance with Noh protocols, the narrator notes:

> Okuni's body refused to stoop or bend the way Sankurō ordered, not because she thought the dance movement was old-fashioned, but because she rejected the subservient spirit the basic Noh posture expressed—a person of the lower classes crouching obsequiously before a samurai lord. . . . Sometimes, Okuni thought, I wish my body could fly or I could leap as high as the stage roof. I won't listen to Sankurō's drum pulling me back to earth. I want to dance my own way, not the way Noh was hundreds of years ago (Ariyoshi 1994:197).

In terms of Okuni's desire to dance for the masses, while there is a tendency for the *mai* of Noh to be performed in closed exclusive spaces for an audience of elites, the unfettered glory of *odori* makes this the perfect fit for large, outdoor group performances such as the summer festival dance.

The above account of diva resistance resonates remarkably with aspects of Muñoz's work. In his discussion of queer performance, Muñoz (1999:xi) refers to the work of New York performance artist Jack Smith, whose art railed against those whom Smith regarded as "pasty normals." These are individuals who either impose, or support the imposition of, control. Okuni holds in contempt the "pasty normals" of her era, those seen using extreme deference toward the samurai.

Recalling the emphasis given to the "lie" at the outset of the narrative, she also despises those who claw their way to power through deceit and deception. It is no coincidence that the obsequious and deceitful were often the very people who set out to destroy her. Challenging and dismantling the norms that permit the obsequious and deceitful to thrive is nothing less than a survival imperative for diva Okuni.

Like many authors who write historical fiction, Ariyoshi surely used her text to make a statement about the situation that prevailed at the time of the text's production. As noted above, the author was herself a bona fide literary diva, who was forced to push back hard against dismissive assessments made by male members of the literary community of the time (Hartley 2017). Performing her craft of popular writer in the face of these attacks was her personal historically situated struggle. Although not a radical, Ariyoshi had a strong political conscience. She organized a pro-bono Japanese performance of the 1968 anti-Vietnam War play, *The Trial of the Catonsville Nine* (Miyauchi 1995:76–77). She also campaigned, with young activist Kan Naoto (b. 1946), for the election to the Diet of woman's suffrage icon Ichikawa Fusae (1893–1981). The latter experience features in what is possibly Ariyoshi's most significant work of social critique, the novel *Fukugō osen* (Compound pollution, 1975). Serialized in *Asahi Shinbun* between October 1974 and June 1975, this trenchant analysis of the environmental consequences of government-promoted agricultural policies of the time is often cited as the inspiration for Japan's now extensive organic farming movement (Nakamichi 2010:35). In this sense, Ariyoshi surely identified with Okuni's rejection of the demands of the elite and with the dancing diva's desire to establish a relationship with commoner audiences who were marginalized by the power brokers of the time.

EXOTICISM

As noted above, invoking the exotic, particularly the Southern Barbarian European costume adopted by fashionable men around town, was one strategy by which Okuni, in Ariyoshi's telling, connected with her fans. Readers learn that "the craze for exotic dress" began after Alessandro Valignano's visit to Kyoto (Ariyoshi 1994:132). While those serving Hideyoshi had been the first to take up these fashions, this fad soon spread among "foppish young samurai, sons of officials, and well-to-do commoners" (Ariyoshi 1994:132). This type of "outlandish combinations of European and Japanese dress" (Ariyoshi 1994:104) is a feature of a samurai procession that makes its way through Kyoto:

> The kimonos of the warriors were made of exotic foreign silk filigreed with gold, and the ends were tucked into ballooned European-styled trousers. Broad white collars and rosaries with cruxifixes made of polished wood encircled their necks. Portuguese-style capes of brown velvet fringed with gold tassels fluttered around their shoulders as they rode forward (Ariyoshi 1994:104).

The sight of this gorgeous procession is made even more riveting by the presence of Okuni's "breathtakingly handsome" future lover, Nagoya Sanza, wearing a "purple velvet sash," with "trailing ends" that "flew in the air behind him" (Ariyoshi 1994:104).

The notion of exoticism features strongly also in Muñoz's (1999:x) discussion of performance artist Jack Smith. Initially concerned that, with its "images of Latin spitfires and cheesy Hollywood renditions of Scheherazade," Smith's work negatively exoticized the women referenced, Muñoz eventually concluded the opposite. For ultimately, Smith's

> underground genius utilized these fantasies of the other in a reflective fashion . . . to destabilize the world of "pasty normal" and help us imagine another time and place. In Smith's cosmology, "exotic" was an antinormative option that resisted the overdetermination of pastiness (Muñoz 1999:10).

In discussing the image of an actress playing a lavishly costumed male role devised by Okuni, Kamachi (2004) also argues for the antinormative power of the exotic. The critic notes that the print depicts the impersonation of a deviant *kabukimono* who is protesting against a society which, in stabilizing after war, was becoming increasingly restrictive. Kamachi then concludes that this is "a manifestation of transvestism as an artistic expression of rebellion against the establishment" (2004:24).

The obvious focus of the *Kabuki Dancer* narrative is the diva herself. Nevertheless, in the same way that Smith gave political significance to "images of Latina spitfires" and "cheesy" Hollywood Scheherazades, Okuni's appropriation of Southern Barbarian exoticism permits her to entertain her audience while at the same time to affiliate with those who were in the process of being rendered socially dispensable.

Okuni's performance was not merely that of a woman in drag. Her genius was to incorporate this Southern Barbarian impersonation successfully into the sensuous voluptuousness of her dance routine. This was particularly the case after she spent her first night with Sanza, who, in a somewhat stereotypical move, gifted her his sword.

> That day, [Okuni's] swaggering masculine figure fascinated the audience crowded into the small theater. Sanza's flute called out. Holding the sword against her hip with one hand and a fan in the other, Okuni danced as freely as the air. Moving with the heavy samurai sword took extra energy. But Okuni's body was tireless. She danced lightly, even with the heavy sword at her side. . . . Okuni was transformed. . . . From this night on she became a true samurai dandy, swaggering with a warrior's confidence (Ariyoshi 1994:211).

Kamachi (2004) examines the possibility of European theatrical influence on kabuki development and in doing so pays diva Okuni an incidental compliment of extraordinary power. The critic notes that by playing a *kabukimono* role herself, Okuni made an even bolder contestation of gender norms than Shakespeare's casting young men playing women disguised as men (Kamachi 2004:24). In other words, Kamachi suggests that Okuni's star blazed even more brilliantly than that of the greatest English-language playwright of all time.

CROSS-DRESSING

Cross-dressing, which here complements exoticism, is introduced early in the narrative when Densuke, whose natural comic talents ensure that he is almost as big a hit with audiences as Okuni, astounds the diva with his skillful performance as "a stuck-up woman" (Ariyoshi 1994:61). Okuni's own interest in performing as a man is first suggested when she wears one of Sankurō's kimono. Although Densuke is initially wary of such a move, the diva observes that if audiences respond to Densuke impersonating a woman there is no reason that she should not perform as a man (Ariyoshi 1994:131). And while Okuni's most stunning performances as a dandy occurs after she becomes Sanza's lover, she is aware well before that time of the liberating impact of dancing like a man. Striving to transform "Densuke's female impersonation into a male dance," Okuni found her "arm gestures and leaps" now "unimaginably freer" and her entire body "intoxicated by rhythm and song" (Ariyoshi 1944:203).

Okuni's cross-dressing *pièce de résistance,* however, comes when, bereft at news of the death of her lover Sanza, she devises a routine in which she impersonates his ghost. This zenith, during which she "immersed herself in Sanza's memory," dressed in "his plum-colored underkimono, red cap worn beneath the straw hat, Buddhist rosary, purple velvet sash and red tassels at the waist" (Ariyoshi 1994:255), paradoxically precedes her fall from audience grace. Aware that she was "giving herself, and her life, to this dance," her devoted attendant, Densuke, anxiously wondered what she would do when "people tired" of her routine (Ariyoshi 1994:255).

FAILURE

Ultimately, in a development that speaks to the precarity of the diva, people did tire of Okuni, although this was partly the result of enemies such as Kyūzō relentlessly conspiring to ensure her professional demise. Nevertheless, where the fluid social order that marked the end of the Warring States era supported the activities of a brilliant woman, the rigid social structures that were imposed soon after saw Okuni ostracized as a target of contempt. Toward the end of Ariyoshi's text, a Kanze master dismantles a Noh stage on which Okuni and her troupe might have performed in order "to prevent its contamination by these riverside beggars" (Ariyoshi 1994:277). In this sense, Okuni was ultimately a diva who failed. Once again, it is Muñoz who provides insights into this aspect of Okuni's life.

In a discussion entitled "A Jeté Out the Window: Fred Herko's Incandescent Illumination," Muñoz (2009:147–68) examines the life of the eponymous Herko, a countercultural New York dancer from the Andy Warhol set. Herko is one of a number of figures discussed by Muñoz who would conventionally be classed as failures. Some failed spectacularly, including Herko who, recalling Okuni's wish that "my body might fly" or "leap as high as the stage roof," literally danced out of the window of a friend's Greenwich Village apartment to crash to his death below. Muñoz, nonetheless, urges celebration of these figures for the way in which they unsettle the "flawed temporality" (2009:154) of what this commentator refers to as "straight time" (Muñoz 2009:154). Those who take their own lives are particularly important since they "help us to look at queer life and cultural labor as resonating beyond traditional notions of finitude" (Muñoz 2009:149). The term "queer" here invokes Muñoz's "queer fantasy," which he argues is linked to "utopian longing" and the creation of "conditions of possibility for political transformation" (2009:172).

This approach is useful when considering Okuni, to whom Ariyoshi attributes a persistent streak of self-destruction. She miscarries early in the text after enduring unbearably frigid weather to view the building of Hideyoshi's castle (Ariyoshi 2014:65–71). Alarmingly—given Hideyoshi's brutality when displeased—she refuses an invitation to drink with his favorite consort (Ariyoshi 2014:139–40), enraging the consort and terrifying the men in attendance. The text closes with Okuni dancing for the miners of Iron Mountain, her father's home precinct. Her death is the result of her obsessive determination to set out in freezing conditions to see where her father toiled. Aware of the mortal peril facing them both, the local guide turns back, with Okuni choosing to head into the driving snow alone (Ariyoshi 2014:341–42). As the weather closes in, a boulder careens down the hillside, crushing her leg so that she dies in agonizing solitude on the frozen path. There is an earthiness to the diva's demise in that Okuni returns to the very soil that gave her birth. Only the natural forces of the homeland had the power to extinguish Okuni's indomitable spirit, giving her death a violent mysticism or even a romantic purity.

This discussion has read the sensational life of kabuki's founding diva, Okuni, through Ariyoshi Sawako's *Kabuki Dancer*. Emphasis was given to Okuni's diva determination to live by her own rules and to experience sexual pleasure in a way that nurtured her creative talents. Okuni's life was a sequence of challenges that would have defeated a less willful woman. Although named "best in the world," her dazzling talent generated enmity, constantly forcing her to reconstruct herself. Eventually, notwithstanding her indefatigable will, her body gave out. Returning to her provincial home exhausted and in failing health, she pronounced a death sentence upon herself by recklessly confronting the forces of nature in the heartland of her birth.

I have read Okuni's performance, including her love for the exotic and for cross-dressing, through a queer utopian lens. The notion of queer utopia comes from appropriating something originally designed to con-

19. Izumo no Okuni statue in Kyoto near the Kamo River. Photo by R. Copeland.

strain or injure, such as the term "queer" itself, and having the audacity and the resilience to transform that notion into a site of hope. The diva, too, must have the audacity and resilience to appropriate what is necessary for her performance even in the face of the attacks that her genius inevitably generates. In this sense she is a solitary figure adrift.

Regrettably, all that remains of Okuni's extraordinary spirit is a forlorn statue beside Kyoto's Kamo River (Figure 19). A stone's throw from Minami-za, one of Japan's lavish theaters famous for its male actors, the statue is largely concealed from passing traffic by a subway station entry.

In the closing stages of Ariyoshi's text, we see Okuni confront her personal isolation, representative of the isolation of every diva, by dancing alone at night on a beach:

> The shore was a stage, limitlessly wide. The night sky, too, seemed to her as broad as infinity. . . . Okuni danced and sang in a blackness that obliterated the boundary between earth and sky. Except for the single point where her foot touched the earth, Okuni's entire body reached out to fill the firmament around her (Ariyoshi 1994:296).

This moving passage from Ariyoshi's text surely captures Okuni's defiantly creative challenge to Muñoz's (2009) notion of "straight time" with its implication of finitude. The passage also confirms, without doubt, Okuni's status as a true goddess, or diva, of dance upon this earth.

I noted at the outset that there was no writer more qualified to create the fictional medieval diva Okuni than contemporary literary diva Ariyoshi Sawako. Like Okuni, Ariyoshi knew both the highs and lows of the creative process and the fickle tastes of audience/readers. Her career was characterized by a dazzlingly prodigious literary output that ranged across novels, documentary reports, kabuki, bunraku, and film treatments and scripts. She was also involved in theatrical production and design. Yet, from early in her career Ariyoshi was marked as an outsider, a woman who did not fit the mold. Leung On Yuk's (1993:175) discussion of Ariyoshi's *Izumo no Okuni* cites the author as declaring that "the novel resonates with my own passionate theory of the arts." As Leung (1993:175) further observes, the novel presents Okuni both as a woman and as an artist. Ariyoshi knew only too well the unbearable pressures that act upon women who have artistic talent. Fêted by society for their brilliance, they are nonetheless expected to obediently comply with the suffocating gender restrictions imposed by hegemonic norms. Like Okuni and Maria Callas, they are often isolated in death. One purpose of this volume is to revive the memory of forgotten divas such as Okuni and to unequivocally locate them in the national memory of contemporary Japan and indeed of readers around the world.

CHAPTER 5

From Child Star to Diva

Misora Hibari as Postwar Japan

CHRISTINE R. YANO

In the rainy season of 1989 as Japan's postwar diva Misora Hibari lay dying in a Tokyo hospital bed, a cataclysmic sense of the passing of an era enshrouded the singer and her fans. Like Emperor Hirohito who had passed away only months before, hers was a life lived as much on stage as off, behind closed doors. With over 1,200 recordings and 150 films to her credit, Hibari's was a life filled with hard work that became the basis of her fame. The frail fifty-two-year-old woman who lay dying had been dubbed the "Queen of Enka," a genre of melodramatic popular song with the reputation of expressing *Nihonjin no kokoro,* the heart/soul of Japanese identity. At the same time, Hibari had lived a life shadowed by controversy, whether from her brother's ties to the *yakuza* (Japanese organized crime syndicate) underworld, her overbearing stage mother, her low voice and sophisticated knowingness as a child star, her short-lived marriage to handsome movie star Kobayashi Akira, her hard-drinking lifestyle, her unmistakable brash crudeness, or her putative Korean ancestry. Her fans—both men and women, many around her same age—took notice of these abrasive headlines, but looked the other way as they called out "Hibari-chan!" with affection. They took these flaws—even transgressions—as evidence of her fallibility, her very humanness, even as she performed to superhuman levels. Amid calls of *tensai* (genius) in her musical abilities, she was one of them, a people's singer, and this endeared her to them. Further, they belonged to her, dubbing themselves *Hibari no sedai* (Hibari's generation). The Emperor's death in January 1989 may have marked the official end of the era of Shōwa (Hirohito's posthumous name); but Hibari's death in June of that year marked the unofficial, no less affecting, end of the postwar period. Hibari embodied both the heights and depths, and the many contradictions in between, of Japan as it recovered from the devastation of World War II and gained international heights of economic achievement. That these extremes of defeat and achievement should be laid at the feet of a diva crystallizes the place of Hibari.

This chapter problematizes Japan's premiere diva of popular song. A child star, Misora Hibari (1937–1989) grew up in postwar Japan to become what I consider to be a transgressive diva. What defines this former child star, this singing *shōjo* (young female) on stage? What kinds of gendered negotiations between childhood and adulthood does the child star have to make, in what kinds of historical contexts, and to what effects? And finally, how does the *shōjo*—here, the child star become adult diva—help define the period? If we are critically examining various female icons of Japan in this volume, then I suggest that we look at this *shōjo*, the Misora Hibari who attains divahood in her adult years with remnants of her child star persona continually part of her stage presence. The remnants of the child star give poignancy to her adult divahood as the Japanese public stood witness to her continual transformations. And in witnessing these transformations, I contend that Misora Hibari's star text enacted postwar Japan's supra-text, particularly during the years when she occupied media and stage as the *shōjo* orphan, the "Tokyo Kid" (in a 1950 film by the same title, *Tokyo Kiddo*, by director Saitō Torajirō; see Figure 20). Nation and child star alike performed themselves as spunky orphans—even nascent cosmopolitans, while masking the hard-hitting realities of the period. I include not only the period of the late 1940s and 1950s, when Misora Hibari was credited with boosting the Japanese public morale as the spunky singing orphan, but also the period that followed—the Jet Age of the 1960s and 1970s—as a site of national negotiations of modernity through the images of diva Hibari.

DIVAHOOD AND HER PUBLICS

The figure of the diva draws upon highly gendered notions of spectacle, transgression, and emotion. Inasmuch as the diva supplies the public with morality tales, these swirl around the complex relationships between the staged versus the everyday, the spectacularized image versus the lived

20. Misora Hibari movie poster for *Tokyo Kid* (Saitō 1950).

life, the public virtuosity versus the not-so-virtuous private life. As a larger-than-life figure of a public woman, the diva oversteps the normative patriarchal bounds that might confine everyday women to the private life of the home, and places her frailties and talents on display. Thus the feeding frenzy of the media glare that dogs her becomes both her boon and her bane: she can barely live with it, while she cannot live without it. If nothing else, the diva is a celebrity of accomplishment, a persona even more than a person, a certain class of performer whose reputation rests in both ability and renown. Sociologist Chris Rojek (2001:9) points out the Latin roots of the modern word "celebrity" in *celebrem*, with connotations of "fame" and "being thronged." Thus the phenomenon encompasses a person (or object) within a public relationship predicated upon widespread mediated knowledge (fame) as embodied in the highly emotional reaction of a crowd (being thronged, whether physically or symbolically). These elements of celebrity certainly hound the modern diva, including Misora Hibari, whose constant media attention sustained her as much as devoured her.

The diva is at once the bad girl for her transgressive celebrity lifestyle, as well as the sacrificial good girl for the awe of her public talent. That talent comes at no small expense, drawing upon the waywardness of her lifestyle—in Japan, as far from the celebrated *ryōsai kenbo* (good wife, wise mother) housewife as imaginable. That lifestyle often includes substance abuse, non-marital sexual liaisons, and/or ongoing psychological maladies; vilified in the press, these deviations from the conventional norm become part of a lifestyle built upon excess. In short, the diva's outsized talent matches and draws from the outsized capaciousness of her public life, creating a chicken-and-egg quandary of cause, effect, lifestyle, talent, and persona. The diva represents life lived as spectacularized melodrama.

Richard Dyer's (1998:2) work on celebrity proves useful in considering media stars (including divas) triply as social phenomena, images, and signs. Dyer asks, why, what, and how do stars signify? These questions pivot around the notion of the audience, or more correctly, various audiences, drawn together for their own purposes around the diva. The practices and effects here go both ways: the diva must attract audiences to survive, but in doing so the figure of the diva and her songs also constitute the audience. Both diva and audience need each other. These processes swirl around what Lauren Berlant (2008:viii) calls an "intimate public": "a porous, affective sense of identification among strangers that promises a certain experience of belonging." This is part of the brand promise of the diva and the intimate public she circumscribes: "consumer participants are perceived to be marked by a commonly lived history; its [the group's] narratives and things are deemed expressive of that history while also shaping its conventions of belonging" (Berlant 2008:viii). In the case of Misora Hibari, the intimate public of her fandom takes her star text to define a generation (*Hibari no sedai;* Hibari's generation) and an era (postwar Japan).

CHILD STAR: BRINGING UP DIVA

Although Hibari may be defined and linked broadly to the nation and an era, she had roots specific to a place, social class, gender, and perhaps even ethnicity. Part of what makes her interesting for analysis is the way in which these specificities stand in for larger issues, particularly invoking a sense of national and historic ordinariness.

Hibari's story begins in 1937 with her birth as Katō Kazue, in Yokohama, the eldest daughter of a fishmonger in a working-class neighborhood. (Note the contrast with artist/performer Yoko Ono, born into an elite family, and who developed a relationship with Japan and the larger world far different from Hibari's; see Carolyn Stevens, Chapter 6, this volume.) Hibari was considered a child prodigy, purportedly memorizing classical poems by the age of three; singing at age six at a 1943 send-off party for her father as he left to fight in the war; debuting in 1946 at the age of nine; and then, while touring in concert in 1947 at age ten, nearly dying in a collision between her tour bus and a truck. Upon her release from the hospital, she went to the site of the accident and, praying to Shinto deities at a nearby ancient cedar tree, vowed to become the number one singer in all of Japan. It is this combination of humble beginnings, precocious and prodigious talent, childhood trauma, and spiritual awakening resulting in a life-altering vow that produces the hagiographic narrative of a life for whom divahood (a sainthood of song) seemed like an inevitability.

Furthermore, this narrative takes place amid Japan's postwar turmoil, facing the aftermath of war defeat with the pressures of economic rebuilding and rapid social change. In short, Hibari's pathway to divahood mirrored Japan's pathway to recovery. She symbolized national resources of grit and determination amid Japan's urban scramble of contradictions. And it is within this personal early history and these contradictions that her charisma may be best understood. Charisma—"a certain quality of an individual personality by virtue of which . . . [she] is set apart from [the] ordinary . . . and treated as endowed with . . . exceptional qualities" (Weber 1968:329)—linked this child star to her adoring public engaged in Japan's postwar uphill struggle. She was an exemplary model of spunky optimism. More than the rational struggle against all odds, it was the affective dimension of this child star's appeal that has been credited with spurring the nation to work ever harder in the initial postwar years. This is why her childhood accident and subsequent vow not only to succeed, but to do so as number one in the nation have become critical to Hibari's star text. It is more than sheer fantasy, but the size and scope of the ambition combined with the appeal to traditional Japanese deities, and most importantly, the hard-fought determination of one so young that startle. Hers is a diva originary tale that can be read as a national motivational text, all the more compelling coming from a child.

Dyer's (1998:31) discussion of the charismatic appeal of stars points to periods of social instability as a fertile ground upon which particular stars arise: "One needs to think in terms of the relationships . . . between stars and specific instabilities, ambiguities and contradictions in the culture." Thus the "instabilities, ambiguities and contradictions" of the postwar era found solace and inspiration in the child star Hibari (Tansman 1996:108). She was the Tokyo Kid, and in particular the streetwise orphan, who could sing her way through tough times with an eclectic mix of a variety of genres, from jazz-inspired upbeat numbers to melancholic Japanese ballads.

Film historian Joanne Izbicki (2008) points out the place of the orphan in films of occupied Japan (1945–1952) "as sign, metaphor and solution for . . . the disconnection of the repatriated Japanese soldier from civilian society, and the disintegration of the prewar conception of the family." Orphans represented transgressions of the social order, producing children forced into adult concerns of survival, and without the care and protection of families. Hibari's starring role as an orphan figure thus symbolized the orphan-like state of Japan, severed from the historic national father figure of the Emperor, citizens of an occupied nation without traditional structures of stability. In war defeat, Japan was orphaned from itself. Furthermore, as John Dower (2000) points out, orphans were stigmatized figures of postwar Japan, considered part of the urban blight, human evidence of the nation at its worst, sometimes the result of illicit sexual liaisons. In the face of such stigmatized conditions, Hibari's star orphan represented not so much pathos as spunky optimism and even freedom. She represented a new order of possibility.

Hibari herself travelled as a child star to Hawai'i and California in 1950, as documented in photo books that recorded and publicized her travels (e.g., Hashimoto and Okamura 2003). Photos show just-turning-thirteen-year-old Hibari, dubbed "Tensai Shōjo Kashu" (Genius Girl Singer), traveling for two months with guitarist Kawada Haruhisa, chaperoned by her mother. Boarding an iconically prestigious Pan American World Airways Flying Clipper at Haneda Airport on May 16, 1950, the party of three (including kimono-clad Hibari and her mother) carried bouquets from family and other well-wishers. When they landed in Honolulu, these bouquets were exchanged for wreath upon wreath of Hawaiian flower lei, gifts of welcome from a wildly enthusiastic Japanese American public in Hawai'i, who transported them by motorcade through downtown Honolulu. Specifically, Hibari's time in Hawai'i was sponsored by Japanese American war veteran groups, and thus framed within the structures of American patriotism (Yano 2006:43). This was no vacation; rather, Hibari proved ever the working girl, whether rehearsing, performing, or filming scenes for the eventual movie *Tokyo kiddo* (Saitō 1950). Even when relaxing on the beach, sightseeing, shopping, or at a party, every minute became a photo opportunity for Japanese and Japanese American media, celebrating this child star whose bright cheeriness and obvious talent served to gloss over national animosities and racial tensions. In the hands of a child star (and perhaps especially a female one), memories of World War II took a distant backseat to sheer entertainment, even if of Japanese origin.

The enthusiasm of Japanese Americans for Misora Hibari in the 1950s—only four years after her debut in Japan and five years after the incarceration by the American government of Japanese Americans living primarily on the West Coast—spoke to the significant place of child stars on both sides of the Pacific. Accompanied by guitarist Kawada and the Hawaii Shochiku Orchestra (one of the revived popular Japanese American orchestras playing a mixture of Japanese and American popular songs), child star Hibari performed to overflow crowds on the islands of O'ahu, Maui, Hawai'i, and Kauai (Tasaka 1985:50). Photos show her in various costumes: kimono; tuxedo and top hat, reprising her role in the 1949 movie *Kanashiki kuchibue* (Lonesome Whistle, directed by Ieki Miyoji, which had just been released); or in pinafore, hula skirt, or sequined top. The Japanese American community even introduced Hibari to a local look-alike (*Sokkuri-san; Hawai no Hibari-chan*, Hawaii's Hibari). Photos show Hibari (*honmono*, the real thing) presenting Hawai'i's Hibari with a Japanese doll; other photos show the two dancing side by side, sometimes in matching hula skirts, accompanied by Kawada on guitar. The mimicry extends doubly: Hibari mimics the jazz numbers (including Hawaiian songs, then considered by Japanese as within the jazz genre) of the United States; Hawai'i's Hibari mimics the "real Hibari," paying tribute to her talent, fame, and accomplishment. One might ask, who is the true *honmono* when singing jazz—the Japanese child star or the Japanese American look-alike? Both

Hibaris demonstrate the mobility of the era through song genres that cross the globe, often enabled and practiced by child stars. The precocity of the cosmopolitanism in the hands of this child star was not lost on Japanese audiences; in effect, she could go where they could not, because of travel restrictions that kept ordinary Japanese from traveling abroad until 1964.

This emphasis on child stars and their flexible global domain took center stage later on in the tour in July 1950 when Hibari traveled to Los Angeles and met Hollywood figures, including Bob Hope, Spencer Tracy, and musician Lionel Hampton. More importantly, Hibari met the American child star Margaret O'Brien. The two, born in the same year, posed for photos, sharing their experiences of a young life lived on stage. This meeting eventually resulted in a 1952 Japanese film, *Futari no hitomi* (literally, The Pupils/Eyes of Two People, but given an English-language title, *Girls Hand in Hand*, directed by Nakaki Shigeo), with Hibari as a Tokyo street orphan and O'Brien as the visiting daughter of an American Occupation official, who takes it upon herself to "rescue" less fortunate Japanese children like Hibari. (Ironically, it is O'Brien who dons kimono in some scenes, while Hibari appears in Western dress, including overalls, rolled-up jeans, and Western dresses.) Again, it is child stars who bridge the gap between nations, even while replicating some of the international politics behind that bridge.

Hibari followed her return to Japan with a stage show that emphasized her recent successful tour of Hawai'i and California—"Paramount Show: Amerika Chindōchū" in Tokyo with her fellow traveler Kawada in 1950 (see Bourdaghs 2012:61, fig. 3 for the show's poster). Furthermore, Hibari's subsequent film hit *Tokyo kiddo* included dream sequences of actual footage of Hibari in Hawai'i posing at famous landmarks, such as Diamond Head and in front of the statue of King Kamehameha (Hashimoto and Okamura 2003:38–49). Hibari starred in movies that emphasized her overseas sojourns; she continued to travel as an adult in the decades that followed, eventually purchasing a condominium in Honolulu.

Hibari the child star did not accomplish this alone. Instead, as is not uncommon with child stars, she was strongly guided by persons who, in part, structurally legitimated her achievements—that is, her parents. Although initially guided and promoted by her father, her mother soon took the helm, and as the ultimate in stage mothers, she guided every step of her daughter's career. Photos show the close relationship between mother and daughter, with mother present on all stage sets, standing in the wings at performances. The two physically resemble each other, and photos demonstrate them gazing at each other as mirrored images, gesturing in parallel. The relationship is further displayed in the now-defunct Misora Hibari Museum in Arashiyama, with one large display case reserved for gifts from daughter to mother.

HIBARI'S DIVA CROSSINGS

From the beginning of her career, Hibari performed an eclectic mix of jazz, Western pop, French chanson, and Japanese ballads, the genres reflecting different times and places. In fact, her virtuosity lay in her very versatility, so that chameleon-like, she could seemingly become anything, anywhere. This imitative versatility started from her earliest days as a child star covering Japanese boogie-woogie singer Kasagi Shizuko, including imitating her dance moves, much to the consternation of Hibari's critics. who condemned a child star moving so boldly and sensuously (Shamoon 2009:134). Her precocious mimicry continued into her teen-age and young adult years covering Hoagy Carmichael's *Stardust* (Carmichael 1927), Duke Ellington's *Take the A-Train* (Strayhorn 1939), Harry Belafonte's *Day O, Banana Boat Song* (Unknown 1956), and Edith Piaf's *La Vie en Rose* (Piaf 1947), to provide only a very small sample. The covers extended to newly created songs for Hibari based on these international pop genres (titles here anglicized for ease in recognizing the genres): from rockabilly (e.g., *Rockabilly Geisha*, Yoneyama 1960a) to Latin dances, including mambo (e.g., *Omatsuri mambo*, Hara 1952; *Naki warai no mambo*, Yoneyama 1960b), beguine (e.g., *Bye-bye Beguine*, Yoneyama 1966), bossa nova (*Ai no bossa nova*, Nishizawa 1968), cha-cha (e.g., *Hibari's cha cha cha*, Yoneyama 1956), to rock (e.g., *Hibari's twist*, Komabayashi 1962a; *Blue twist*, Komabayashi 1962b, only two years after the Twist dance craze in the United States had begun).

There are racial ironies to many of these performances. On the one hand, many popular hits that Misora Hibari covered derive from America's own history of racial prejudice, which also lies at the core of the entertainment industry. These include borrowings from African Americans (e.g., jazz, rhythm and blues), Latin Americans (e.g., mambo, samba, bossa nova), or even Native Hawaiians. On the other hand, Hibari herself was the target of persistent rumors of Korean origins. These rumors, of a scorned ethnicity, include *enka* itself; one of its renowned composers, Koga Masao (1904–1978), was known to have spent a significant amount of time in colonial Korea as a young man, where he undoubtedly heard and was possibly influenced by the melodramatic popular songs there known as *trot* or *ppongjjak*. The origin threads for *enka* remain tangled to this day.

When I went to visit Hibari's gravesite in Yokohama, I encountered two unsolicited versions of the rumor about her origins. The taxi driver who drove me to the cemetery claimed to have gone to the same elementary school as Hibari, and disclosed without my asking, "You know her father was Korean, don't you?" Shortly after, the old woman from whom I bought flowers to take to her gravesite said in hushed tones, "Well, her mother was Korean, you know." This origin rumor lends an ironic twist to Hibari's divahood, sensationalizing her life and music further through the specter of a shadow background (cf. Bourdaghs 2012:79–83).

At the same time that Hibari was sampling much of Euro-American popular music, the 1960s and 1970s also represented a period of cultural nationalism during which Japan, inundated by influences from abroad, deliberately and distinctively turned inward. In a bout of cultural nationalism, this included the distillation and naming of the genre *enka,* to set apart popular music of (putative) Japanese origins from that of Western origins. In other words, the Japanese music industry incorporated their own Jet Age appetite for the foreign, as shown through covers and syncretic compositions; at the same time, it developed a deliberate alternative to such foreignness in a genre that purported to express the "heart/soul" of Japanese identity (Yano 2002). Thus, Hibari's versatility included constant pulling herself back to overt performances of "Japan." As Hibari came to more closely and consistently inhabit a Japanese musical space of *enka,* so, too, did her performances include aspects linked to premodern settings.

One such premodern stage practice was cross-gendered performances. At the age of fifteen, Hibari's mother and manager felt that she needed to broaden her stage image, in an effort to bridge the gap between child star and adulthood. Hibari thus performed in *jidai-geki* (period dramas), often in cross-dressed roles as a young sword-fighting samurai, for which she gained widespread acclaim. These roles became a significant means to link Hibari to premodern Japan. It was also a way to demonstrate her versatility and virtuosity. Thus Hibari's cross-gendered, cross-historical performance paralleled her many cross-genre, cross-national performances: multiply crossed on-stage drag marked the coming-of-age Hibari.

Throughout her career, cross-dressed roles in period-costume films and staged performances became one of her hallmarks. So, too, did certain cross-performed songs, most notably the 1964 Koga Masao composition *Yawara* (Judo). In this year of the Tokyo Olympics (with its national pride of judo), Hibari sang this very masculine song, a notable departure from the typical Koga formula known as *Koga merodii* (Koga melody). Instead of the wistful guitar tremolo, melancholy pentatonic minor scale, and words of longing, the song *Yawara* sounds resolutely straightforward, almost militaristic with its 4/4 marching beat and pentatonic major scale. With lyrics alluding to the philosophy and practices of martial arts, and sung in a low, nasal register, *Yawara* became an anthem of Japanese masculinity. And Hibari's performance of it echoed this theme unambiguously. Performed by Hibari in a short wig, dressed in kimono with *obi* (belt) slung below the belly, men's style, and one hand in a fist gesturing strongly while the other hand gripped the opening of the *yukata* (robe), her performance of the song represented the ultimate crossed performance, in period-style *iki* (stylishness). She swaggered as she sung, inhabiting the bodily and vocal gestures of bravado. In many ways, Hibari was singing the roles that she had performed in movies as the sword-fighting swashbuckling young samurai. The song became a huge hit in Japan, earning her the *Nihon Rekōdo Taishō* (Japan Record of the Year) award in 1965, cementing Hibari's place in Japanese hearts as embracing the masculinity of times past (Bourdaghs 2012:69–70).

Japanese notions of *kata* (patterned form), by which the performativity of gender—predating Judith Butler's (1990) pronouncements—can be broken down into recognizable units and perfected as art, which allowed Hibari-as-samurai to cross fully and gloriously (Yano 2002:25). Although the crossing spans historically from the premodern (e.g., kabuki, in which male actors take on both male and female roles; Mezur 2005) to the modern (e.g., *Takarazuka*, in which female actors take roles either as men or women; Robertson 1998), the modern evocations allow the actor's biological gendering to shade through as part of her inherent "thirdness" appeal. By contrast, in premodern crossed genres, the assumption of *kata* is even more thoroughgoing and complete. Thus the premodern crossed stage assumes the androgynous nature of all human beings, the inherent *yin* and *yang* within each person providing a wellspring of contrasts that could be drawn upon, both for uncrossed and crossed performances (see Barbara Hartley, Chapter 4, this volume). The androgynous nature of crossed-diva Hibari, then, was not so much queer, in a Japanese context, as a naturally occurring, inevitable drag.

When I attend the yearly Tokyo fan club video celebrations of Hibari's birthday on May 29, among the performances that receive the most enthusiastic female response are those in which Hibari played boys or men, such as *Yawara*. One fan showed me her favorite portrait of Hibari, as *wakashu* (young man), *yukata* slightly parted, eyes looking directly at the camera. It is enough to make at least this one fan, in her sixties and dressed conservatively, swoon. In an interview I conducted at a teahouse with several female fans in their sixties and seventies, the women spoke girlishly, even giddily, about Hibari. They recalled how their hearts fluttered when they saw her (in Japanese, they use the verb *au*, "to meet")—whether on the distanced stage or in person on the street). One woman talked of falling backward ("knocked her off her feet") when she saw Hibari, and demonstrated as we sat on *tatami* (mat) on the floor so that she ended up flat on her back, laughing uproariously. What these women talked about included her singing, her voice, her movies, her concerts; but more importantly was their deep emotion for her, akin to love, expressed as *horechau* ("falling rapturously in love").

This is diva Hibari whose drag heats up as she mimes not modern men, but men of the past. Here Hibari sets in motion a certain kind of yearning for premodern sexuality, even as she performs premodern stereotypes of machismo. This premodern sexuality encodes ancient Japan, quite specifically. The samurai that Hibari depicts nostalgically represents the prototypical Japanese warrior, held to a code of honor from a feudal past when Japan did not have to contend with the West. The retro-poignancy of her cross-gendered performance distills Japan as not only premodern, but more importantly, pre-Western.

Hibari's cross-gendering may pull her fans back in time through its retro-poignancy. However, what pulls Hibari undeniably closer to their shared core is the timelessness of her tears (Yano 2002:99). This heart's tug, in fact, forms the basis of Hibari's charisma. As Edward A. Shils (1965:201) argues, "The charismatic quality of an individual . . . lies in what is thought to be his [sic] connection with (including possession by or embedment in) some very central feature of . . . existence. . . . The centrality, coupled with intensity, makes it extraordinary. "

Thus, Hibari's tears, both in their centrality to her public image and performance, as well as their intensity, well up as the source of her charisma. This holds true particularly in the midst of Japan's postwar cataclysmic social change. Tears have been the source of her imaging, from her earliest childhood films, such as *Kanashiki kuchibue* (Lonesome Whistle, Ieki 1949) in which her tears flowed from the onions she peeled, to her final heroic Tokyo Dome performance months before her death. Tears became her trademark feat, surpassing other key liquids such as alcohol and sweat. In this liquid world of heightened sorrow, amidst national material accomplishments, Hibari's tears embodied the contradictions of the times. Known by the 1970s as the "Queen of Enka," Hibari performed to greatest acclaim in Japan in the genre whose hallmark lies in the intensity of emotional expression.

Take her signature song, *Kanashii sake* (Lonesome Sake), written by Koga Masao (1966). With lyrics expressing the searing loneliness of a broken heart, Hibari's reputation rested on her ability to cry, apparently during every performance. Expressions of heightened emotion on the concert stage, in fact, became more pronounced as she grew older. A comparison of early- and late-career performances of *Kanashii sake*, for example, shows ways in which she sang with progressively greater artistic and emotional license, slowing down the tempo considerably, milking the musical moment to heighten the dramatic effect. Whereas earlier performances may have kept a relatively steady beat, in later performances she varied the speed, slowing parts of it to a near-halt, and filling those spaces with vocal embellishments. In short, she asserted her tear-filled diva crown onstage with ever greater authority.

COMPARATIVE DIVA GAZING

Although a comparative perspective is not essential for analyzing celebrities, in the case of Misora Hibari, the comparison with American pop diva Judy Garland (1922–1969) provides important insights. Their parallel lives and careers afford us the possibility of theorizing divahood transnationally. Consider that both began their career as child stars in films and recordings, both suffered private lives of substance abuse and marital strife, and most importantly, both occupied diva status through the intensity and emotionalism of their singing. Both also died relatively young—Garland of suicide (after repeated attempts) at age forty-seven, Hibari of liver disease (after several hospital stays) at age fifty-two. Although death came to both prematurely, both singers had been, in effect, dying before the public eye for years, in and out of hospitals, living lives of emotional and physical instability. According to sociologist Jane O'Connor (2008:2), the different parts of the narratives of their lives—child star, suffering, diva, death—follow an interconnected public logic that becomes part of the purported tragedy of the figure of the child star in Western popular imagination. Garland (along with Shirley Temple, Jackie Coogan, Mickey Rooney, and others) were part of the child star era in Hollywood films of the 1920s and 1930s, although the phenomenon of performing children well preceded them. What the child star offered the newly media-saturated public, in Hollywood, as well as Tokyo, was "their power to symbolize all of the 'good' attributes of childhood such as innocence and natural wisdom" with preternatural abilities, often considered transgressive or freakish (O'Connor 2008:5). In fact, the freakery of child stars as prodigies lies exactly in their very precociousness that confuses categories. Child stars overstep the very bounds of childhood (O'Connor 2008:79; cf. Bourdaghs 2012:55). Lori Merish (1996:190) describes the link between child stars and adults of abnormally small stature: "Part of the pleasure of watching precocious child and 'little person' perform derived from how they unsettled, in a contained but dramatic fashion, the conventional boundary between child and adult." Thus Hibari and Garland, girls with big adult-like voices, represented the transgressive freakishness of the child star, performing themselves as both child and adult (cf. Standish 2005:197). Notably, neither performer as an adult was very tall in stature (both under five feet), in effect visually allowing the possibility of continuing identification with their childhood star status. Besides the occasional negative reaction that both got from the general public, Hibari herself suffered famously: a well-known story about the young girl Hibari takes place at an amateur public song contest (Nippon Hōsō Kyōkai, National Public Broadcasting Corporation singing contest) during which Hibari received less than the highest remarks as a result of the judges' displeasure that she sounded too little like a child and too much like an adult.

Both Hibari and Garland built adult careers of divahood in part by a mixture of suffering and grit. Importantly, although not exclusively, both shared a certain public iconicity among gay male fans. Note that this does not discount a strong lesbian following, but lesbian fandom may be far less public or may be subsumed, at least in the case of Hibari, as part of normalized same-sex relationships of emotional intimacy. In comparing Hibari with Garland, I am not attempting to compare gay male subcultures in the United States and Japan, which is beyond the purview of this writing; rather I am focusing on the shared aspects of both divas' star texts.

To a surprising degree, Richard Dyer's (1986) analysis of Judy Garland as a diva with a significant gay fandom parallels what might be said of Misora Hibari. Writing as an insider and scholar of gay subculture, Dyer (1986:155) analyzes Garland's particular appeal: "Garland works in an emotional register of great intensity which seems to bespeak equally suffering and survival, vulnerability and strength, theatricality and authenticity, passion and irony." In short, Garland, like Hibari, performs her own contradictions, and these find particular resonance in their gay fans, especially linking them to social suffering and performativity. Other female Euro-American singers who also enjoy a gay male following, such as Edith Piaf, Billie Holiday, and Barbra Streisand, may share some of these qualities, but according to Dyer, only Garland (and here, Hibari) possesses all of these and more.

The intensity of expression parallels the intensity of Garland's personal life, resulting in what Dyer (1986) calls a "comeback phenomenon" of repeatedly falling down and then picking oneself up that characterized Garland's later career. In Garland's case, falling down included suicide attempts for which she was hospitalized, as well as swings of weight loss and gain. Dyer (1986: 152) writes: "This comeback, going on going on, suffering and strength quality could even be read in the performance of the songs, especially towards the end of her career. In the later concerts, the sense of the trials of her life was no longer offstage . . . but could be seen in the frailty of her figure, heard in her shortness of breath and shaky high notes. . . . Yet she was still carrying on with the show." Hibari did much the same thing, with her most notable performance being her last, taking place at the Tokyo Dome only months before her death. In spite of a doctor's recommendation to cancel the show due to poor health and overall frail condition, Hibari took to the stage, looking alarmingly thin. But she refused to perform her own frailty. In true diva style, she propped herself into position (with backstage assistance), grabbed the microphone, and sang song after song, covering her hits from childhood (*Tokyo Kid*) to her latest *Kawa no nagare no yō ni* (Like the River Flows, Mitaki 1989), which has since become an anthem of her diva stardom. Like Garland, she carried on with the show, and did so dressed in gowns laden with sequins, donning elaborate headdresses of plumage and jewels, miming the movements of the songs that had placed her exactly where she belonged on that stage. She would have it no other way. Fans who I spoke with remember this performance not so much for her singing, which inevitably showed the ravages of her condition, but for her heroism. In Japanese terms, they invoke her spirit of *gambaru* (perseverance), but they share with Garland fans an appreciation of the melodrama of the moment. Here is performance as self-sacrifice, in effect, for their pleasure. Audience and diva lock arms within the tightened circle of the sacrificial lamb, both spent.

Dyer (1986:156) goes on to note three critical aspects of Garland's persona that contributed to her gay fandom: ordinariness, androgyny, and camp. And it is in this complete list that Hibari and Garland become eerily comparable bedfellows. Dyer (1986:156) writes of Garland: "The insistent ordinariness of her MGM [early film] image is a prerequisite for the gay male reading. It cannot be overstressed just how dominant the image was, and we should also remember the degree to which ordinariness was offered as the ultimate moral attribute of the American way of life." The ordinariness in Garland lay in her early portrayals of the typical small-town girl-next-door, or in the case of her most famous role as Dorothy in *The Wizard of Oz* (Fleming 1939), an orphan living with her aunt and uncle on a small farm in the middle of the United States. Garland's ordinary girl-next-door image parallels that of Hibari as *shōjo*, singing from the apple orchards of northern Japan to the alleyways of Tokyo as the optimistic can-do orphan. Hiroshi Aoyagi (2005:16) writes of the Japanese public's strong desire for *tōshindai* (ordinariness), in the portrayal of girl-next-door (or boy-next-door) by its young entertainment idols. Although Aoyagi was describing the entertainment machine of young teen idols primarily from the 1960s on, the aesthetic he describes provides apt reference for Hibari, as well. The ordinary represents not only attainability and accessibility, but most importantly, familiarity; in Japanese terms, she is part of *uchi* (inside, social in-group; contrasted with *soto*, outside, stranger). The star on the Japanese stage is thus most beloved because she represents "one of us." Notably, both Garland and Hibari retained a sense of the ordinary, even as they led and performed extraordinary lives. And yet, the ordinariness of their fundamental persona became part of the attraction, creating a framework of contradiction of an ordinary girl doing extraordinary things. They were both the girl-next-door placed on a national stage, *shōjo* faced with all-too-adult problems and situations. The tensions between ordinary and extraordinary cloaked both divas with an air of vulnerability.

Androgyny presents possibilities of cultural differences between the Japanese and Euro-American entertainment worlds, even as they demonstrate overlap. The overlap exists with shared cross-dressing elements of the twentieth-century entertainment stage that features girls and women in tuxedoes (albeit sometimes with short shorts and net stockings) and top hats, or other boys'/men's clothing, on both sides of the Pacific. The difference lies not so much in this modern cross-dressed display, but in the premodern cross-dressed roles discussed earlier. Whereas Garland developed a tramp androgyne onstage persona through short hair, open-collar men's shirts worn loosely with tails out, and slacks, Hibari fully adopted premodern, sword-brandishing samurai splendor with appearances in *chambara* (swordfight movies) and on-stage, singing men's songs of valor, strength, and stalwartness.

Camp—that tongue-in-cheek approach to comedy by juxtaposing opposites—speaks to the contradictions within divas such as Hibari and Garland, as well as the particular place of such humor in twentieth-century Euro-American gay men's subculture. Dyer (1986:178) describes camp as a "characteristically gay way of handling the values, images and products of the dominant culture through irony, exaggeration, trivialization, theatricalization and an ambivalent making fun of and out of the serious and respectable." Even if appreciation of camp goes well beyond gay subcultures, Dyer asserts that a particular affinity for subversion that dwells in a play of illusion and reality finds a welcome home within many Western gay men's circles, at least in the late twentieth-century of his writing. However, if we were to decouple camp from gay subculture, we would still be left with a relationship to the dominant culture that carries its own combination of wit and savagery. Thus Euro-American camp is not just ironic, but drippingly so; it is not merely exaggeration, but winkingly so; it is not just subversion, but derisively so. In camp, laughter becomes the ultimate judgmental expression.

According to Dyer (1986), camp encompasses late twentieth-century gay male subcultural expression in the West. However, on the Hibari stage, camp (that is, irony, exaggeration, trivialization, theatricalization, and making fun of the serious and respectable) exists as aboveground cultural expression through the concept of *asobi* (play). In short, the overlap between Hibari and camp rests not so much in the wicked savagery of the Euro-American diva stage, but in the far gentler, more ambiguous playground of *asobi*. The respected cultural position of *asobi* as the fount of creativity, invention, interaction, and expressivity, allowing one to artfully *kata-yabureru* (the breaking of *kata*, pattern, considered the height of creative achievement and knowledge) evidences a different approach to what might be considered camp (Yoshida, Tanaka, and Tsune 1987). And Hibari's performances abounded in *asobi*/camp. Sometimes the *asobi*/camp takes the form of a sexual come-on, especially with her female audiences. For example, during a sultry summer performance in 1981 marking the thirty-fifth anniversary of her debut, Hibari took out a handkerchief from the bosom of her gown, casually wiping the sweat from her armpits, neck, and chest, and suddenly pauses to look up at the audience, slyly asking "*Iroppoi desu ka?*" (Am I sexy?). The (mostly female) audience roared. Here is the wink of camp as pure sexual tease, woman to woman, nudging the nudge. In

Japan this kind of foreplay would not work as effectively for a male audience. The come-on would be interpreted as too direct, too overtly sexual, and thus not quite capturing the spirit of *asobi*. However, within a same-sex all-female context, the purported suggestiveness of Hibari's sweat could drip as an element of ambiguous humor—whether camp, erotica, or otherwise.

ON HIBARI AS BAD-GIRL/GOOD-GIRL DIVA

In a 2002 book, *Disruptive Divas; Feminism, Identity and Popular Music,* Lori Burns and Melisse Lafrance analyze four female musicians (Tori Amos, Courtney Love, Me'Shell Ndegeocello, and P. J. Harvey) for the ways in which each "disrupts" the boundaries of acceptable female music-making. Their choice of female artists and use of the concept of disruption is based upon the following four attributes: "marginal, countercultural positions in and through their creative work"; ability of the music to "disquiet and unsettle the listener"; "manipulations of conventions and styles"; and personal involvement in "the technical and creative operations of music making" (Burns and Lafrance 2002:2–3). Based on these definitions, I cannot include Misora Hibari (or Judy Garland, for that matter) as a "disruptive diva." Hibari worked far too much within a restrictive music industry as one of a stable of musicians at Japan's major recording company, Nippon Columbia. Her goals were always and only to succeed, not to challenge. That she became Nippon Columbia's biggest star is testament to her ambitions, founded in childhood and realized through talent and grit. In the process, she hardly asserted her will: the story goes that even toward the end of her career when she wanted to position a particular song as the A-side of a single, her producer would not allow her to do so. In short, her diva status lived primarily on stage, not necessarily off. And thus, as the hard-working, more-or-less obedient studio singer who did, and sang, what she was told, Hibari was a good girl. In general, she worked to please.

Nevertheless, I find the phrase "disruptive diva" intriguing and provocative, because even this good girl had a bad side. Part of it rests in the transgressions of her career, from the young girl with the too-low voice singing boogie-woogie and dancing jazz numbers with immodest abandon, to the hard-drinking hospitalized diva who defied doctor's orders to rise from her seclusion to perform once more on the sacrificial stage. Transgressions dovetailed with rumors to produce a diva shrouded in personal secrecy, as well as a diva defiant in confronting the negative publicity of her *yakuza*-linked brother.

If we are to consider Hibari as a disruptive diva, then we must place her within the disruptions of her era. Here is the Tokyo Kid made good, just as orphan Japan succeeded beyond anyone's expectations to rise from the ashes of war to international economic ascendancy. Just as stunning, Hibari accomplished her declaration, made when a young ten-year-old girl at the base of an ancient cypress tree following a near-fatal accident, that she would become the number one singer in all of Japan. Here I do not mean to add to the hagiographic narrative of Misora Hibari, elevating her to a prescient Queen of Postwar Japan. Rather, I suggest that we examine her star text and her diva status as a morality tale that Japan may tell of itself to itself (possibly as a tale oft told). In parallel with Misora Hibari's life, career, and death, postwar Japan itself may stumble as fraught icon, from the pedestal of accomplishment only to pick itself up time and again. In the end, that is the story of diva-hood, reaching the highest heights from stumbling through the lowest of lows. In short, Misora Hibari, like postwar Japan, may be viewed specifically through her transgressions. This is exactly the position from which she could be heralded as the "people's singer," only as fallible as they are, in a classed, generational, and national position of badness. Her tears flow as one whose suffering parades her vulnerability, shared with "the people," an era, and a nation.

These contradictions frame Hibari's postwar divahood. Challenged by wave after wave of new sounds and images from abroad, she eventually became rebranded as the queen of things fundamentally common and Japanese. It is the juxtaposition of the two—fundamentally common and Japanese—that levels the social playing field into one of intimate access. In the 2000s, that juxtaposition has been memorialized through numerous televised and concert tributes, statues in various parts of Japan, museums, postage stamps. She returns in the form of holograms, robots (such as the 2007 Misora Hibari Little Jammer Pro from Bandai), and endless performances of her songs by professional and amateur singers. If Misora Hibari emerged as a poster child of things Japanese in the Jet Age, then that version of Japan included ironic admixtures of ethnic minority positions and nostalgized retreats into premodern forms. The child star divahood of Misora Hibari, however, represents more than retreat. Rather, it represents triumphal mimicry—even appropriation—while maintaining one's Japaneseness, the nation's *shōjo,* singing in and of complex times. Misora Hibari as postwar Japan suggests the bad-girl/good-girl divahood that encompasses the contradictions of the era. This heady admixture of transgression, glitter, and melodrama disrupts the very structures of an era and a nation. Thus, in that rainy season of 1989, people's tears flowed for the passing of an era, simultaneously mourning and celebrating the diva who lay dying.

CHAPTER 6

Yoko Ono

A Transgressive Diva

CAROLYN S. STEVENS

Before the Internet, and before the "Cool Japan" era, Yoko Ono was arguably the most famous Japanese person outside of Japan. A Japanese artist, musician and peace activist, Ono found worldwide fame in the 1960s and 1970s through her relationship with the famous Beatles band member John Lennon. Despite her significant body of visual and recording work, and her political and environmental activism, she is best (or perhaps worst) known as the woman—a Japanese woman—who broke up the Beatles. She came from a privileged background, yet experienced isolation and hardship as a child; as an adult, she married one of the most famous men in the world, but was despised and publicly ridiculed for her relationship with him. Then, she lost him in the most horrific circumstances. Not all critics have seen her work as complex or meaningful, but her life story, as it has been publicly performed in her art and as covered by the global media, is a narrative of great peaks and valleys, representing a singular experience of Japanese womanhood during a time of great social change.

For this reason, Ono represents a certain kind of diva: a Japanese woman who has lived her life beyond set geographic, social, political, and aesthetic borders (and as we see in other contributions to this volume, these borders can be quite rigid within Japanese society). As an international public figure, Ono has been often labelled with a variety of names—and sometimes epithets—yet she is a Japanese national, a woman, an artist, and a political activist. Unlike a "stereotypical" (read:

submissive) Japanese woman, for much of her life Ono did not conform to expected feminine roles such as wife and mother. She married three times, but each relationship was marked by independence and partnership equality. As a proponent of peace, she was the target of direct and indirect verbal and physical violence on many occasions. Some biographers present her as a highly creative but also at times manipulative individual (e.g., Hopkins 1987, Goldman 1988, and Riley 2011) while others write more admiringly and respectfully of her persona and experiences (see essays in Munroe and Hendricks's 2000 retrospective, Norman 2009, Carver 2012, Kulwicki 2011, Mackie 2012, and Zoladz 2015). Ono is a woman of many public (and private) faces, one who has been simultaneously revered and reviled consistently over her many decades in the global media.

This chapter argues that Ono's life and work contributes to our understanding of iconic Japanese women through her distinguished artistic and political work. As a public figure, however, she is different from some of the other Japanese women profiled in this volume. When imagining an icon for Japanese femininity, foreigners might rely on conflated Japanese mash-ups of the orientalist geisha girl and/or the postmodern *kawaii anime* (cute animation) heroine as a baseline for what a Japanese woman might look and sound like, or how she might live her life. Yet Ono's legacy (and current activism) presents a different image of Japanese femininity to the rest of the world. She is both "Japanese" and "not-Japanese." She is an artist who has been both critically acclaimed and dismissed. Her early migration overseas and her relationship with a global superstar mean that Ono's story is an exceptional one, but it is through this exception that her life's work has gained traction with a global audience. One of the few Japanese divas well known outside of Japan, she has had an impact, at times negative and at times positive, on the world's perception of Japanese women since the 1960s. Yet, in embodying these many contradictions, her life story demonstrates an honest and sometimes fallible humanity which transgresses gender and cultural borders. This chapter first outlines Ono's formative years, before she was thrust into the global gaze. Then, I review Ono's art, music, and film work through selective examples that demonstrate her views on gender and society. Lastly, I look at how she and critics have come to terms with her life story after Lennon's premature death. Her status as a Japanese woman living overseas, as a feminist, and as an independent woman makes Yoko Ono a transgressive "diva of Japan."

ONO'S EARLY LIFE AS A GLOBAL CITIZEN

*Genzai no watashi no seikatsu o hitokuchi de hyōgen sureba, shakai no
henken o mushi shite, "jibun" ni narikiru to iu koto o negatteiru seikatsu da.*

If I were to express my current lifestyle in one word, it would be a life that
wishes for one to ignore social prejudice and be completely one's own "self"
(Ono 1974:237).[1]

In the 1960s and 1970s, a time of great social change for women around
the world, Ono's story represented a truly progressive and international
vision of Japanese women. Under a global gaze, she is undeniably "Japanese," despite her long association and residence in London and New
York. Yet, from Japan, she is seen as somehow "foreign," illustrated by
the Japanese press's habitual use of *katakana* syllabic script to write her
name as if she were a foreigner, not the characters her parents used to
register her birth in Tokyo on February 18, 1933. The meaning of Yoko's
given name was translated into English by Lennon as "ocean child" in the
1968 Beatles song *Julia,* but the Chinese character used for *yō* in her
name also means "Western," or "Occidental" (as in "across the ocean").[2]
From her birth, Ono was an individual with broad horizons.

Yoko Ono is the great-granddaughter of Yasuda Zenjirō, the founder
of the Yasuda *zaibatsu* (large industrial monopolies which were disman-
tled or reorganized during the postwar period) on her maternal side, and
the great-granddaughter on her paternal side of Saisho Atsushi, one of
the leaders in the battle to end Tokugawa rule in the 1860s (Munroe
2000:14; Clayson 2004:11). Because Saisho's daughter—Ono's paternal
grandmother—was an only child, her father invested heavily in her education (Hopkins 1987:6), and she received more opportunities than
other young women might have at that time. Saisho Tsuruko studied
English and then converted to Christianity, a religion she passed down
to her son, Ono's father. Yoko Ono is said to have been brought up as
"half Buddhist, half Protestant," and this bicultural set of values was
strengthened by her experience living in the United States from 1933 to
1937, and again in 1941 to 1942. Her father, an aspiring pianist, gave up
his ambitions for a musical career when he married Ono's mother, and
went into the more stable profession of international banking (Munroe
2000:14–15). As his grandfather had done before, Ono Eisuke invested
in the academic and musical education of Yoko, his firstborn child,
despite his being away on foreign postings for much of her childhood.

Ono, in a recent interview in Sydney, reflects on her childhood and
says that as a young girl she always had felt that she "would like to

change the world . . . I was going to say to fix the world, but I don't know, was it to fix the world or change the world? It's a very delicate difference" (Contemporary Museum of Modern Art 2013). Precocious at a young age, she would have been one of the first *kikokushijo* (returnee students), even before the term became widely used in the 1980s and 1990s. From an early age, this "ocean child" was surrounded by international intellectual traditions and values. As a small child, she attended a Christian school, Keimei Gakuin, where she studied English and Bible studies. In her autobiographical essay, she writes of her childhood as being lonely. Her early memories of Japan, she states, were when she was about five or six years old, and she was living alone in a house in Kamakura with servants, as her father was overseas for work and her mother was busy in Tokyo (Ono 1974:240). She was aware from an early age that her social privilege isolated her from bonding with other people:

> [When a servant] was supposed to play with me, they would say in an unpleasant tone "What would you like to do? (*nani o surun de gozaimasu ka*)." Even a child could understand that attitude of dislike. . . . [Even when a classmate came over to play], I would say, "I'll play whatever you want to play!" but the girl's answer was the same: "no, whatever the young lady likes is fine (*iie ojōsan no nasaritai koto de ii*)." That was so lonely (Ono 1974:241).

Ono later wrote that she learned to manage her childhood feelings of loneliness and boredom through the study of music and literature. These stories give us some insight into the formation of her social and emotional independence, seen later in her unconventional marriages and her views toward motherhood. Given this experience, it is understandable that she became an adult who had little patience for conforming to the social status quo. While she admits her mother came from a more progressive family, in general the Onos were a conventional, "establishment" family, and she wrote that as she was growing up she learned that "running underground and being unconventional was delightful" (Ono 1974:241).

During some of her father's overseas postings, Ono attended school in San Francisco and New York (Clayson 2004:20–21), before returning to Japan in 1942. Her Tokyo education was interrupted by her family's wartime evacuation to Karuizawa in 1945, where the three Ono siblings survived by trading their Yasuda and Ono family heirlooms to local farmers for food (Sayle 2000:53). After the war ended, she returned to Tokyo and entered Gakushūin, a high school and university associated with the aristocracy in Japan. Her classmates at that time included then Crown Prince Akihito, and his younger brother Prince Masahito, with whom she developed a friendship (Hopkins 1987:11). Another famed classmate at Gakushūin was the writer Mishima Yukio (Munroe 2000:15). After graduating from its secondary school, she was admitted to Gakushūin University's philosophy department in 1952, the first Japanese woman to do so in its history. At university, she first came into contact with left-wing ideas that confronted her own social and economic privilege, and these ideas sat uneasily with the high expectations placed upon her as a descendent of two high-ranking families (Munroe 2000:15–16). She left this program after studying there for only two semesters, and joined her family who were at the time living in Scarsdale, New York. She enrolled at Sarah Lawrence College, which at the time was seen as a relatively progressive and even "permissive" school for upperclass young women (Clayson 2004:26).

Ono suspended her study at Sarah Lawrence in 1955 to marry Ichiyanagi Toshi, who studied at Julliard and was an associate of John Cage (Munroe 2000:15, 17). The couple moved to Manhattan, and during this period (the mid-1950s to the early 1960s), Ono developed her ambitions to create art, both static and performed (as a kind of "happening") in New York. This was a time that has been described as both inspiring and impressive, due to her proximity to the flourishing creativity of Cage and Fluxus founder George Maciunas (Munroe 2000:13, 17; Hopkins 1987:22) as well as difficult and even soul-destroying, as the newlyweds lived in relative poverty, having declared their independence from Ono's family wealth (Hopkins 1987:23). Ichiyanagi and Ono's music and art found limited audiences, but in 1961 she did hold her first "concert" at Carnegie Hall, not in the main auditorium but in a smaller room in the building (Clayson 2004:33). This event drew little attention; discouraged, Ono returned to Japan and worked with Ichiyanagi on various productions (including the first art installment named *Cut Piece,* detailed below), but to little acclaim. The marriage broke up not long after their return to Japan.

In Tokyo, she met American Anthony Cox, who was to be her second husband. In early 1963 she married Cox, and their child, Kyoko, was born later that year. In 1964, the small family returned to New York (Munroe 2000:26–27). Cox and Ono then moved to London in 1966, and in November of that year Ono met John Lennon for the first time at the Indica Gallery in the fashionable St. James section of London. There, as famously recalled by many hangers-on and observers, Lennon is said to have been impressed by the optimism expressed in several installations and paintings in her *Unfinished Paintings and Objects,* Ono's first major London exhibition. In particular, he was enamored with the *Painting to Hammer a Nail* piece, which invited the observer to participate in the creative process. He also felt they shared the same sense of humor; when John scoffed at the price of the participation (five shillings), he asked Yoko if he could pay an imaginary price for an imaginary nail (Munroe 2000:31). He also cited the simple but effective *Ceiling Painting (YES Painting)* as having a particularly positive impression on him (Clayson 2004:55). In this piece, the viewer is invited to stand on a chair and gaze at the ceiling, from which a magnifying glass was suspended. Expecting some wry or sarcastic surprise, Lennon was delighted to find only the tiny word "YES" written there.

At the start of her relationship with Lennon, much of the criticism leveled against Ono was racially tinged, but her nationality and race were not the only disruptive factors. The very public fact that Lennon was a married man with a small son did not facilitate their blossoming romantic and creative relationship and instead she was viewed as an immoral home wrecker. This was not the first time a celebrity affair had been outed, however. More importantly in this case was that even as "the other woman," Ono did not conform to the public's image of what an "other woman" should look or act like. Not only did she not conform to British (white) standards of attractiveness, Ono did not mesh with Western stereotypes of Japanese femininity in either her behavior or appearance (Figure 21). Her previous marriages, her vocal manner (her accented English could veer between saccharinely childish to irritatingly screechy) and fuzzy, unfashionable hairstyle didn't fit with their image of a well-bred and attractive Japanese woman—one who should present a modest manner and appearance, and speak in gracious and harmonious tones. Her Japaneseness was "foreign" to the extent that British and American reporters could not place her in a continuum of tropes that expressed Japanese feminine identity as they understood it: she was no geisha, nor was she a "good housewife and wise mother," nor a "well-bred miss" such as Asada Mao (see Masafumi Monden's Chapter 10 in this volume). Even Japanese writers at the time saw her as an atypical example of Japanese womanhood, as in a popular manga at the time, which portrayed Ono as a shape-shifting, oversexualized being who not only breaks up the Beatles but also draws Lennon into a farcical protest about the Vietnam War (Oikawa and Terayama 1997). The Japanese media at the time often referred to her as a "*hapunisto*," loosely translated as a person who conducts "happenings," a term used in the 1960s not only to refer to avant-garde performance art that was emerging at the time, but also referenced the "loose morals" sometimes seen at such events (Ōmura 2016:381).

21. Yoko Ono from a pamphlet for *Yoko at Indica* (1966), held at the Indica Gallery, 6 Mason's Yard, Duke Street, St. James, London (photo courtesy of the Rare Books Collection, Monash University Library).

After her 1969 marriage to Lennon, Ono's work was scrutinized more heavily, and the couple found the negative media attention upsetting (as demonstrated in their film *Rape*, detailed below). After a few more years in England with Lennon, the two emigrated to the United States, and continued their musical and political activities despite fighting several prolonged legal battles: the first with her ex-husband Cox over custody of their daughter, and the second with U.S. immigration, over Lennon's rejected application for a green card. Ross (2000:56) writes of this period that "both were targets, not only of continuous FBI harassment . . . but also of those whose inner hatreds and reliance upon violence defined them." Despite this, Lennon and Ono had some creative success, including Lennon's singles with Yoko such as *Instant Karma!* (1970), *Power to the People* (1971a), *Imagine* (1971b), and *Whatever Gets You thru the Night* (1974).

Lennon and Ono separated for about a year during this time, but they reunited in late 1974 (Hopkins 1987:193). The couple then went into a kind of artistic hibernation, with Ono focusing on developing their business portfolio, which included not only managing John's financial affairs but also taking on new projects in real estate, the acquisition of art and antiques, and dairy farming (Norman 2009:772–75). Their son Sean Taro Ono Lennon was born soon after Lennon's green card was granted in 1975, and the family continued to live in relative media seclusion for some years after their son's birth. In 1979, Lennon decided to return to the studio, resulting in the LP *Double Fantasy* (1980), titled because of its dual approach: the album consisted of alternating tracks composed and performed by Lennon and Ono. Only weeks after this comeback record was released, however, John Lennon was fatally shot by Mark David Chapman at the entrance of their apartment building in Manhattan. Overnight, Ono was transformed from the part she had played since 1968 to a new role, from the "woman who broke up the Beatles" to the "world's most famous widow." In this new role, Ono has gone on to release more music, such as the single *Walking on Thin Ice* (Ono 1981a) and the album *Season of Glass* (Ono 1981b), which is probably her most commercially successful work. She continues to live in Manhattan, working to curate the legacy of her husband's music, artwork, and writings. The most notable project in this vein would be her release of a number of demos which allowed the three remaining Beatles to create new music for the 1995 documentary and six-CD set *Anthology* (The Beatles 1995). Her own work has been featured in museums and galleries around the world in a variety of retrospectives that also include new pieces and reinterpretations of her past work, and she is active in promoting political causes such as Artists Against Fracking (2013).

As an artist and an activist, Ono's work has a wide reach, considering her period of activity from the mid-1950s to the present. Given her prolific output, to summarize her life work is a difficult task, but in the context of this chapter's charge to understand her work as an expression of her "transgressive" diva status, I focus on two major themes: Ono as a feminist and Ono as a peace activist. Through these thematic groupings, we can analyze her work as viewed as transgressive in the era in which they were presented. While her work today may be seen as close to, if not wholly, mainstream art and politics, we must remember that in the 1960s and 1970s, Ono's message was on the edge of what was considered acceptable, both artistically and socially.

YOKO ONO AS A FEMINIST ARTIST

Despite her association with "foreignness," Ono is still considered an early proponent for feminism in Japan. Her image and story are included in the 2015 "First Feminists of Japan" calendar, an annual publication of a feminist press (JOJO Kikaku 2015). When John Lennon sang, "I gotta ask you comrades and brothers/how do you treat your own woman back home?" in his 1971 song *Power to the People,* many understood these lyrics as inspired by Ono, who had been probing mainstream definitions of femininity and sexuality for many years. Sayle (2000: 53), in his discussion of Ono's life and work, writes that her feminist perspectives are rooted in her Japanese heritage, as her international background allowed her to understand differences in women's rights in the United States and Japan. Raised in a family of highly educated and independent women, Ono would have found restrictions against her (in Japanese, American, and British society) difficult to accept. In her performance, film and musical works, we see distinctive strands of Ono's feminist beliefs expressed. There are many examples to choose from, but here I offer a discussion of a few seminal works: *Cut Piece* (1964), *Rape* (1969), and *Sisters, O Sisters* (1971) to demonstrate Ono's ideas about the strength and vulnerability of women in contemporary society.

Cut Piece *(1964)*

One of the most famous examples of her feminist artwork, and of her performance work in general, is *Cut Piece,* first staged in 1964 in Kyoto, and again from 1965 to 1967 in Japan and New York (at the Carnegie Recital Hall, Munroe 2000:158). During this performance piece, Ono sat "in a traditional Japanese female position . . . with her face mask-like" (Munroe 2000:28) while audience members were instructed to cut off pieces of Ono's clothing with scissors. How far would the audience members go to provoke a response from the artist? Sitting in silence, motionless, Ono made a blunt and discomfiting statement to the audience about the relationship between art and gender. She, as a potentially naked female body, could only shock the audience as much as they desired, forcing them to acknowledge the active role audiences play in marginalizing feminist art. Ono's statement distributed to the audience at the time contained a section that eerily foreshadowed her treatment by the press after her relationship with Lennon went public:

> People went on cutting the parts they do not like of me until there was only the stone that remained of me that was in me but they were still not satisfied and wanted to know what it's like in the stone.[3] y.o. (Ono 1966:n.p.)

In a 1974 essay, she recalled the details of the early *Cut Piece* performances and how they were received at the time:

> The idea is that I sit on the stage wearing western clothes, and the audience cut and destroyed my clothes with scissors, snipping away. Previously, artists had made something of themselves and presented that to an audience. I wanted to give a present of myself rather than a thing as a gift . . . I wanted to create something that had no pride and was on the border of selflessness. . . .
>
> I went on stage wearing my best suit. Wearing something cheap that would cut easily would go against my intent. To perform this piece while I was poor was painful! . . . I really felt that the audience saw me as a true offering. They were totally silent. I could hear their breathing . . . long moments of time passed, with the audience taking pieces from around my body until it was gone. Then, I was down to my brassiere. The moment the strap was broken, without thinking of course I pressed my hands to my chest. Some people criticized me afterwards, saying "Covering herself like that—that's not 'pure'" . . . [Even though] the event was criticized but it cultivated in me a sense of quiet success. I went on with all my might following the art that I believed in (Ono 1974:246–47).

Striking here is her physical description of the performance: the need to use thick material to emphasize the effort of the cuts; the uncomfortable silence revealing the breathing sounds of the audience; and the instinctual modesty that arose when her breasts were uncovered. Many years later Alexandra Munroe, curator at the Guggenheim, wrote that

> *Cut Piece* expresses an anguished interiority while offering a social commentary on the quiet violence that binds individual and society, the self and gender, alienation and connectedness (Munroe 2000:28).

Today *Cut Piece* is seen as one of Ono's more successful "events" where she saw her art as not static objects passively presented to an audience, but instead as "an immediate social event . . . and an aesthetic commentary on the complicit relationship between individuals and the social body as a whole" (Munroe 2000:158).

Rape *(1969)*

Ono's feminist concerns are also represented in her many film projects, which focus primarily on "concern with the body, women's rights, personal freedom and political activism" (Iles 2000:205). *Rape* (1969) is 75-minute film that reveals several aspects of Ono's experience as a woman and as a sudden celebrity in the late 1960s. The title "rape" is an inclusive one, which refers to the sexualized and personalized interest the mass media takes in women as well as men. As Norman (2009:597) writes, "the rapist in the film is the television camera, which followed [the] character everywhere with the same remorselessness that such devices once had stalked the Beatles—and now the newlywed Lennons." But it is no coincidence that the Lennons chose to portray this invasion of personal space through the representation of a solitary young woman's experience. At first, the actress accommodates the camera's presence in an awkward but sociable way, but soon the young woman's patience is worn down, and her body is on display for public consumption, regardless of her consent.

The film begins in a graveyard, showing the woman being followed. At first she smiles and tries to communicate with the cameraperson in German and Italian, before admitting she doesn't speak English. Her attempts at speaking to the camera/audience are not translated, which forces the audience to rely on her facial expression and body language, rather than words, for meaning. The graveyard scene, despite its bleak landscape, has a relatively benign level of intrusion, but the followed woman begins to show irritation when she is rebuffed with silence after trying to engage the cameraperson by asking for a light for her cigarette. The chase accelerates as the woman is followed next onto a London street complete with iconic red double-decker buses. The sound of her increasingly urgent footsteps and those of the camera crew following her are set against ambient environmental sounds and the woman's untranslated protestations. The woman goes back and forth between two strategies: ignoring the intrusion and confronting it, which are symbolized through shots of her back as she walks away from the camera, and close-ups of her face as she turns to protest. A half an hour into the film, she becomes fed up and seeks escape by calling a friend, and then taking a taxi (but the crew merely take the next taxi and follow her). As the chase wears on, the woman appears older, as her tear-stained mascara creates dark circles under her eyes in contrast to the wide-eyed smiling look she had at the start of the film. Indoor shots of her (presumed) flat show an unmade bed, underscoring the sense of invasion of privacy of one's inner sanctum, and at this point, the woman begins to try to block the camera's gaze with personal possessions from the room and she begins to shout: "*Das ist genug!*" (that's enough!). She attempts to use the phone but it seems there is no one to call for help. No one intervenes on her behalf, demonstrating that the personal safety of a woman is portrayed as her own sole responsibility and solitary experience. Whether she is outside or inside a building, she is not given reprieve. The woman speaks to the silent camera (which makes itself visible at various click points in the film) but given that there is no answer, she seems to be talking to herself, hinting at the edge of madness to which the pursuit drives her: she screams "*Weg! weg!*" (away!). Late in the film, the woman covers her face with her hands; sitting in a chair, she bends down and assumes an almost fetal position, her long hair covering her head and face. She uses the telephone again and after repeated attempts finally gets through to a female voice on the other end of the line—she asks for the police's help, because—she then breaks into English, saying "My passport is expired I have to go to the Austrian embassy." Her eye makeup is smeared and as we hear the other end of the line drone on with a seemingly unhelpful response, the screen goes blank except for one word: RAPE.

This short film was broadcast on Austrian television in March 1969 and received some exposure and good press in Canada and England (Norman 2009:597), where critics praised it as Kafkaesque. While this film portrays the physical and emotional invasion both Ono and Lennon felt throughout their careers, it is important that a female, rather than a male, actor was chosen to portray this sense of vulnerability. Of interest is also the portrayal of the woman as young and beautiful at the start of the film, but her appearance (along with her well-being) disintegrates as the film's tension mounts. Women are always vulnerable to, and are deeply hurt by, the invasive gaze of the media, and of society in general. This is still true today, where women are more often than not the target of online harassment and abuse. Despite this film's negative message, it serves as evidence of Ono's personal strength arising from her experience; she said, "Having been so severely attacked and laughed at by the whole world, I feel I became wiser, stronger, and more creative for it" (cited in Wenner 2004:60).

Sisters, O Sisters *(1971) and Other Writings*

Besides performance art and film, music is the other main artistic mode that Ono has used to express feminist messages. Though trained as a classical musician as a child and married to a Japanese musician from 1956 to 1963, she did not focus on musical performance much in her early career. After partnering with John Lennon, however, her musical output gained momentum, though some of these works are co-credited with Lennon. An example of Ono's only composition credited to her alone during John's early post-Beatle career is *Sisters, O Sisters*, a song performed in 1971 by Ono, Lennon, and others at a benefit concert for prisoners who had been injured during riots (Clayson 2004:88–89). It was released as the B side to Lennon's A-side single *Woman Is the Nigger of the World* in early 1972 and also included on Lennon's *Sometime in New York City* album. *Woman Is the Nigger of the World* featured John on vocals but the composition was co-credited to Ono, and Norman (2009:698) writes that the title of the song was originally Ono's "pioneering feminist slogan." American media censors banned the song on radio stations, but Lennon and Ono were able to draw attention to the song's intent and meaning when popular talk-show host Dick Cavett allowed them to discuss the song and perform it on their 1972 appearance on his show (Norman 2009:698–99).

Linked by their positions on the single, the two songs are an inseparable pair, giving the celebrity couple each a chance to express their views on women's rights. While the A side tune is a bluesy mid-tempo piece and has more cynical tone ("we make her paint her face and dance"), Ono's B side is more positive. The song starts out with Yoko's *a capella* statement: "male chauvinist pig engineer," which is quickly followed by John's response: "right on, sister." Its lyrics are relatively simple and even repetitive, using environmental images to communicate the loss of status women currently experience. The song is a wake-up call to women to reclaim their "wisdom" and "knowledge" to rebuild a "new world." Despite the darker notions of femininity expressed in *Cut Piece* and *Rape*, this song is more optimistic, for she sings "it's never too late" for the struggle to begin.

Sayle (2000:53) writes that both these songs were inspired by Ono's personal experience of despair in the immediate postwar period for "what her humbler sisters had once been driven to, just for survival." Both Ono and Lennon had unhappy childhoods: Lennon had been separated from his divorced parents from a young age, and Ono retained bitter memories from being surrounded by emotionally distant servants. Unsurprisingly, in their adult lives she and Lennon chose to identify with the politics of the working class; Lennon portrayed himself as a *Working Class Hero* for much of his career, despite this not being actually the case (while Ono had the more distinguished pedigree, Lennon's family was solidly middle class, Norman 2009:651). Nevertheless, Ono recognized the creative and social stagnation of the establishment classes and relied on class-based intersectionality to make their message regarding feminism relevant to a wider audience.

About the time *Sisters, O Sisters* was released, Ono was also especially active as an essayist. Her biographer Hopkins (1987:165) writes that the early 1970s was her "most feminist period" when she submitted several articles in national and local presses. Her 1972 essay "The Feminization of Society," reprinted in the *New York Times,* is probably her most well-known, and gives us a sense of the politics that lay behind the *Woman Is the . . ./Sisters, O Sisters* single (Ono 2014). In it, Ono again makes an intersectional statement, equating women's status with slavery, and chiding elite professional women for "kicking our sisters on the way up." She also warns that equality in some areas of society (the military, for example) is a "con" and that buying into "male perversions" will not bring about true equality. Some of her statements today seem out of sync with contemporary understandings of women's politics and sexuality (e.g., her view that "lesbianism" is a major contributor to the women's movement because it is a "rebellion" against the "existing society"), but Ono asks still important questions, such as:

> The ultimate goal of female liberation is not just to escape from male oppression. How about liberating ourselves from our various mind trips such as ignorance, greed, masochism, fear of God and social conventions? [. . .]

> Childcare is the most important issue for the future of our generation. It is no longer a pleasure for the majority of men and women in our society, because the whole society is geared towards living up to a Hollywood-cum-Madison Avenue image of men and women, and a way of life that has nothing to do with childcare. We are in a serious identity crisis. This society is driven by neurotic speed and force accelerated by greed, and frustration of not being able to live up to the image of men and women we have created for ourselves; the image has nothing to do with the reality of people. How could we be an eternal James Bond or Twiggy (false eyelashes, the never-had-a-baby-or-a-full-meal look) and raise three kids on the side? In such an image-driven culture, a piece of reality, such as a child, becomes a direct threat to our false existence. [. . .]

I am proposing the feminization of society; the use of feminine nature as a positive force to change the world. We can change ourselves with feminine intelligence and awareness, into a basically organic, noncompetitive society that is based on love, rather than reasoning. The result will be a society of balance, peace and contentment. We can evolve rather than revolt, come together, rather than claim independence, and feel rather than think. These are characteristics that are considered feminine; characteristics that men despise in women. But have men really done so well by avoiding the development of these characteristics within themselves? (Ono 2014)

The essay closes on a both realistic and hopeful note: "As mothers of the tribe, we share the guilt of the male chauvinists, and our faces are their mirrors as well. It's good to start now, since it's never too late to start from the start" (Ono 2014).

Reading her work from the 1960s and 1970s today, it is striking how many issues she has identified that have not yet been resolved; for example, intensified by the prevalence of social media, the "Hollywood-cum-Madison-Avenue" image of men and women is still a negative influence in the lives of many women. Despite its lasting message, Ono's feminist art, music, and writing have met with mixed responses: as noted by Ono herself, *Cut Piece* was seen at the time as an attention-seeking stunt; *Rape* was critically well received but never saw exposure outside a limited European run. Her music with John Lennon had the most global exposure, but she was often criticized there for taking advantage of his fame to further her career. One might also argue that while her relationship with John Lennon widened her exposure, it also hampered her ability to be taken "seriously" as an artist due to his commercial "pop star" status. In this sense, Ono was arguably one of the earliest and most visible examples of the 1970s' catchphrase "the personal is political"—she both benefited from this but bore much criticism when her personal life was at the forefront of her art.

AT LAST . . . WAR IS OVER? ONO AS THE WORLD'S MOST FAMOUS WIDOW

Ono's art and music has been strongly criticized over the decades, though it is often unclear if the criticism is in response to the work itself or of her relationship to, and influence over, John Lennon. Most would agree, however, that after years of being seen as "transgressive" as an attention-seeking strategy, criticism of Ono has waned. This has likely occurred in sympathy to her transition into her new public role as the world's most famous widow. Despite her desire to be seen as an independent artist both during Lennon's lifetime and after his death, a significant proportion of Ono's work today focuses on preserving Lennon's legacy, both musical and political. In these pursuits, she has received more favorable press: the *New York Times* reviewed her recent work sympathetically, saying

> The unrest in the Middle East, the economic downturn in Europe and the political challenges here at home, they say, have made people more receptive to her simple, unironic message about loving one another and doing your part to bring about social change (Bernstein 2012).

Some of the retrospective exhibitions featuring Ono's work include "Yoko Ono: War Is Over, If You Want It" (Sydney, 2013) and "Yoko Ono: One Woman Show 1960–1971" (New York, 2015). Regarding the title choice of the Sydney show, the museum curators wrote that Ono and Lennon's phrase, while belittled as naïve in 1969, "decades later, those words still resound, they have meaning and currency today, and . . . they still speak to a younger generation" (Contemporary Museum of Modern Art 2013). The press release for Ono's 2015 MoMA exhibit tells the story of a 1971 unofficial event that she performed there, where in avant-garde guerrilla form, she "infiltrated the Museum's walls and the consciousness of its visitors without having any work on display" (Graham 2015)— with affection rather than sarcasm, demonstrating the slow shift toward acceptance of Ono and her work.

Ono (2012) has written about emotional resilience and staying true to herself in a *Rolling Stone* essay, where she relates a story during Lennon's final recording sessions. During a break, she tells how they went shopping and purchased wrap-around sunglasses. Ono writes that Lennon stared at her when she put them on, and explained why she continues to be photographed wearing similar shades today.

> It reminded me of the first time I saw him gazing at my "Painting to Hammer a Nail In" in the Indica gallery. This time he was gazing at me wearing the glasses he picked for me. "Why?" I asked with my eyes. . . . I immediately forgot the incident totally. Later those were the glasses I wore to face the world. I heard John saying "Keep your chin up. Never let them know that they got you!" So even after his passing, he was still protecting and helping me (Ono 2012:91).

Ono does on occasion defend herself in the press. One early example of this is an essay submitted to the *Village Voice* in 1971, which was then expanded and republished the following year in the magazine *Sundance* (Ono 2014). In this evolving essay, Ono called out her critics not on sexism or racism, but on intellectualism, stating that most music writers have "lost the ears to understand the type of music" that she and Lennon played, which was intended to reach the masses, not a small elite (Hopkins 1987:161–62). "The ears to understand" Ono's work, however, also includes a sensibility and an openness to new perspectives, which challenge patriarchy and unsettle the establishment. Men are not her only detractors, however, demonstrating that the "sisterhood" that Ono wished to create is still not realized. For example, social/art critic Camille Paglia (1992) has famously sided against Ono in an evaluation of Lennon's *oeuvre*. Situating Lennon in her discussion of great rock musicians who "emerged from art schools," giving them cultural legitimacy, she then critiques his "lesser" solo work as being overinfluenced by Ono's "infantalising" (Christy 1999).

Ono is not silent in the wake of these continuing judgments. She maintains an active online presence; in early 2015, Ono posted a black-and-white photograph of herself sitting in the middle of an instillation of the *Half-a-Wind* exhibition, presumably at its opening in 1967 at the Lisson Gallery in London. Wearing an androgynous outfit of a black top and black pants, she sits cross-legged on the floor, her hands clasped and gazing directly at the camera. The caption reads:

> I see a woman who is rather calm because she doesn't know what is waiting for her in her life after this. I was still not "that woman" who was hated by the public. I was an artist with fresh ideas. yoko (Ono 2015)

The blunt honesty of this statement asks the audience to consider the separation of her intertwined identities: how would she be viewed if we could separate "that [other] woman" from the "artist with fresh ideas." Her caption for this photograph is nationless and ungendered, defining herself as a person first with "fresh ideas," rather than as the "destructive Japanese witch" who tore apart the most beloved pop band in the world. Ono's vision here should be integrated into our understandings of the meaning of Japanese femininity as she looks back at herself in 2015, conquering the world in 1966—this sense of creativity and originality could belong to anyone and at any time. Being a Japanese woman does not preclude a global outlook.

NOTES

1. This quote comes from her lengthy 1974 essay in the literary magazine *Bungei Shunjū*, entitled *Waga ai, waga tōsō* (My Love, My Struggle, Ono 1974). In this essay, Ono writes about her sense of alienation from her natural self

through social rules and structure; her work as a struggling artist in New York and London (prior to meeting Lennon); her feelings about her childhood and motherhood; the ups and downs of her relationship with John Lennon; and her views on feminism.

2. The transliteration of Ono's given name is technically Yōko, but given that her name is well known in the international media without the diacritic, this chapter conforms to this convention.

3. The text here is reproduced as it was originally written, without internal punctuation.

CHAPTER 7

Transbeauty IKKO

A Diva's Guide to Glamour,
Virtue, and Healing

JAN BARDSLEY

Strut, don't stroll. Flaunt your originality. Embrace your own inner diva. Want to see how it's done? Catch an online clip, a fashion layout, or a book cover featuring IKKO, Japan's celebrity make-up artist and author of numerous beauty guides. A tall, compelling presence, IKKO is a diva like no other. No wonder she renders her name in caps. Yet fame came relatively late in her life. IKKO was in her mid-forties in 2007 when she became synonymous with the exuberant catchphrase *Dondake!* ("What the . . . ?"/"Who the hell do you think you are?"), turning this irreverent expression from Tokyo gay-bar culture into one of the year's top ten trend-setting phrases (Maree 2013:107). By 2008, two of IKKO's early beauty books had sold over 300,000 copies, and in 2009, she was named Ambassador for Tourism to Korea. Open about her double-gender experience—living as a woman in a man's body—IKKO encourages her fans, too, to accept themselves, while pushing them to strive for continual growth through discipline and positive thinking.

In this chapter, I show how IKKO uses her personal story and beauty expertise to encourage all women to find their inner diva. In turn, her influence in Japan raises important questions for this volume: How does IKKO's success connect to neoliberal trends in Japan that celebrate individual risk and achievement over collective action? How does her celebrity status illuminate the paths open and closed to gender-variant individuals in Japan? And, ultimately, what does it mean to be a citizen of IKKO's diva nation? Although open about her transgendered identity,

IKKO is not on the front lines of political protest and much of her advice reinforces normative gender and consumerist rhetoric. Nevertheless, as a diva active in multiple performance modes and platforms, IKKO does not shy away from encouraging fans to follow their own paths wherever this may lead, opening the possibility of transgressive choices.

Following IKKO's career through her published work and perform-ances, we find a diva of many voices: she easily alternates among speak-ing as the funny, high-spirited entertainer, confident make-up artist, sis-terly lifestyle advisor, and enthusiastic travel guide. Although her speaking style changes to suit diverse venues, her message remains remarkably the same: through beauty work and overcoming timidity, all women can achieve the same self-confidence and happiness that IKKO has obtained after decades of struggle. Here, Eva Illouz's (2003) work on American talk-show star Oprah Winfrey, another multitalented diva, proves useful to interpreting IKKO's construction of her own public persona. Winfrey's openness about personal troubles (in her case, poverty, abandonment, sexual abuse, drugs, and weight problems), and her self-presentation as an everywoman plagued with the problems endured by numerous others, rather than as an extraordinary superstar, have helped her forge bonds of sentiment with mass audiences of viewers. Illouz explains how Oprah's story becomes a "therapeutic biography," a model narrative of an ordi-nary person overcoming adversity through self-awareness and effort. Winfrey "became famous not *in spite of* having been abused but *because* she was abused and because she publicized that fact" (Illouz 2003:34). IKKO also employs a language of recovery. She repeatedly claims in her guides that she would not be who she is today without having had to face her own personal challenges, including gender-variance, bullying, social clumsiness, panic attacks, and weight gain. Accordingly, whether by per-forming, writing, or doing interviews, IKKO advises her fans, too, to pursue self-cultivation as a path that leads toward polishing one's beauty and engaging the world from an aesthetic stance. As we shall see, this call to a personal aesthetics of virtue and beauty can lead to social change, even when the diva does not seek political action.

To explore the aesthetic and social dimensions of this diva's influence, I take up IKKO's work in quite different performance moments, begin-ning with her narration of the therapeutic biography by drawing on her best-selling 2007 volume *Onna no hōsoku* (Law of Woman) and high-lighting how she presents the most formative points in her life journey as personal challenges requiring personal solutions. Next, I look closely at how IKKO develops her persona in other moments: the performance of her 2007 hit song *Dondake no hōsoku* (Law of Dondake, IKKO and Okada 2013); a televised visit to a girls' high school in 2007; and her transnational debut as a promoter of travel to Korea in 2008–2009. In conclusion, I show how IKKO's appealing public persona and message of personal achievement link to neoliberal narratives of success for women in Japan by focusing on a cameo role she had in a 2011 TV miniseries that enacted a kind of therapeutic beauty biography of its own.

THE HEALING BIOGRAPHY OF A DIVA AS LIFESTYLE GUIDE, DANCER, AND BIG SISTER

IKKO's glossy lifestyle guides offer readers advice, often in maxims and anecdotes, based on her personal life lessons. Although the format of the guides vary, IKKO is consistent in the way she presents her life story. For her, the realization of her gender-variant identity and her efforts to come to terms with it defined her childhood and youth. Overcoming loathing for her own body was her first struggle, but not her last. Born in 1962 in a coal-mining town, now incorporated as Fukuchi, in Fukuoka Prefecture, Kyushu, IKKO grew up as Toyoda Kazuyuki, the only boy among three sisters (the stage name IKKO is actually a different reading of the two characters used for Kazuyuki). IKKO relates the sense of dislocation that came from feeling like a girl in a boy's body. Other children teased her, using the pejorative *okama* (fag), and to this day, IKKO speaks out against using this word. Isolated from other children and adept at neither academics nor sports, IKKO found a safe zone in her mother's beauty salon. It was here that she developed her love for cosmetology, deciding that even though she could not be a beautiful woman herself, she could create beauty. Although IKKO often wished she had been born female, and even once considered surgery, she tells her readers that she has come to a place of truly joyful self-acceptance (IKKO 2007:11). Like Oprah, she expresses gratitude for the hardships that have made her who she is today.

No doubt her readers can identify with the pain of feeling out of step with peers and idealized norms. In IKKO's transgendered case, the wide gap between her reality and the norm created an equally great challenge, and in turn, her achievement of self-acceptance can provide an inspiring model. Notably, narrating her story does not move IKKO to call for school awareness programs or any other reforms. Nor does she refer to any sort of academic or medical literature on transgendered youth. Rather, she confines her narration to personal anecdotes and the expression of feelings. Choosing to view her gender-variance as simply the harsh fact of her early life, IKKO invites readers to see their own disadvantages similarly as hurdles to overcome. Not giving up and taking to heart her advice, which can range from beauty and exercise tips to ideas about goal-setting and positive thinking, will be the first steps on their own journeys.

IKKO's description of the career-building decades of her twenties and thirties emphasizes employment as a means to self-cultivation and personal growth. Although IKKO relates how hard she worked to build her professional skills, like Oprah, she places most importance on character-building moments of self-awareness. In IKKO's case, this meant learning to navigate relations in the workplace. Dreaming of working in the beauty field at the highest levels, IKKO moved to Yokohama at age nineteen to train at the elite Sawaii salon, working under the supervision of the awarding-winning Sawaita Hiro for several years in the 1980s. Proud of the association with IKKO, the Sawaii salon posts a picture of her on its website.[1] IKKO recalls practicing her trade compulsively at this time, going home every evening to practice even more. Yet, she also remembers this period as a time of constant stress borne of her inability to work well with others. Having spent so much time alone in her youth, IKKO did not find the workplace easy and often misinterpreted her workmates' suggestions as bullying. Reflecting on this period years later in her books, IKKO saw her Sawaii apprenticeship as a time when she needed to overcome her stubbornness to learn from others. IKKO uses this experience to advise her readers to develop their own self-awareness, set and pursue goals, and cultivate kindness to improve relationships. She does not hold up her professional life as an extraordinary one requiring unique talent, but as a series of challenges on the road to maturity and self-acceptance. Also like Oprah, IKKO avoids giving information about her intimate life in her guides, though she mentions having boyfriends (*kareshi*) and promotes romantic love.

Nearing thirty in the early 1990s, IKKO opened her own salon, Atelier IKKO, and made a name for herself as a make-up artist and hairstylist to well-known actresses, becoming known for her skill in creating the right look to complement kimono. As her fame as a beauty expert became established, she appeared in magazine articles, store promotions, advertisements, and commercials. Managing the salon was far from easy, however, and IKKO remembers feeling an overwhelming sense of responsibility for her staff and clients that led to debilitating anxiety. This new hurdle seemed insurmountable, worse than any she had experienced previously. She undertook expensive acupuncture and massage treatments to ease her panic attacks, but it was years before she could overcome them. Again, the key was self-awareness and adjusting her behavior. Although I have not found instances where IKKO uses the phrase "coming out" (*kamingu auto*) in relation to her gender identity, she does use it to underscore her reluctance to let anyone know about her anxiety for fear of hurting the salon's business. Her book *Onna no hōsoku* has a special section that explains anxiety and panic attacks (Law of Woman, IKKO 2007:117).

In her early forties, IKKO became a television personality. She credits the documentary-style show *Soromon-ryū* (Solomon Style) for featuring her as a renowned beauty expert in January 2006 as her lucky break (IKKO 2007:119). This led most famously to her featured role in the program *OnēMANS* (Kaneda, Itoi, and Matsubara 2006–2009). Aired on Nippon TV and somewhat in the style of the U.S. show *Queer Eye for the Straight Guy* (Collins and Metzler 2003–2007), *OnēMANS* featured IKKO and other queer-identified hosts as lifestyle experts able to advise cisgender celebrities on everything from fashion to interior design and even sports (Abe 2010:117; Maree 2013:99). The entertainment industry, including theater, bars, and cabarets, had long been one of the few welcoming spaces to gender-variant people in Japan (McLelland 2003). But this televised promotion of transgender and gay individuals as lifestyle experts was novel. As stars of the show, IKKO and others embodied a new kind of *onē-kyarakutā* (older-sister-characters, or *onē-kyara*, for short), performing gender-variance as "queen personalities" (Maree 2013:98). They made entertaining use of *onē-kyara-kotoba* (queen's language), an irreverent mix of the *onē*'s use of stereotypical aspects of feminine, formal speech and malicious wit, as Hideko Abe (2010) and Claire Maree (2013) have discussed in detail. The program *OnēMANS* also opened lucrative opportunities for IKKO and other show regulars to author guide books, becoming models of "transformational beauty" that simultaneously endorsed and transgressed "the boundaries of normative gender and sexuality" (Maree 2013:98).

Despite this embrace of her queer identity on TV, IKKO does not provide many details about her sartorial male-to-female transition. Viewing photos of IKKO from the 1990s and 2000s shows her evolution from an attractive young man to an *OnēMANS* diva who wears dramatic eye makeup, short skirts, and high heels. Although her guides, especially the early ones, include lots of glamorous photographs of IKKO, she does not write about this exterior transition or mention how anyone from family to fans received it. In her 2007 *Onna no hōsoku*

(Law of Woman), IKKO does write that it was during her early TV career that she became comfortable wearing chic body-revealing clothing, which she equates with exposing a "true self rather than a clumsily crafted one," and remembers that life became easier at this point once "everyone recognized that IKKO equals *onē-kyara*" (IKKO 2007:122).

In December 2007, IKKO capitalized on her *onē-kyara* association with the expression *Dondake!* by releasing the song *Dondake no hōsoku* (Law of Dondake, IKKO and Okada 2013). A fast-paced catchy tune that blends salsa with J-pop, the song cheers on listeners with IKKO's trademark advice. Adopt healthy habits like IKKO's morning walk, enjoy beauty treatments like the sauna, and remember that stress is bad for your skin. Love, while painful at times, is essential, so don't give up (*meganai! meganai!*) even when you're dumped (*furareta*). The song urges the listener to love herself and to find the job that she *must* do as that will produce the "smiling self that shines" (*kagayaku jibun no egao*). Bid a hasty farewell to a life that is nothing but a copy and to timidity about being an ugly duckling. Yet, for all this upbeat emphasis on seizing the day and the exuberant shouts of *Dondake!,* the song also sounds somewhat desperate. At one point in the song, IKKO asks, "Am I cute? Am I? Am I?"

Looking closely at a music video of IKKO performing the song, we find an erotic play with gender and race (IKKO and Okada 2013). The video captures something of the range of modes with which IKKO experimented as she developed her public persona. Styled in an overtly sensual and androgynous way, IKKO wears a silver lamé mini-dress over short black pants that fit like underwear. The deep décolleté of the dress accentuates her flat boy-chest, the high hemline and high heels emphasize her long slim legs. IKKO's big, curly, reddish wig is brushed Afro-like into a frizzy halo about her head. Her face is carefully made-up, her pink lipstick matching the polish on her long fingernails. Dancing behind her and almost hidden in darkness are two young men, one black, the other Asian. Interspersed in the colorful dance video are scenes in black and white with IKKO in the forefront, apparently nude, with her legs and arms crossed, artfully covering herself from chest to groin. In these scenes, the frizzy wig is gone, and IKKO wears her usual short, straight hair, parted in the middle. She looks seductively at the camera, as a man's muscled chest appears behind her, the two bodies blending into sinuous sculpture of gleaming muscle. IKKO's arms appear lean and muscular, but her pose makes her appear feminine in contrast to the (faceless) male body moving behind her. In the style of a

high-fashion perfume ad, such erotic scenes sensationalize the transbody and are at odds with her peppy performance in the main scenes.
Moving on to IKKO's frequent appearances on variety shows, we see
the earnest sobriety of the lifestyle author and the allure of the *Dondake!* dancer fall away. Comfortable with slapstick humor and jokes at
her expense, IKKO plays her *onē-kyara* to the hilt on TV. In 2007, at the
height of her *Dondake!* celebrity, IKKO participated in a TV special
installment of the variety program *Gakkō e ikkō!* (Let's Go to School!),
a series that featured celebrity visits to high schools. In the special we
see a fascinating mix of laughter and curiosity about the transgendered
body and appreciation of IKKO as a beauty expert and approachable
big sister (Tashiro, Tokadama, Watanabe, and Genta 2007). Taking a
close look at this performance sheds light on another side of IKKO's
popularity, her appeal to young people, and some of the ways mainstream television approaches gender-variance.

As her TV special (*Gakkō e IKKO*) opens and two young male emcees
introduce IKKO, we hear the bouncy refrain of the Culture Club (1983)
song *Karma Chameleon* as she makes her entrance. The line "Karma,
karma, chameleon" draws comic attention to IKKO as *okama*. She laughs
at the emcees' joke about the song and their comic reference to the
"appropriateness" of the school's name—Kamata (Kamata Girls High
School, Tokyo). She adds that she detests the word *okama,* but this comes
off as a joke, too. (In her writing and in other televised moments, IKKO
has condemned its use.) Wearing a bright red jacket over a navy-blue
jumper and a crisp, long-sleeved white shirt, IKKO almost has an air of
the schoolgirl about her, except for her high heels. The emcees show
IKKO the mountain of questions, solicited in advance, which the students
have written for her. Asking about how she looked when in her school
days, the emcees produce a photo of IKKO as a student with a regulation
buzz cut and boys' uniform. Although she makes a great show of trying
to retrieve the photo, IKKO jokes about hating that haircut. which earned
her the nickname "the nun." Although still in good humor, she admits to
having been a *hikikomori* (shut-in) in high school, a reference to youth,
most often male, who withdraw from social engagement, some even to
the extent of confining themselves in their rooms for years. This frank
recognition of her transbody and painful history coupled with her lighthearted attitude set the tone for the visit.

Smiling broadly, and on the arms of the emcees, IKKO enters the high
school courtyard to the cheers of hundreds of girls leaning out the win-
dows of all five stories of the building. Shaking the hem of her dress to

and fro like a dancer, she greets them with a loud cry of *Dondake!* The visit includes a variety of different interactions between IKKO and the students. She is literally game for anything, playing badminton (badly, and for the first time in thirty years) with one group, dancing to the song *Macho Man* (Village People 1978) with another, and in more serious moods, leading a workshop in elaborate cosmetics application and addressing a gym-full of students with some life lessons from her youth. But most revealing—and the segments apparently given the most air time—are her visits to some of the classrooms. At each visit, excited students greet her with screams, applause, and cries of *Dondake!* Then the emcees call out the names of selected students, inviting them to speak to IKKO. Students are eager to ask personal questions. They want to know about IKKO's preferred type of men (boxer types with nice skin and bodies) and her first love experience (as a first-year elementary school student, she had a crush on a boy and her teacher). Asked if she ever liked a girl, IKKO adds that in high school, thinking she should make an effort to be "normal," she had dated a girl, but the relationship never went past friendship since IKKO felt no romantic spark. When one student asks for a hug, an emcee jokes, "You do know that even though she looks like this, she's really a middle-aged man (*ossan*)." This gets a laugh from the class, but everyone seems envious as IKKO walks up to give the girl a hug. Commenting that she always had girl friends, not boy companions, growing up, IKKO emphasizes that she likes girls "as members of the same sex (*dōsei to shite*)," thereby stressing her own identity as a woman.

Curiosity about transgendered people often centers on the body—the extent to which it may have been altered and how it affects the most basic acts of daily life. This program is no exception. In fact, the first student question IKKO receives brings up one of the common problems faced by transpeople: "Which bathroom do you use?" Replying that she is frequently asked this and without missing a beat, IKKO explains she never finds this easy and her decision depends on the situation. She prefers using the women's, and if no one else is in there, she enters without hesitation. When she uses the men's, she always enters a stall, adding comically—"because I don't stand up," to which everyone laughs. She adds that since it is hard for her to enter either restroom, she can end up really perplexed. Building on the humorous moment, one of the emcees quips, "Because there isn't one for 'middle (*chū*),' right?" To which IKKO replies with another *Dondake!*, shaking her finger at him as the classroom erupts in yet more laughter.

For all the jokes about IKKO as an *okama* and a spectacularized gender oddity, the show presents her as a much beloved celebrity. Emcees and students alike listen with respectful attention when IKKO, in a sober, authoritative voice, leads the cosmetics workshop. The diva's self-acceptance, honesty, and humor open a space where students feel comfortable asking questions that reveal their own concerns about beauty and relationships. Like *OnēMANS*, this and other TV programs, despite their obvious problems, have brought visibility to the concerns of gender-variant people in Japan (Mackie 2008:420). They may in some measure have contributed to the progress made in 2015, for example, when the Ministry of Education "urged local boards to ensure that schools to do more to cater to children who believe they were born the wrong gender" (Murai 2015).

THE JAPANESE DIVA GOES TO KOREA

The diva is not one to stay cooped up. As IKKO demonstrates in her promoting beauty travel to South Korea (hereafter, Korea), the diva lives large, enjoying multiple avenues for self-expression and self-discovery. But she is not operating in a vacuum. Championing Korean culture places IKKO within a fraught historical framework that includes ongoing diplomatic tensions between the two nations on the divided peninsula (Tokita 2010:03.1–2). Narrating her enthusiasm as a beauty story, however, and one that encourages personal communication among Japanese and Korean women, allows IKKO to sidestep overt reference to politics. This position also links IKKO with the embrace of Korean popular culture displayed by numerous Japanese women since the early 2000s and their fondness for travel to Korea for beauty treatments (*esute*) since the 1990s (Miller 2006:198–99). By taking up IKKO's travel writing and the significance of her official appointment as a tourist ambassador, we see how the diva helps create a fresh image of Korea in the Japanese imagination. Although IKKO avoids reference to political disputes, one can read her work as fashioning an alternative politics of cultural engagement that places women at the center as powerful consumers.

In 2008, IKKO, a longtime fan of Korean cosmetics and television dramas, and a frequent visitor, published a glossy travel guide to Seoul. The guide's title is transnational in itself, mixing Japanese with English, *IKKO: no kirei o migaku in Kankoku* (IKKO's Guide to Polishing Beauty in Korea, IKKO 2008; see Figure 22). It is subtitled in English as *IKKO's Beautiful Days in Korea* and promoted as "a guide to Korea for women who want to become more beautiful." By 2011, the book was

22. The cover of *IKKO's Beautiful Days in Korea* (IKKO 2008).

in its eleventh printing. Narrated in IKKO's voice and in the style of her early beauty guides, *IKKO's Beautiful Days* models how to shop for cosmetics and fashion, enjoy unusual beauty treatments, and dine on all kinds of Korean cuisine from gorgeous formal dinners to tasty street food. A fan of spicy dishes, IKKO writes that she makes Korean food at home every day, too. The vivid color of the book jacket, the tiny flowers and butterflies ringing IKKO's name, and the abundant photos inside package this guide as a fanciful, feminine journey all in itself.

IKKO's Beautiful Days takes one through Seoul as she experiences it. Photographed for the guide's cover, IKKO looks every inch the trendy traveler. Clearly, this is not a tourist outfitted for sweaty hikes or dutiful learning tours, but a diva looking for fun. Similarly, photographs of IKKO inside the book show the festival of fashion that awaits the Japanese woman traveling to Korea. We see IKKO in glittery mini-dresses for evenings, sporting youthful fashion found in local boutiques, relaxing in her hotel suite and walking the hotel grounds in expensive leisure outfits, and, when introducing Korean products, wearing the traditional Korean woman's *hanbok,* its full, wraparound skirt (*chima*) in deep red topped with a multicolored jacket (*jeogori*). Although she is no doubt traveling with an entourage, most photos depict IKKO alone, emphasizing her role as the celebrity guide here, but also welcoming other women to imagine traveling abroad on their own, too. Such images promise safety as well as luxury. They not only make such indulgence permissible, but code such trips as responsible missions of self-care. Refreshed, the savvy beauty tourist arrives back in Japan "from her exotic experience with her own body as the souvenir" (Miller 2006:198).

Beauty guides published in Japan, as in the United States, often promote travel to European capitals, especially Paris, as the preferred destinations for the beauty consumer. Photos in such guides take the reader vicariously through elite hotels and cafes, shopping in boutiques and consulting with fashion professionals, while soaking up the city's historical sites and chic atmosphere. IKKO celebrates the pleasures of traveling to Seoul in exactly the same ways. She writes reverently of beauty advice gained by conversations with Korean experts, delights in her discoveries, and takes energy from the vitality of all the women, but particularly older ones, that she meets through the course of her trip. She praises Koreans for retaining their traditional culture and seeks to learn their beauty secrets. Like typical beauty guides' depictions of Paris, IKKO's portrait of Seoul is a romantic one and her journey one of pleasure and self-discovery.

IKKO's 2009 appointment to the honorary post of tourism ambassador by the Korea Tourism Organization (KTO) was seen as a bold, even risky choice. It also made good commercial sense for the promotion of Japanese travel to Korea. According to the English-language edition of the Korean newspaper, *The Chosun Ilbo* (Daily news from Korea), the "IKKO effect" meant that products she recommended became instant bestsellers. For example, "Japanese tourists in Korea bought over 3,000 tubes of cream a day" after IKKO promoted the product, a blemish balm called BB Cream, on a talk show (*The Chosun Ilbo* 2009). The *Korea*

Times reported that IKKO had inspired a "Korean boom among Japanese youngsters" and that the cosmetic brand Étude had "made an exclusive contract" with IKKO (Rahn 2009). For her part, IKKO responded by describing how much she loved Korea, from its television dramas and food to the healing properties of *ondol* (the Korean system of floor-heating). IKKO was not, however, the first transwoman to star in beauty promotions in Korea; the transwoman performer and model Lee Kyung-Eun, better known by her stage name Harisu, had famously made her 2001 debut in a cosmetic commercial for the Korean corporation Dodo. Although Harisu has been vocally supportive of transpeople's rights and successfully battled to change her name and gender legally, her celebrity, like IKKO's fame through *OnēMANS,* also points to corporate use of gender-variant people as means to capture attention through exploiting novelty while also attaining approval for the progressive inclusion of gender-variant bodies (Ahn 2009; Davies, Davies, and Cho, 2010).

Although age forty-seven at the time of her appointment, IKKO initially had been attracted to Korean culture years earlier, as were many women of her generation, in part by the miniseries *Winter Sonata* (*Gyeoul Yeonga,* in Korean and *Fuyu no sonata,* in Japanese translation; Yoon 2002). Nicknamed *Fuyusona* by Japanese, the drama produced enormous numbers of female fans in Japan in 2004. Their appreciation of these and other Korean pop-cultural products associated women with *hallyu,* the Korean Wave, and fuelled "a rush of Japanese tourism to Korean locations from the drama" (Tokita 2010:03.2). The handsome, young male star of *Winter Sonata,* Bae Yong-joon, affectionately dubbed "Yon-sama" by Japanese, became a favorite; five thousand fans reportedly went to Narita airport to greet him when he visited Japan in April 2004 (Tokita 2010:03.2). Critics in Japan responded with ridicule. They ignored the actual range of viewers among all ages and both male and female who had responded with even more enthusiasm in 2005 to the historical drama *Jewel in the Palace* (*Dae jang geum,* in Korean; Lee 2003–2004); *Kyūtei jokan changumu no chikai* (The vow of the palace court lady Jang Geum, in Japanese; Miller 2008a:20–21). Moreover, despite the fact that, as Hyangjin Lee (2010) has demonstrated, female fans of the Korean Wave comprised a range of age, class, and employment backgrounds, critics depicted them as uninformed, unremarkable, interchangeable "middle-class, middle-age" women. Not only was this categorization sloppy, it failed to capture women over thirty, "a formerly denigrated and neglected market segment," in their new role as "active cultural agents" (Miller 2008a:17). In the early 2000s, Japanese women became active consumers on various fronts, traveling to Korea on luxury and budget trips, forming interest groups, and taking Korean-language classes. Lee finds that while these fans may be "largely apolitical," the "impact of their cultural consumption" can be seen as "surprisingly political in that they have improved the popular image of Korea and Korean residents in Japan" (Lee 2010:07.2).

By promoting beauty travel to Korea for Japanese women, IKKO displays this same enthusiasm and contributes to this positive image. In her guide, she modestly acknowledges that many readers will know more about Korea than she does, but that her book introduces the "charms of Korea" with a focus on enhancing one's beauty (IKKO 2008:4). In this fashion, IKKO enfolds herself in a consumerist quest understood as thoroughly feminine. Without apology, she takes on all the contempt and envy women's interests can inspire, and emphasizes her own identity as a woman. Her guide to Korea includes introductions to twenty of her favorite Korean dramas. Photographed in *hanbok* for this section, IKKO writes that she takes courage from the way they depict people overcoming adversity, connecting the dramas with her own therapeutic message of self-care. She also finds herself inspired by the "power of pure love" portrayed in these programs (IKKO 2008:140–43). Also in the guide, IKKO advises women to pack at least one dressy outfit for a night on the town, not only to add the spice of variety to their Korean trip but also because this might be their chance to meet a "charming man," making the experience "much, much more enjoyable" (IKKO 2008:138). Although buried at the end of the book, this comment recalls Japanese women's reputed fantasies about Korean men like Yon-sama as romantic partners and their implied dissatisfaction with Japanese men. IKKO's guide concludes by voicing the hope that readers understand that "you can become beautiful just by traveling," narrating this journey as a personal beauty story available to all women (IKKO 2008:158). In the same way that Japanese women's involvement in the Korean Wave has become "surprisingly political," one can argue that IKKO, too, through her promotion of beauty travel to Korea has made a difference.

WINNING THE BATTLE FOR BEAUTY

Tracing different moments in IKKO's career illustrates how she employs the language of recovery to encourage her fans, establishes an alternative politics of transnational engagement through promotion of beauty travel to Korea, and uses her transgendered status and diverse performance styles to reinforce and subvert gender norms. In conclusion, to show how IKKO's message upholds common narratives of women's success in contemporary Japan, I discuss her cameo role in the 2011 TV mini-series *Bara-iro no seisen* (Rose-colored crusade), subtitled in English, *The Future is in Our Hands* (Yokochi 2011). By appearing in this drama, IKKO lends support to the "therapeutic biography" of the fictional character Miki Makoto, described as an "absolutely ordinary housewife and mother of two," who transcends domestic boundaries to become a sought-after fashion model. The pursuit of beauty radically upends Makoto's life, pushing her to leave a constraining marriage and to brave single motherhood. In the end, her beautified appearance and inner strength complement each other as Makoto wins the "fight for beauty." It is IKKO, among others in the drama, who cheers her on this path. Analyzing *Rose-colored Crusade,* we see how this beauty story, like IKKO's guides, endorses the rhetoric of neoliberal Japan: the courageous, enterprising individual "invests" in herself, risks competition, and defines her predicaments as personal problems requiring personal solutions. At the same time, she is willing to defy conventional norms of feminine behavior and overturn her comfortable life to seek personal happiness.

As the story opens, we see thirty-year-old Miki Makoto, played by Fukuishi Kazue, from behind as she trudges downhill on the way back to her comfortable, suburban condo. Everything about her is lackluster, from her nondescript appearance to the shapeless bag of groceries drooping at her side. The narrative overlaying this scene invites skepticism of Makoto's life, asking rhetorically what the housewife receives in return for an uneventful life that brings no particular recognition and robs her of beauty. Makoto's drive to become beautiful begins when she discovers that her husband, Miki Atsushi (Hasegawa Tomoharu), a junior banker on the fast track, has had a fling with a pretty, young coworker. Apologetic at being caught in his affair, Makoto professes his love for Makoto as the perfect mother and homemaker, though as Makoto and viewers soon learn, he has clearly lost interest in her as a romantic partner. In response, Makoto promises that she will do her part to reignite his desire by becoming more beautiful. Atsushi laughs at this proposal, seeing no need for a mother to do beauty work, but Makoto is determined. In the end, the beauty for which she strives comes to encompass more than physical attractiveness, becoming the demand for recognition that pushes her to fight Atsushi for the right to pursue a career and ultimately, to divorce.

IKKO enters the story in the first episode of the drama when Makoto has won a makeover and modeling opportunity by excelling in a contest to represent a new diet-drink supplement. In a sense, IKKO plays herself, assuming the role of famed hair and make-up artist Yukiko, one of the contest judges. Warmly supportive, she sympathizes when Makoto confesses to the judges in an interview that her husband no longer "sees her as a woman." During the makeover, the camera zooms in as she transforms the housewife and then exclaims, "Makoto, how *lovely* you are." The scene makes "Yukiko" clearly recognizable as IKKO, picturing the make-up artist with her trademark Louis Vuitton make-up case and her neat rows of cosmetics. (To simplify hereafter, I will refer to her as IKKO in describing this performance.)

IKKO plays a major role in depicting the launch of Makoto's beauty project. Following the makeover, Makoto enjoys her first photo shoot, working alongside the diet-drink campaign's lead model, the rail-thin sophisticate Akaneko (Takizawa Saori). Afterward, as all involved in the shoot gaze happily at the session's photos, Makoto is taken aback at her own beauty. Intuiting that Makoto has long been self-conscious about her height, IKKO urges her to celebrate her body, exclaiming, "Hide any part of your body, it becomes a flaw; show it off, and look what an asset you've got!" Akaneko chimes in, proclaiming that "women are . . . *finished* goods (*kakōhin*)." *Kakōhin*, a word used to describe processed foods such as lunch meats, is intended here as a positive way to communicate the work Makoto needs to do to achieve womanly beauty. *Kakōhin* also resonates with a phrase from IKKO's song *Law of Dondake,* alluding to the line, "*Dondake!* Men's words of love make dreamy seasoning!" At this point, the camera zooms in for a close-up of IKKO, looking meditative, as she agrees with Akaneko. She turns to Makoto, exclaiming, "Without any seasoning, pork tastes terrible, but spice it up with salt or pepper, and you have a first-rate pork steak! You've got bacon!" IKKO delivers this last line in the spirited style of *onē-kyara-kotoba.* Makoto rushes over to Akaneko, admitting that it was her advice to the contestants that "beauty was a battle" that had inspired her to keep trying when she felt discouraged. In turn, Akaneko assures her that, with effort and no matter her age, there is no end to a woman's potential to achieve beauty. "Do not forget that *beauty!*" orders Akaneko, and then reciting the catchphrase from the diet-supplement campaign, she adds, "Women must wear the rose always." She delivers this line without a hint of irony, reminding Makoto of the effort and skillful consumerism that she must expend.

Throughout *Rose-colored Crusade,* Makoto must struggle to overcome adversity. In the end, wise and completely transformed, she fully embodies a new maturity. This new confidence is on display in a scene depicting Makoto walking thoughtfully in the city. She moves slowly and with assurance as though unconsciously turning an ordinary street into a diva's runway by her sheer presence. In short order, she has become a top model known for her creativity, developed a new sense of self, and gained the confidence to divorce her husband, who has never accepted her career, offered to take on child care, or felt a rekindling of desire for her. She decides on divorce when she realizes that, while any woman would do as Atsushi's wife, only she could live the one life of Miki Makoto. In the last scene with Atsushi, she is amused when he finally refers to her as Makoto rather than as "Mama." But this recognition of her personhood comes too late, and she walks on. Strolling amid a cascade of rose petals in the final scene, diva Makoto has emerged as a winner in the "battle for beauty," a woman clad in roses.

Rose-colored Crusade, much like IKKO's guides, presents a narrative of beauty that entwines tackling personal challenges with beauty work, but stops short of envisioning social change. Although at one point Makoto asks her father why men can have both a home life and career while women cannot, this ends up a rhetorical question. The program also offers some sympathy for the pressures constraining the male breadwinner in scenes where we see Atsushi in his own war with the rigidity and competition of the corporate workplace. Ultimately, the drama implies that brave women like Makoto can go their own way despite social disapproval, but it does not show how she will handle child care or whether she can earn sufficient income in a profession as age-sensitive and unstable as modeling, although we do see that she has supportive parents. The drama implies that the strong woman has the ability to find her own solutions. Analyzing Makoto's story against the backdrop of contemporary Japan, however, shows that she is not in fact an ordinary woman, but an unusually privileged one. She enjoys an elite, comfortable lifestyle as a full-time homemaker, and when she decides to work, she joins the alluring world of fashion modeling. The reality in Japan is not so rosy: whether in full-time regular positions or flexible ones, women earn far less than their male counterparts, and they are far more liable than men to end up in temporary jobs and much less likely to achieve leadership positions (Allison

2013:32; Macnaughton 2015:4). Women who opt out of paid employment temporarily for motherhood find it difficult to re-enter the work force except in low-wage, often part-time and temporary work. While Makoto's improbable tale of overcoming adversity may inspire viewers, she is not voicing a call to collective action. The change in her own life, however, is dramatic and ripples outward to others, in some sense making her pursuit of beauty personal as well as political.

Like *Rose-colored Crusade,* IKKO's therapeutic biography, too, communicates to her fans that the future is in their hands, inspiring change as personal, not societal. Viewed against the broader landscape of contemporary Japan, IKKO's focus on transformation through beauty work reflects a rational response to the pressures of living in a neoliberal, free-market society that places enormous responsibilities for self-care on the individual while diminishing social safety nets. It is a competitive environment that blurs the "borderline between personal 'consumption' and 'investment'" (Standing 2011:123). By blending self-cultivation with consumerism and, like the fictional model Akaneko, urging the individual to develop herself as a "first-rate brand" and "finished" goods, IKKO promotes the familiar message of endless self-optimization alive in millennial Japan. References to the shining (*kagayaite iru*) woman, which have become ubiquitous in Japanese popular culture, also capture this message, and appear both in the song *Law of Dondake* ("smiling self that shines") and when Makoto speaks of her hopes to become a shining mother to her children. This reference cannot be separated from Prime Minister Abe Shinzō's much publicized "womenomics" policies that, although resulting in few concrete changes, promise to create an environment where all women can "shine" by contributing to the economy and taking on leadership roles (Abe 2014; Macnaughton 2015:1).

Yet, for all her apparent support of neoliberal rhetoric, IKKO, as a transwoman, brings something new to the meaning of the shining woman. Although her projects to achieve womanliness endorse convention, the visibility of her transbody highlights the performative aspects of gender and questions the alleged naturalness of the binary sex-gender system. She is also subversive in her role as another "middle-aged woman" promoting tourism to Korea, offering an alternative path of engagement across diva-nation borders. Still active on many fronts, IKKO remains a diva in the making. As a celebrity beauty expert in her fifties, IKKO will no doubt have much to contribute to conversations about growing older in Japan, a rapidly aging society, especially as she confronts aging as a transwoman. How she continues to carve out a space for difference and social bonding makes IKKO a diva to watch for many years to come.

NOTE

1. Sawaii salon website online at http://sawaii.net/company [accessed 7 July 2016].

CHAPTER 8

Seizing the Spotlight, Staging the Self

Uchida Shungiku

AMANDA C. SEAMAN

In 2011, manga artist Uchida Shungiku wrote a provocative installment of her regular column in the newspaper *Yūkan Fuji*. Its subject was the Tenga, a three-dimensional silicon vagina marketed to men as a sexual aid. On a dare, Uchida explained, she had repurposed the device, turning it inside out and adding some lubrication in order to transform it into a vibrator. The column, while in part a paean to Uchida's creativity and manual dexterity, also offered an extended discussion of masturbation, including Uchida's blunt assertion that she felt far more sexually satisfied when she could stick something inside herself (Shimanaka 2016).

This column's cleverness, frankness about sexual matters, and willingness to comment on Uchida's own sexual practices are nothing new. Instead, they are hallmarks of one of Japan's true divas, a woman who has carefully performed and crafted a reputation for sexual directness, social nonconformism, and artistic iconoclasm. Uchida, who was born in Nagasaki in 1959, got her start as a manga artist in 1984 and published her early work in *Garo,* an avant-garde manga magazine, before becoming more mainstream. She became popular in a relatively short period of time, leading to opportunities to write about her life, the travails of women's lives in Japan, and gender relations in major women's magazines such as *an-an* and *More* (Shigematsu 2005:572). Her career leapt forward in 1994 when she was awarded Bunkamura's Deux Magot award for two very different 1993 publications—a lurid bio-novel about how she was sexually assaulted by her stepfather as a teenager, *Fazā fakkā* (Father fucker, Uchida 1996a); and *Watashitachi wa hanshoku shite iru* (We are breeding, Uchida 1994; commonly shortened to *Wata-han*), the first in a series of manga about giving birth to her children and raising them on her own. From this point onward, Uchida steadily published manga, fiction, and essays, while also branching out into a variety of other fields such as acting (her best-remembered creation may be as the Tokyo Electric Company's energy-efficiency mascot, Denko-chan) and creating craft manuals.

In a country where idols roll steadily off the pop culture assembly line, this kind of diva persona is rare. If idols are industrial and fungible, divas are artisanal and particular. This is particularly true of Uchida Shungiku, who raises diva-ness—hyperaudible, hypervisible, and hyperartificial—to new heights. Unlike run-of-the-mill idols, Uchida is a wide-ranging, multimedia phenomenon, variously performing as a singer, actress, manga artist, novelist, and cultural critic. In doing so, Uchida has also brought the character of the diva into the twenty-first century. In addition to exploiting traditional media fora—weekly magazine columns on provocative topics, appearances on television, and live shows around Tokyo—her canny awareness of technology allowed her to move onto the Internet before many other writers, creating a website to advertise and expand upon the early and most popular volumes of a manga series about her pregnancies (Shamoon 1999). Her social media savvy, in turn, allows her to keep fans closely engaged with the details of her life, either by sharing seemingly intimate snapshots in her articles or by blogging about everything from her newest artistic endeavor to pretty things she has seen to the triumphs and tragedies of her own children and her romantic partners.

As one would expect of a diva, Uchida embodies allure, aura, and eroticism (Doane 1991:138). It is the latter quality, however, that takes center stage across her many platforms, where Uchida's diva performances loudly and often flamboyantly flout gender roles and expectations that restrict or suppress women's agency. In particular, Uchida uses her many stages to dramatically and confrontationally rewrite, redraw, and reperform the roles traditionally assigned to Japanese women, particularly in the sexual realm. Rather than being an empty signifier that people can project their own desires upon, moreover, Uchida defines and deploys her own sexuality as a key element of personal self-realization as well as family life and relationships.

Uchida's embrace of dramatic performance and styles across a variety of media highlights her particular mode of diva-ness, the focus and material of which is Uchida herself and the stories of her life. The foundation of this narrative persona is staged personal trauma (child abuse, sexual assault, ectopic pregnancies, a breech birth, and multiple messy breakups), trauma that she has presented as the impetus for and foundation of her transgressive approach to sex, marriage, and motherhood. By repeating the same stories across different genres—first in her debut novel *Father Fucker* (*Fazā fakkā*, Uchida 1996a) again in the early volumes of *Watahan* (Uchida 1994), and yet again in S4G: *Sex For Girls* (Uchida 2007), a highly personal sex education manual—Uchida has been able to shift perspective and highlight different aspects of the same events, recycling them to make new points or shed new light on old ones. In turn, Uchida over the years has assumed a series of different roles in her own self-narratives. This process of auto-dramaturgy, in which life is repackaged as fictional product, helps Uchida to engage new audiences by carefully redefining and representing herself as different kinds of woman, a tactic employed (albeit in different ways) by Misora Hibari and Yoko Ono (examined elsewhere in this volume by, respectively, Christine Yano, Chapter 5 and Carolyn Stevens, Chapter 6). Uchida's various roles chart a progression in her self-presentation vis-à-vis her own past, her partners, and her family, a progression from tragic victim to transgressive heroine to wise (but still sexy) matriarch.

WOUNDED WOMAN

Uchida's first and most (melo)dramatic role was that of the wounded woman, elaborated and performed in the pages of her debut 1993 novel *Father Fucker*. Set in Nagasaki in the mid-1970s, the novel tells the story of Shizuko (Uchida's given name), a young girl who lives with her mother and her younger sister, Chieko. The mother, a bar hostess whose husband has abandoned the family, takes up with another man when Shizuko is six years old, a traveling pharmaceutical salesman (referred to simply as Stepfather) whom we later learn has a wife and children in another city. Over the following years, Shizuko finds herself the focus of unwanted attention, both from the men on the street as well as from her own stepfather, experiences ignored or denied by her family. After being groped by a man in a record store, the middle-school-aged Shizuko is lambasted by her sister for complaining: "there you go," says Chieko, "getting all glum-faced again!" (Uchida 1996a:127) Things become far worse when Shizuko accidentally gets pregnant with her high school boyfriend. Despite her attempts to keep her condition a secret, she is found out by her mother and then savagely beaten by her outraged stepfather, who rapes her in a perverse act of retributive "justice." After undergoing a late-term abortion, she returns home and endures continued sexual abuse at Stepfather's hands until finally summoning the courage to flee and live on the streets of Nagasaki as a teenaged runaway.

The wounded woman in this novel is a victim, in part, of Japanese patriarchy, represented in the beginning by her biological father and in the end by Stepfather. Along the way, young Shizuko is traumatized by a number of people in her life, whose motives she cannot understand and whose abuse she cannot resist, due to the negative images of female sexuality imparted to her from an early age. It is this treatment, and these images, that Uchida sees as the root of her later sense of worthlessness and self-loathing. In the widely quoted opening of the novel, the narrator tells us:

> People often tell me that I have the face of a prostitute . . . Until yesterday, though, I had completely forgotten that I *was* a prostitute. My whorehouse was in a place to the west. My pimp was the person who raised me until I was sixteen—my actual mother—and my john was her lover, the father who raised me (Uchida 1996a:5).

Notably, however, Uchida's anger in the novel, and in a number of later works, is directed less at the men in her childhood—Shizuko's stepfather, for example, is presented in *Father Fucker* as a rather onedimensional, sociopathic cypher—than at women, including her sister and especially her own mother. In particular, throughout the novel it is Shizuko's mother's actions, inactions, and betrayals that are called out and described repeatedly. Indeed, although Shizuko reports that she has few memories of what happened when she was young, her mother constantly dredges up the past, recounting troubling stories from her childhood, "self-serving and full of clichéd drama," that remain with her long after she has run away from home (Uchida 1996a:8).

From the outset, Shizuko is bewildered by her mother's words and actions, which impart profoundly mixed messages about appropriate behavior, and even more significantly about female sexuality. Unable to make her daughters breakfast due to her work hours, for example, the mother gives them money and tells them to buy whatever they want, only to later scold them harshly when the school complains to her about the children's diet (Uchida 1996a:41). As a bar hostess, moreover, Shizuko's mother lives in a sexualized world whose mores often spill over into her home. Racy stories and jokes from work were part of the family argot, but since they were never contextualized or sanitized for the children, Shizuko is left with little sense of what is (or is not) appropriate material for discussion in social situations. Likewise, although Shizuko's mother's armoire contains red, frilled underwear and a naked picture of herself (Uchida 1996a:34), she berates Shizuko for lying on the veranda clad in shorts, lest someone see her underpants (Uchida 1996a:40).

Far worse than such contradictions, however, is the mother's unwillingness to support or encourage her daughter. While still a young girl, Shizuko tells her teacher that she wants to be a manga writer when she grows up, an aspiration that the teacher encourages by providing her with a ream of blank paper. Shizuko, who is used to drawing on the back of advertising circulars, is thrilled. When she reports this windfall to her mother, however, she is harangued for being a foolish dreamer, and told to return the paper at once (Uchida 1996a:56). Her mother and Stepfather continue to mock her and her teacher for encouraging frivolous pursuits, ultimately leading to Stepfather's use of humiliation and verbal abuse (described dryly as the "Spartan way of education") whenever Shizuko's grades or activities do not meet his expectations.

This maternal neglect and disengagement becomes even more damaging when Shizuko enters puberty. Stepfather begins to take a prurient interest in his maturing ward, squeezing and fondling her growing breasts and commenting critically on their size. When Shizuko appeals to her mother for help, however, she refuses to intervene, instead simply remarking that "Father is naughty, isn't he?" In turn, despite the respite offered by Stepfather's increasingly long absences from the family, and the mother's admission that "it is better when Father is away," she cannot or will not break with him, instead running to the door to greet him whenever he returns. Recognizing that her mother's allegiance lies with Stepfather rather than the children, Shizuko stops confiding in her altogether, even when she becomes pregnant in high school. Unable any longer to hide her growing belly, she finally is forced to admit her situation. After a visit to the doctor confirms that she is six months along, her mother responds not with compassion or concern, but rather with scorn: "You thought you could keep this to yourself? If you'd said something earlier, I could have gotten you an abortion . . . Well, this isn't just some bad dream you'll wake up from" (Uchida 1996a:146).

Her mother's words, recalls Shizuko, were like a "wall of hard, cold air" between them, yet another example of the disdain she had faced "ever since I was a child." She adds, "Everything bad was always my fault" (Uchida 1996a:147). This lesson is reinforced when Shizuko returns from the hospital and must endure repeated sexual assaults by her stepfather. Despite her pleas for her mother to intervene and make the assaults stop, Shizuko is told that she is getting what she deserves: anyone who would engage in "abnormal" (*futsu de wa nai*) sexual behavior (i.e., premarital sex with her boyfriend) should not be surprised when men like Stepfather seek her out. Besides, she adds, "the first time he did it, he said it didn't hurt you (*zenzen itagarakatta*)" (Uchida 1996a:188). Now that Shizuko had lost her virginity, pain would not be an issue; besides, since she had decided to jump the gun and have sex like an adult, she clearly was "asking for it."

By the end of the novel, Shizuko-*cum*-Uchida has learned an important lesson, performed upon her as well as by her for her readership. Women's sexuality in *Father Fucker,* that is, is a fungible and often violently manipulated commodity controlled by family and society. Learning how (or if) to speak about sex, much less engage in it, are activities fraught with danger for a young woman like Shizuko, who is punished not simply for what she says or does, but for simply being female. To be good, in Stepfather's eyes, is to be pure and asexual; thus, Shizuko's sexual maturation ensures and perversely justifies abuse and sexual victimization. In turn, her own mother's casual and instrumental treatment of sex as a professional and financial tool coexists in paradoxical ways with puritanical and condemnatory attitudes about her daughter's sexual nature and behavior, allowing her to offer Shizuko's body to Stepfather as compensation for her own sexual dalliances while blaming this state of affairs on Shizuko's "perversion" and "immorality." As the curtain closes on *Father Fucker,* then, Uchida's debut role as "Shizuko" has established her credentials as the victim *par excellence,* yet one whose ability to make it through—and beyond—this tawdry tale defines her above all as a survivor with many more stories still to tell.

It is crucial that Shizuko/Uchida is understood as a survivor because the articulation of her trauma allows her to rise above the circumstances of her youth and the abuse heaped on her by both her parents. By locating the source of her trauma in the figure of her mother, Shizuko is able to wrest control of her life and to take the power from her victimizer. This allows her to move beyond the narrow world of female roles and to craft a new persona that can unabashedly articulate her own goals and agenda—most pointedly, by being a loving mother with a healthy and active sex life, a central theme in Uchida's later works.

WONDER WOMAN

In stark contrast to the dark and violent tone of *Father Fucker*, the manga series *Watashitachi wa hanshoku shite iru* (We are breeding, Uchida 1994; shortened title, *Watahan*) is generally lighthearted and humorous, albeit with serious interludes such as an ectopic pregnancy and a breech birth. In these manga, the victimized girl-turned-wounded woman of *Father Fucker* has taken on a new role: that of Wonder Woman, someone who has children, spends quality time with them, and still finds time to pursue a fulfilling career. *Watahan*'s protagonist (and Uchida's alter-ego), Gigi, depicted throughout the series with long blonde hair, perky breasts, and an impossibly slim waist, shares the panels with a growing number of offspring, identified simply as Son 1, Daughter 1, Daughter 2, and Son 2 (a naming system used to protect the identities of Uchida's children, allowing her to skirt the boundaries of autobiography and fiction).

While the *Watahan* series has now reached its fifteenth volume, it was with the first three installments (appearing in 1994, 1996, and 1999) that Uchida gained her greatest readership, and elaborated the iconoclastic and polemical persona with which she came to be most identified (Shamoon 1999:88).[1] Notably, the elaboration of her persona took place not simply through the manga's own narrative and illustrations, but through a series of interspersed essays woven into each volume, laying out her arguments for decoupling childbearing from marriage and for rejecting the traditional notion of the mother's role in Japanese culture. These essays, including "Does Everyone Want to Get Married?," "Enough with the Unmarried Mothers," and "I Never Thought I Would Be a Mother," work in tandem with *Watahan*'s chronicle of Gigi's life, which depicts her as a sexy and sexually adventurous, ambitious and career-oriented, intellectually and emotionally independent woman who also is devoted to motherhood and child-raising.

At the heart of this "have it all" depiction of female agency is Uchida's rejection of either-or choices, stereotypes, and traditionally mandated gender roles. Clearly, Gigi loves her children and spends time with them. Many of the manga's episodes are set in her home, and she is depicted as an engaged and demonstratively affectionate mother, hugging and kissing her children, playing games and singing songs, and watching children's videos with them. Nevertheless, she refuses to become pigeonholed as a "mother": she still maintains her career (although we are not told explicitly what she does), taking her children with her rather than staying home with them, and she cultivates a rich social life involving friends as well as lovers. Gigi thus embodies the conviction expressed by Uchida amidst the frames of the *manga* story: "Although I might be 'mom' to my child, I am myself to myself . . . while I might have a child now, I still can say that I haven't changed one bit" (Uchida 1994:187).

Significantly, Gigi does not fall prey to the commonly held Japanese notion that women, once they become mothers, are no longer sexual beings. In contrast to conventional, asexual images of mothers, Uchida depicts Gigi on numerous occasions engaged in an active and pleasurable sex life with a variety of partners—scenes in which a child is often present, reinforcing the compatibility of motherhood and sexual fulfillment.[2] Just as importantly, from the very beginning of the manga series, Uchida emphasizes that Gigi is a working mother. In the opening pages of the first (yellow) *Watahan* volume, her partner drives her to the hospital, where she was admitted and prepped for birth.[3] The next few frames show her in the grips of a terrible contraction. When the pain ends, however, she looks around and says, "I have some free time now," retrieves her laptop, and begins to work (despite scolding from the nurses) until her contractions finally overcome her "will to work" (Uchida 1994:22–23). Later that same hospital stay after her son is born, the laptop quickly returns. As Gigi dryly remarks to the nurses, it seems pointless not to keep busy: "It's not like I'm in the hospital because I'm sick, right?" (Uchida 1994:159).

In the pages that follow, Uchida depicts Gigi taking her baby to parties and to dinners; as Gigi remarks, "I've gotten good at eating with one hand," despite the occasional dollop of food that ends up landing on her son's head (Uchida 1994:82). She continues to meet people for work (Uchida makes a point of identifying them by name), encounters that also allow Gigi to poke fun at their discomfort with children and, in contrast, to highlight her own ability to balance the demands of career and parenting. When a colleague tells her that he would be happy to babysit any time, for example, her son immediately poops, forcing him to admit that he either cannot or will not change the proffered infant's diaper—a comic episode that draws attention both to the disjunction between workplace and home and to the gender expectations at the heart of Japanese child-rearing. Uchida explicitly depicts Gigi as interacting with the world outside of her home in contrast to the conventional image of the stay-at-home mother.

Elsewhere, Uchida challenges these expectations more directly, poking fun at cultural norms for mothers that she considers pointless, sexist, or intrusive. In one set of panels, depicting a teenager and her boyfriend watching Gigi with her infant son, the girl's infatuation with the cute baby turns to consternation at Gigi's long hair. "Don't most women cut their hair short when they become mothers?" she asks, alluding to the expectation that mothers should cut their hair short to avoid getting it in their babies' faces (Uchida 1994:63). The large final panel offers a quite literally "in your face" reply: "My son loves long-haired women," declares Gigi, her face framed by long hair in the clutches of her son's chubby hands (Uchida 1994:63).

While the protagonist of *Watahan*'s debut volume is rather light-hearted, blending breezy (if often pointed) feminist self-assertion with vignettes worthy of sketch comedy, the Gigi we encounter in the following two installments offers a fuller and more serious performance, one that dramatizes the difficulties of childbearing as well as Uchida's conviction that women must take control of their own bodies and relationships in order to ensure that both remain safe and productive. The first of these dramas, concluding the second (pink) *Watahan* (Uchida 1996b) volume, concerns Gigi's failed attempt to have a second child with her then-husband. Racked with pain due to what she suspects is an ectopic pregnancy, Gigi decides to go to the hospital, making sure beforehand to put the final touches on a manuscript she's writing (Uchida 1996b:251). A number of scares and painful examinations ensue, before Gigi eventually recovers.

As Uchida's staging and casting of this bio-drama make clear, Gigi is not simply the star, but the hero overcoming daunting circumstances. Doctors blunder in and out of the scene in often farcical fashion, while Gigi's face and reactions—subsequently irritated, anguished, and relieved—dominate the manga's panels. In turn, Gigi's partner—who begins as a bit player, leaving her to insist on medical intervention—becomes her adversary rather than her helpmate. Upon awaking from her surgery, Gigi had been alarmed to see herself fitted with a urinary catheter. Although the device was inserted due to the loss of a fallopian tube, Gigi is convinced that she has lost an ovary and been rendered infertile. As Uchida reveals in the volume's closing essay, it was her (now ex-) husband who had passed along this false information, an act that she attributes to his bitterness over their impending divorce but also to his desire to stymie her sexual and reproductive autonomy.[4] Here as well, Gigi/Uchida emerges triumphant: "A woman's history is the history of the uterus" declares Gigi at the manga's conclusion, assuring her young son that she will "continue to persevere" (Uchida 1996b:288).

The story of Uchida/Gigi's perseverance, and the cultivation of her can-do persona, continues in the third (blue) *Watahan* volume, as Gigi carries her second child to term (Uchida 1999). Upon being told by her obstetricians (Drs. Sawa and Okubo) that they have discovered that her placenta no longer can safely support the fetus, she chooses to forego a C-section in favor of induced vaginal labor, despite the fact that the baby is in a breech position (in her case, the baby's feet rather than head are positioned at the entrance to the birth canal). She carries through successfully and relatively cheerfully with her daughter's delivery, despite a variety of potential dangers (including excessive amniotic fluid leakage and the baby's entanglement in the umbilical cord). This successful labor and birth epitomizes Uchida's dominant self-fashioning in *Watahan* as the woman who can have, and do, it all, setting the agenda for her own life and carrying it out. Gigi's admission to the hospital is timed to fit into her busy performance schedule, yet as Uchida makes clear in the volume's afterword, having children (even under fraught conditions) is just as much her "life's work"—a fact confirmed by the other children she would go on to raise, produced with yet another romantic partner (Uchida 1996b:224).

WISE WOMAN

Annette Geiger's (2014:164) observation that a diva is both a public and a private figure at every time of the day is particularly true of Uchida Shungiku. From the publication of *Father Fucker* in 1993 to the present day, there has been no part of Uchida's world that has not been visible, ranging from her naked body (in pictures of herself taken while pregnant, and published in the book *Anata mo ninpu shashin o torō* (You too can take pregnant pictures, Uchida 1998) to her troubled past, to her children's births, growing years, and relationships. This hypervisibility extends to Uchida's sex life—including pre- and postpartum sexual congress, coitus when her kids are outside the bedroom door or even in the bed, and the challenges of sex as a perimenopausal woman. In many ways, Uchida's dominant persona has been that of a woman who challenges and frequently violates the social and sexual norms of Japanese society, and who asserts her own identity as a counterexample to such norms.

As Setsu Shigematsu (2005:571) notes, Uchida's project of sexual liberation has been an essentially privatized endeavor, rather than a politically or socially activist one. Indeed, her frank depiction of sexuality, and in particular its transgressive qualities, seems to "rely on a perpetuation of the very modern mores and boundaries that she seeks to breach" (Shigematsu 2005:573). As Uchida flouted one social norm after another, her very way of being transgressive was one unavailable to most other women, making it solitary and almost solipsistic. Shigematsu (2005:578) points out: "The act of transgression does not dismantle or destroy social institutions, but relies on a reinscription that marks the insurgent moment and the boundaries that are crossed." This certainly is true of Uchida's recent foray into dramatic writing, *When Will Yuko's Dream Start*, which premiered in December 2015 under the direction of Peter Goessner (Uchida 2015). Here, Uchida steps away completely from the use of alter-egos or autobiographical stand-ins, focusing on a woman who gives herself over wholeheartedly to sexual pleasure, gleefully embracing the chaos this causes for family and society alike.

Over the last decade, however, Uchida has tended to take on other and more complex roles, ones played under softer lighting and in more intimate spaces. After the early success of the *Watahan* series, in the mid-2000s Uchida turned her attention to other projects, including writing books on crafts, honing her acting career, and building a lavish house. In 2002 she married the actor Takahashi Yūya, who had fathered her third child and with whom she became pregnant with her fourth (and last), a son. Five years later, Uchida (2007) published *S4G: Sex For Girls*. As Uchida explains in the introduction, when she was asked by her editor to write a sex education manual, she originally demurred because she thought herself ill-suited to such a project: "I love dirty jokes, and when I write I am not serious. Besides, I don't have the technical know-how, so how could I teach anyone else?" In the end, however, she decided to give it a go, with the caveat that "I will write about what I know" (Uchida 2007:2).

The character who emerges from this text, while just as outspoken and attention-grabbing as her *Father Fucker* and *Watahan* incarnations, offers us a new iteration of Uchida: the didactic diva. *S4G* is a manifesto about the need for honest, accurate, and straightforward education about the female body and its reproductive functions, one prompted and narratively anchored by Uchida's recollections about her own childhood in 1960s Nagasaki and the faulty views which she was allowed to form of her own body and sexuality. Motivated by the fact that her own sexual education was based on misinformation and half-truths hampered by conservative attitudes her own mother laid on her, Uchida wants to ensure that no one—neither her daughters nor other young women—grows up under the same delusions. Mothers, she insists, need to provide a positive image for their daughters in order to ensure that they will grow up to be successful and self-sustaining members of Japanese society. In this context, Uchida presents herself—in the guise of her alter-ego Gigi—as a flawed but compelling role model, a source of hard-won insights and lore whose wisdom can help both mothers and daughters to overcome misinformation and debunk persistent stereotypes about women and women's bodies. Her clear articulation of the assaults both major and minor are highlighted to teach women that rather than accept the abuse as status quo, women should stand up and acknowledge sexual assault for what it is.

Uchida's most bravura performance as the didactic diva in S4G takes place in her treatment of Gigi's ectopic pregnancy. This event is one familiar from the second volume of her *Watahan* series (Uchida 1996b:249–88). In *Watahan,* the story focuses upon the discovery of the tubal pregnancy, the extremely painful emergency surgery Gigi undergoes to fix the damage, and the emotional turmoil surrounding the removal of her fallopian tube (including her mistaken belief that she had lost one of her ovaries). Here, however, the story serves distinctly pedagogical ends: the emphasis is not upon the pain of the event, or its effect upon Gigi's psyche, but upon the fact that the failed pregnancy was caused by a chlamydia infection contracted after being raped in an elevator (a fact which Uchida had not revealed in earlier iterations of the story). As Gigi goes on to explain to her young interlocutor, the statistical likelihood of tubal pregnancies (around 10 percent) becomes far higher in women suffering from pelvic inflammatory diseases like chlamydia, an ailment that not many people realize they have contracted.[5] Rather than ending the episode with the removal of her fallopian tube, Gigi continues to expound on the potential hazards of having a tubal pregnancy, including the obstacles it can pose to future pregnancies. Uchida's life story, in other words, has been reframed in the guise of edifying example, rather than explicit exposé.

Uchida's S4G however, is more than just a guide for girls or a confessional advice manual. It also is a reflection upon motherhood—its responsibilities, its potentials, as well as its pitfalls. While the episodic arrangement of S4G seems at first glance to be haphazard, abruptly leading the reader from practical discussions of ovulation, fertilization, and menstruation to autobiographical exposé (including the story of Uchida's childhood abuse), Uchida's storytelling is organized around a central theme—namely, the critical role which mothers play in the education and upbringing of their daughters. At the heart of this pedagogical dynamic, Uchida makes clear, should be the female body: a mother must teach her daughters how their bodies work, and give them a positive body image, in order for them to realize their full emotional and sexual potential as women.

The lesson is driven home with stories taken from Uchida's own life—many of them first recounted in *Father Fucker*—which demonstrate how her own lack of bodily knowledge and outdated sense of how women ought to behave damaged her emotional and sexual development. As Gigi/Uchida was growing up in Nagasaki, she received contradictory messages about a woman's sexuality from her mother, whose traditional (or perhaps old-fashioned) notions about female behavior stood in seeming contradiction to her work within the *mizu shōbai* as a bar hostess, where she served drinks, flirted, and entertained in bars largely frequented by men.[6] From the time she was a little girl, Gigi talked about sex in an open and candid way—a habit likely learned from her mother, who "used to tell me funny erotic stories from her work," but whose cramped sense of social propriety led her to treat sex as something which was best left undiscussed, and who went so far as to punish Gigi for showing guests her parents' bed (she was proud of the coverlet that her mother had knitted) (Uchida 2007:88).[7] As Gigi recalls, "My mother said things like 'I am a good mother, but this daughter of mine is a problem child who makes lewd (*etchi*) remarks,'" criticisms which the young girl found contradictory and confusing (Uchida 2007:89).

Another example of such mixed messages occurred over what kind of contact from other people was permissible. When she was six or seven years old and had rarely been hugged as a child, an older male neighbor grabbed her hand for a few seconds as he walked past her. After telling her mother, she was treated to a tirade about "perverts" (*chikan*) and excoriated for allowing herself to be touched by one. Unaware of the meaning of the term, Gigi had to look it up in the dictionary, where the too-formal definition perplexed her. Uchida also revisits an incident familiar from *Father Fucker*, where the young Shizuko/Gigi/Uchida was scolded by her mother for lying on their porch because passersby might see her underwear, peeking out from her shorts.

Such anxiety- and shame-ridden attitudes toward the female body and female sexuality only became more acute as Gigi entered puberty; when she first had her period, her mother simply showed her where the sanitary napkins were kept without any further explanation, while her teachers discussed menstruation in only vague and embarrassed terms:

"I was told that the menstrual blood was there to nourish the baby . . . There was no mention of eggs, sperm or fertilization" (Uchida 2007:19). As a result, she wryly notes, "I had the unpleasant image of a blood-drinking baby in my head" throughout her adolescence, despite the sex education that she subsequently received in school (Uchida 2007:20). Intent on sparing her own children from the same ignorant childhood, Gigi intersperses her reminiscences with a series of lighthearted family discussions about sexual intercourse and the body's reactions when aroused. She is careful to frame each of these conversations within the context of reproduction when talking with her younger children, and takes care to ensure that the level of discourse is appropriate for them and presented with good humor.

Her own birth family's failure to embrace this kind of honesty, and the silence and shame with which the adult world treated her maturing body, is associated by Uchida with a far more sinister outcome—namely, her abuse at the hands of her own stepfather, "the biggest pervert of all" (Uchida 2007:93). This traumatic period, first chronicled in *Father Fucker*, is revisited in *S4G*, but this time in a way that emphasizes the barely pubescent Gigi's innocence and lack of knowledge. Fondled by her stepfather and told that he would "snatch your virginity and make you my wife," Gigi has to look up the meaning of "virginity" in the dictionary (Uchida 2007:94). Here we are not shown the horrific abuse described in Uchida's novella; instead, we are confronted with a faceless male figure and the language with which he dominates his stepdaughter, until the beaten face of young Gigi appears in the next-to-last frame.

While Gigi's tale of abuse is horrific, its role here is not simply to shock, but to serve Uchida's larger goal of demonstrating the critical role of mothers in educating, and thus protecting, their daughters when they are young. The story's emotional climax in *S4G*, therefore, occurs *after* its actual narration. As her oldest son weeps at his mother's treatment, Gigi explains that there is a greater lesson to be learned—namely, the pernicious effects of "the kind of thinking that says that 'the woman asked for it' in cases of rape" (Uchida 2007:96). Her own mother said the same kind of thing to her, and made her feel like she was responsible for the abuse she received. Gigi's mother's attitudes, moreover, were not simply a matter of her mother's misplaced loyalty to her husband. When Gigi was groped by a man in a local record store, she felt powerless to do anything about it, for despite her shame and anger at the attack she realized that her mother and younger sister would hold her responsible for it. The adult Gigi, looking back at her younger self in the previous frame, concludes that "I wasn't bad—I was pitiable," before grabbing her own two daughters tightly and declaring, "I won't let you feel that way!" (Uchida 2007:99).

Uchida's portrayal of her mother in this affair as a black outline, spewing abuse outside of the traditional discursive space of the word-balloon, is a clear iconographic analogue to the way in which she depicts her stepfather earlier. As such, it further emphasizes in negative terms the importance of mothers for their daughters' healthy development. Without an engaged, informed, and informing mother, girls like Uchida/Gigi are rendered susceptible to men who want to take advantage of them or to make them feel worthless. Such mistreatment, Uchida points out, does not have to be as extreme as Gigi's first rape; instead, it can stem from something as simple as insulting comments on their physical appearance by fathers, boyfriends, and even husbands, disinterest in their physiology beyond the basics needed for sexual gratification, or the implication that a girl's body is somehow dirty simply because of her sex. In this vein, Gigi recalls always having to bathe after her father, who was offended by the very fact that she was female; during her period, in fact, he banned her from the bath altogether, forcing her to shower outside.

The form and content of S4G clearly is motivated by Uchida's sense of a crisis of sexual self-image among Japanese girls and women in the twenty-first century. Much of Gigi's concern about how women are treated is rooted in, and expressed in terms of, Uchida's own upbringing and experiences as a Japanese woman. These experiences, however, are now understood as object lessons (both positive and negative) for Uchida's own offspring, whom she wishes to spare from abuse and degradation—not only the explicit and personal mistreatment she endured, but the relentless objectification and diminution of women's sexuality that pervades Japanese society in general, and makes life-histories like her own possible. This sense of urgency and helplessness comes up again and again when Gigi pokes fun at the way women are portrayed on television ads with "bōyō" (lost sheep) expressions and high-pitched voices (Uchida 2007:99–100). Reflecting on why they talk and look this way, she realizes that such depictions are meant to stereotype women as "helpless, so that they can be chosen by men and colored by men's lust" (Uchida 2007: 100). This truth, however, is one that she struggles to communicate to her daughters, who look up at her with hopeful, wide eyes. Standing between them, with her eyes shut, she simply says, "It's complicated," realizing that they are still too young to understand (Uchida 2007:100).

Although *S4G: Sex For Girls* addresses many of the same issues as her earlier works, it also represents a significant change in Uchida's self-presentation and self-fashioning. As before, she writes in a uniquely personal and even confessional style, freely sharing her loves, her fears, her enthusiasms, and her pet peeves. Nonetheless, after more than a decade spent defining herself as a "transgressive woman," fearlessly challenging the social taboos surrounding sex and violence and redefining the traditional roles of daughter, mother, and wife, Uchida Shungiku here begins to focus her energies and talents upon something beyond, if still close to, herself—her daughters. In large part effacing the separation between herself and her alter-ego Gigi (*née* Shizuko), Uchida uses her own past as a daughter not as a subject in itself, but as a way to reflect upon what it means for her to be a mother. Talking about the past, therefore, becomes more than an act of self-definition and self-promotion: it is a labor of love, an attempt to explain what had been societal norms in order to teach her daughters what they should and could become. For this reason, *S4G* can be read as "sex education" in a much fuller and more complex sense of the term, combining biology and biography to teach what it might mean to positively understand oneself as a young woman—a woman, that is, who by knowing her body knows her worth, and by knowing her worth can participate freely and confidently in the world around her.

Over the course of her career, Uchida has remained a diva—a transgressive figure who, like every woman chronicled in this volume, plays by her own rules, boldly blazes her own trail, and takes center stage. What sets Uchida apart, however, is the degree to which both sexuality and motherhood define her dramatic persona and performances, themes whose depth and breadth this chapter has tried to elucidate. Notably, Uchida's performances frequently are fueled by anger at the hand that women have been dealt in contemporary Japan today, an anger also found in Kirino's *Goddess Chronicles* (2008, and explored by Rebecca Copeland in Chapter 1). As she grows older, Uchida's unique blend of indignation, humor, and sexual bravado is being channeled into new and largely untapped territory, in particular the sexual identity and needs of "mature" women in a culture where sex and aging (like sex and motherhood) long have been seen as antithetical. Uchida continues to demand her close-up, to be sure; all the same, as we see in works like *S4G: Sex For Girls,* the diva has changed costumes, slowed down the tempo, and begun to sing a new, more intimate tune.

NOTES

1. As Deborah Shamoon (1999) has noted, the first volume of *Watahan* generated so much interest among readers that they crashed the comments section of Uchida's website, forcing her to create a separate site dedicated solely to the series.

2. The common Japanese practice of co-sleeping with children while they are young means that unless the couple avoids sexual intercourse, the child will be present (although usually asleep) when the parents are intimate. Uchida's portrayal of her baby son waking up while she and her partner are making love is meant to be amusing, and does not have the perverse connotations that might be felt by a non-Japanese viewer. Rather, Uchida's humorous point is that the child, although awakened, is not perturbed by what interrupted his sleep.

3. The most popular volumes of the *Watahan* series have been reprinted in *bunko* (paperback) format, and are distinguished by the colors of their dust jackets—yellow for volume one, pink and blue (respectively) for volumes two and three.

4. This divorce was chronicled in Uchida's book *Inu no hō ga shittobukai* (The dog's jealousy is deep, Uchida 2002).

5. Chlamydia trachoma is a sexually transmitted disease that also can manifest as trachoma or a bacterial infection of the eyes. It is only rarely found in developed countries.

6. For a detailed study of the hostess industry, see Allison (1994).

7. Unlike Japanese futon, which traditionally are stored out of sight during the day, her mother slept on a Western-style double bed. The mother's reaction thus seems to be rooted in the metonymic association between sexual relations and the bed, an association made visible and tangible by the freestanding furniture but literally out of sight in the case of futon. This symbolic point clearly was lost on the young Shizuko.

CHAPTER 9

The Unmaking of a Diva

Kanehara Hitomi's Comfortable Anonymity

DAVID HOLLOWAY

The literary depictions of Japan's gap-widening social
condition and the increasing displacement of the salaryman
class by classless individuals, may be a kind of social
barometer for the cathartic literary expressions of precarity.

—Rosenbaum 2015:14

In 2003, a twenty-year-old Kanehara Hitomi took the literary world by
storm, winning the prestigious Akutagawa Prize with *Hebi ni piasu*
(2004a; translated by David James Karashima as *Snakes and Earrings*,
2006b), a brief narrative concerned with sex, violence, substance abuse,
body modification, and, according to some, not much else. Critics saw
the text as a window into the lives of Japan's disaffected youth, and the
press heralded it a grimy anthem for Japan's "lost generation." Kanehara
was almost immediately construed as the spokesperson for a generation
of restless, aimless, and "lost" Japanese who had missed out on earlier
postwar affluence. She was writing for the subaltern, the press said, for
those who hated school, their parents, and themselves, for those who had
drifted too far from center and too far away from the social institutions
of family life, educational pedigree, and career advancement that defined
postwar Japan. Her novella sold out immediately after it went to press, to
the delight of some critics and to the irritation of others.

In this light, Kanehara was simultaneously idealized in the press as a
"teen idol" writing for fashionistas who like to read, and criticized as the
embodiment of all that was wrong with Japanese youth in millennial
Japan (DiNitto 2011:454). As has been well documented, Kanehara

created a "commotion" by showing up to the otherwise staid Akutagawa Prize ceremony in grand fashion: high heels, short skirt, designer handbag, colored contacts, multiply pierced ears, and dyed hair (Hosogai 2004:93). In contrast to the modestly dressed and demure nineteen-year-old Wataya Risa, with whom she shared the Akutagawa Prize, and whose outfit caught the eye of nobody, Kanehara came off as a rebel, an antibookworm, a diva. It was as though Kanehara—whom Mark Driscoll (2007:183) suggests had, at the award ceremony, the aura of "a hybrid of fashion model and adult video actress"—was there by accident, having wandered off the streets of Shibuya, where such attire is common, and stumbled into the middle of a celebration of Japan's most promising literary talent (Saitō 2004:71). Indeed, what business did Kanehara, with barely a middle-school education, have sharing the stage with the studious, Kyoto-bred Wataya, who was in her second year of college at the time?

Both authors were praised for capturing the pulse of their generation and confronting readers with the difficulties of growing up in post-postwar Japan:

> [These were] the first writers to clearly emerge from Japan's post-bubble generation. Born at the height of this country's economic might in the mid-1980's, this is the first generation to have come of age after the bubble burst, in a Japan that has been questioning almost all aspects of its society, from its educational and political systems to its companies and military (Onishi 2004).

It was Kanehara, however, who seemed mired in the kind of life she captured so vividly in *Snakes and Earrings,* the kind of life void of education, politics, and even family, the kind of life you want to read about. In an interview after the initial success of *Snakes and Earrings,* Kanehara commented on the half-empty outlook that is typical of her generation: "I never knew the bubble era, so my way of looking at things can't help being different. Since I was born, I've never experienced a time of prosperity" (Onishi 2004).

In other words, her own life experiences seemingly authenticated the story she was telling: she dropped out of school, spent time on the streets, lived with boyfriends (something not often done in Japan), cut herself with razor blades, and fought with her parents (*Bungei Shunjū* 2004a:320). Furthermore, press reports following the award ceremony were quick to remind readers that she was a *furiitā,* a temp worker (Saitō 2004:71). She was "just an ordinary girl" with an ordinary life and ordinary problems (Takii 2010:22).

In concert with social concern over and infatuation with Japan's "youth problem" (DiNitto 2011: 456) and academic interest in "the wild child" of millennial Japan (Arai 2006:216), Kanehara fit right in. In true form, when asked why she decided to quit school, Kanehara replied: "The uniforms were hideous . . . There was no way I'd go to school looking like that" (*Bungei Shunjū* 2004a:321). Kanehara was clearly exaggerating, having also commented on being bored in school from a young age (*Bungei Shunjū* 2004a:320). But her carefully constructed words suggest a certain nonchalance and cavalier attitude toward Japan's education system—of great cultural importance since the end of the war—and perhaps even toward broader Japanese society in general.

In interviews following her initial success, Kanehara maintained this aura, insisting that because she writes from experience, her protagonists are stylized versions of herself. To be sure, *Snakes and Earrings*—and most all of her publications to date—deploys the first-person perspective, and protagonist Lui shares a number of personality traits with the author, such as multiple piercings in her ears and a fondness for designer goods (in the text, Lui claims that her name is short for Louis Vuitton). These discursive techniques allow Kanehara to readily conflate the textual and extratextual and further propagate the diva narrative that has circulated around her. The "encoded author" (Sakaki 1999:5) gives authority and urgency to her subject matter: alcohol, suicide, sex, violence, body modification, and self-harm. In encouraging a specific mode of reading, Kanehara (intentionally or not) drew upon the tradition of the self-referential *watakushi-shōsetsu/shi-shōsetsu,* or I-novel, that became a prominent literary movement in the early twentieth century. According to Tomi Suzuki (1996:6), an I-novel depends on "the reader's expectations concerning, and belief in, the single identity of the protagonist, the narrator, and the author." Critics and general readers have responded to Kanehara's *Snakes and Earrings* in this manner, with the expectation that it is a "barely fictionalized self-portrait" of being down and out in Tokyo (Driscoll 2007:182).

At the same time, the candid nature with which Kanehara has spoken about leaving home, dropping out of school, and flirting with suicide has similarly allowed her to maintain proximity to her characters and connect with her readers (Saitō and Ishizuka 2004:30). The eagerness with which readers consumed her novella, combined with savvy media marketing of Kanehara's personal narrative, put Kanehara on the fast track to success and diva-ness. Since then, however, she has gradually stepped back from the fanfare of her early years. As I demonstrate below, Kanehara's deliberate construction of her own diva-ness can be matched by a deliberate retreat from that same persona. As Christine Yano demonstrates in Chapter 5 on Misora Hibari in this volume, sometimes a diva is "a persona more than a person." Over a decade has passed since Kanehara's face was plastered on magazine covers and subway posters (Onishi 2004; DiNitto 2011:461), but the public perception of the author remains grounded largely in her early fame and the adolescent defiance of *Snakes and Earrings*. For example, only her early fiction seems to interest scholars: namely *Snakes and Earrings,* but also *Asshubeibii* (Ash baby, Kanehara 2004b) and *AMEBIC* (Kanehara 2005). And her only works to be translated into English are *Snakes and Earrings* and *Ōtofikushon* (Kanehara 2006a; translated by David James Karashimas as *Autofiction,* 2008). Even the film adaptation of *Snakes and Earrings* (Ninagawa Yukio 2008), while returning Kanehara briefly to the spotlight, underscored the fact that she may be forever bound to and perhaps overshadowed by her literary debut and the persona that came with it. The continued visibility of *Snakes and Earrings* is a gentle nod to Kanehara's place in what Amanda Seaman in chapter 8 of this volume calls Japan's "pop culture assembly line," which churns out celebrities with great frequency.

My interests in the rest of this chapter are in the processes of diva construction that transformed Kanehara into millennial Japan's bookish bad girl, and, more importantly, in the ways in which she has since removed herself from the public eye. In contrast to some of the other divas discussed in this volume, who are pledged to a life of diva-ness, Kanehara seems tired of the spotlight. This chapter is thus an attempt to broaden the scope of Kanehara's biography and to distance the author from the image that was constructed for her and the novella that continues to follow her. It is an attempt to offer a more complete portrait of both *Snakes and Earrings,* which Driscoll suggests reads like "reality fiction" (2007:183), and Kanehara the writer, and to work toward a space where her fiction is allowed to speak for itself. Ultimately, this essay offers new ways of thinking about Kanehara and her oeuvre by focusing not on who she was as a teenager, but on who she is today: a married mother of two living in Paris. In other words, Kanehara wants to be left alone, having found what her protagonists find elusive— stability in an increasingly unstable world. Ever the outsider, Kanehara has made her way back to the fringes, even if that means leaving Japan behind.

KANEHARA'S DIVA CITIZENSHIP

Divas are by nature unstable and unpredictable. They live according to their own impulses toward agency and insurgency and "put the dominant story into suspended animation" (Berlant 1997:223). At the heart of diva construction is an implicit challenge to normative ways of living that transcends gendered boundaries and expectations—a bedeviled and unruly femininity. At the same time, the term *diva* itself does what it wants. Initially used to identify "a heralded opera singer," the term has now expanded to describe several attributes: "a powerful and entertaining, if pushy and bitchy woman" who is "immensely talented but selfishly driven and difficult to deal with" (Springer 2007:255–56). The contemporary signification of "diva" splices artistic abilities with "rampaging female ego" (Tyrangiel 2002): powerful, entertaining, and talented, *but* pushy, bitchy, and selfish. Diva construction thus depends on a gendered way of interpreting the personal lives of female celebrities and icons. Seemingly untethered and unmediated, divas are captivating for the ways in which their personal lives—in contrast to their public lives—are incongruous with normative conceptions of femininity. In other words, the "politics of respectability" that govern women's lives are deconstructed and trashed (Springer 2007:258). And the media and fans cannot look away. Women who act outside of societal expectation or in accordance with their own desires are sometimes considered selfish. This is especially the case in Japan where self-sacrifice is critical to the female—that is, maternal—archetype (Ohinata 1995:205).

Because of the importance of motherhood in the popular consciousness, women's bodies are especially susceptible to public ridicule and surveillance (see Rebecca Copeland's Chapter 1 in this volume). The figure of the diva is grounded in women's positions and performances in the public eye—in performing as divas, women act, using their bodies and voices (for writers, the pen may act as a voice). For Lauren Berlant (1997:223), performance—"flashing up and startling the public"—can have immense political repercussions. She theorizes about the notion of "diva citizenship," in which marginalized people might upset "social and institutional practices" by narrating stories of oppression and abjection through public performance (Berlant 1997:223). This kind of political model is useful for considering the ways in which *performance* is instrumental in diva construction: performance as ability or talent, and performance as persona. The ways these two manifestations of performance unfold on the female body offer insight into contemporary configurations of the diva.

Snakes and Earrings became Kanehara's passport to diva citizenship. An antinarrative of Japanese social life, the text exposed threads in the social fabric in which people like her—with little chance of upward mobility—frequently get ensnared. Nineteen-year-old protagonist Lui has fallen through the cracks, as have all of the other characters. As Norimitsu Onishi observes:

> [In the text,] the institutions that built postwar Japan—the family, school and companies—are noticeable by their absence. In a nation known for its social cohesion, the characters have no interest in playing a role in society, but only in finding personal satisfaction among themselves. Unlike Japanese in, say, their 30's, the characters in the novel are not disillusioned at Japanese society, since they had few expectations to begin with (Onishi 2004).

Although Lui and her boyfriend Ama are teenagers, there is little textual reference to their families or even friends, and all of the characters embrace strategies of mediocrity: none attend school, and of the three primary characters, only Lui's illicit lover Shiba, the owner of his own tattoo/sex shop, has a tangential role in Japanese society and the economy. With nothing to do, then, the characters turn to their own bodies and the bodies of each other. They live according to Kanehara's logic that because "there are many people who don't expect anything from society . . . they [look] inward or to the people closest to them" to fill a void (Onishi 2004). In other words, Lui spends her time drinking, having sex, and getting tattoos because she has nothing else to do. She lives off of the meager wages Ama earns at a secondhand clothing store. After he is murdered, she moves in with Shiba, knowing that he is the man who killed Ama.

The presumption was, given Kanehara's supposed proximity to her protagonist, that the author was writing, at least partially, from experience. In other words, she was an outlier, an accidental celebrity; she should be taking your order at Starbucks, like so many other young Japanese who are trapped in part-time work, rather than writing popular works of fiction. Her very presence at the award ceremony was a reminder that "a seismic change in the body politic has taken place in recent years: from a society with a vast . . . middle class to one that is now . . . downstreaming, bipolarized, and riddled by class difference" (Allison 2013:5). Older readers saw the world she captured as unfamiliar, alien (Saitō 2004:71; Onishi 2004; *Bungei Shunjū* 2004a:121), even "completely incomprehensible" (*Bungei Shunjū* 2004b:315); younger readers saw it teemingly alive, just below the surface.

Admittedly, part of the attraction was the text's subject matter and the "indifferent" and "detached" narrative voice that has little quarrel with potentially upsetting themes such as murder, recreational sex, and violence against women (Matsuura 2007:19). Passages such as the following are commonplace:

> Shiba-san stubbed out his cigarette in the ashtray and stepped up toward the bed, undoing his belt as he walked. He stopped at the edge of the bed and pushed me down roughly with one hand, then brought his palm up against my neck. His fingers traced my veins and his grip tightened until his fingertips began to dig into my flesh. . . . The veins on his right arm bulged to the surface. My body was screaming out for air, and I began twitching. My face tightened and my throat felt like it would crack. . . . Shiba-san looked down at me with a blank expression, grabbed hold of my hair, and pulled on it in a rough rhythm—fucking my face. I could feel myself getting wet, though he hadn't even laid a finger on me (Kanehara 2006b:35–36).

Male critics were intrigued not by what was said necessarily, but rather by who said it. After all, masochism had been thematized before, by literary giants such as Tanizaki Jun'ichirō (1885–1965) and Kōno Taeko (1926–2015), who was an Akutagawa Prize winner herself. An attractive young woman writing so openly about the body, its sensations, and its limitations, however, was perhaps for male intellectuals a source of fascination.

Furthermore, the text's emphasis on the body echoed provocative theories put forth by intellectuals such as Miyadai Shinji who, in the midst of the "lost decade," argued that the body could serve as the new cornerstone of millennial identity and purpose. It could be tailored and changed, and even shared with others. Accordingly, Miyadai and Suzuki Takayuki (1988:27) argued that the body is "the last controllable environment, the modifiable exterior. This is why there is no problem with the body being consumed by others." In a milieu in which nothing mattered, Miyadai argued, the body was all that mattered. The text's pursuits of the "evanescent pleasures" of the body thus spoke to the hedonistic zeitgeist of millennial Japan (Driscoll 2007:185).

Since at least the postwar era, the body in literary works has been portrayed as a site of contestation and protest, through which writers might advocate "a return to the immediacy of the physical" (DiNitto 2011:465). Rachel DiNitto observes that *Snakes and Earrings* "can be contextualized within a history of postwar writing that has employed the body as a vehicle for resisting various dominant ideologies" (DiNitto 2011:465). The carnality and hedonism celebrated in the immediate postwar works of the "flesh writers" emerged from a milieu in which the physical body had been broken down during the war and subject to intense coercive measures by the state. With the end of the war came a sense of reprieve but a simultaneous looming awareness of a mass starting over. For some writers of the time, such as Tamura Taijirō, the body was all that remained and needed to be the locus for a new postwar identity. "Only the body is real [*jijutsu*]. The body's weariness, the body's desires, the body's anger, the body's intoxications, the body's confusion, the body's fatigue—only these are real. It is because of all these things that we realize, for the first time, that we are alive" (Tamura 1978:62; translated in Slaymaker 2004:47).

In Tamura's writing, characters are driven by sexual instinct and impulse. The "group of feral prostitutes" around whom the novel *Gate of Flesh* (Nikutai no mon, 1947) revolves pledge to a life of sex and money, but never love (Orbaugh 2007:470). When one of the prostitutes, Maya, falls in love, she is suspended from the ceiling and beaten. Maya dies, but not before experiencing a carnal renewal: "Maya was struck with the idea that even if she were banished to Hell, she would not be separated from the pleasure of the flesh she experienced for the first time. She felt that a new life was beginning" (Tamura 1978:52; translated in Slaymaker 2004:60).

Snakes and Earrings shares a special affinity with the hedonistic pulse of Tamura's novel. The text flaunts the sexual female body and, following Tamura's work, positions it between the contradictory yet complementary sensations of pleasure and pain. Lui's initial sexual experience with the sadistic Shiba leaves her in a state of purgatory: "I felt a strange combination of relief and excitement, like I'd been released from Hell, but exiled from Heaven at the same time" (Kanehara 2006b:40). In *Gate of Flesh*, Maya is reborn through sexual violence, even if that means eternal damnation. Her liberation into Hell is similar to Lui's liberation from Hell, if only because both women are confronted with a quasi-religious awakening through sexual violence. Lui's sexual relationship with Shiba is predicated on her desire for a tattoo—"one fuck" per session (Kanehara 2006b:34)—but as the narrative progresses, any pretense to Lui's sexual pleasure is sublimated to physical and ultimately emotional pain. Shiba is ruthlessly violent, but Lui finds that that is exactly what she needs, at least for the short term. In his analysis of the text, Driscoll places the sexual aspects of Kanehara's novella within the broader context of sexual politics in contemporary Japan. Driscoll notes that since the 1990s, the political right has condemned nonreproductive sex, among other activities, as a hobby of "at risk" youth who have turned their backs on "the Japanese nation state" (Driscoll 2007:185). The anxiety surrounding the falling birthrate has brought strict focus on those "at risk" Japanese who, like Kanehara's Lui, embrace the body at the expense of nationalistic discourse and ideology.

The Akutagawa Prize ceremony revealed to the public Kanehara's own interest in the body as a site of performance, spectacle, and rebellion. Flanked by Wataya, Kanehara was offered up as all body. To this end, Saitō Juri explained that Wataya, in a skirt that stretched tastefully below her knee, appeared ever the *ojō-sama,* or upper-middle-class daughter from a good family (Saitō 2004:71). Saitō could not say the same for Kanehara, and instead commented on how short her skirt was, what parts of her body were showing, and how many earrings were in her ears (Saitō 2004:71). Hosogai Sayaka followed suit, commenting on Kanehara's stilettos and colored contacts (Hosogai 2004:93). "If I had had more confidence in myself, maybe I would have worn something more formal—like a dress or something. But I didn't, so I left the house like usual," Kanehara explained when pressed about her outfit (Hosogai 2004:93; see also DiNitto 2011:462).

This kind of attention to her body would follow Kanehara for years to come. The magazine *Hon no tabibito* (Literary traveler), for example, interviewed and photographed Kanehara in 2010, after the release of *Trip Trap* (Kanehara 2009a), an anthology of short stories. The title of the photo spread, and its accompanying interview with Kanehara, is "Hinichijō de deau onna to iu jibun," a clunky turn of phrase that can be rendered "I'm Just an Ordinary Girl" (Takii 2010:22). Kanehara appears wearing thigh-high leather stilettos and a short denim skirt. In an empty room, she sits on a chair, which sits on a rumpled sheet (Figure 23). Her eyes are subdued, contemplative, unconcerned with the camera's intrusive gaze. Her hair hangs provocatively. It is the same image of Kanehara as before— cool, fashionable, sexy—that presents the same conundrum: her words are not allowed to speak for themselves. Visibility, embodiment, and performance are crucial in the construction of the diva aesthetic. Even a woman writer, who supposedly lives at her desk, must be *seen* and must be subject to public scrutiny. Again, praised for her ordinariness and appearance, Kanehara is revealed to be anything but ordinary; if she were truly ordinary, nobody would care; she would be in the shadows.

To be in the spotlight is to be extraordinary, as the dynamics of one's private life extend into national culture. Kanehara's ascent to literary fame was timely in this respect, for her personal life, as exhumed in interviews, was a reflection of the breakdown of Japanese social life and illuminated the precarious state of Japan's youth and the tremendous

23. Kanehara Hitomi photograph by Hongo Yuji (Takii 2010). Image used with permission of the Kadokawa Corporation.

existential pain they endure (*Bungei Shunjū* 2004b:120). She used to be ordinary: broke, rebellious, apathetic, authentic—which is what the media liked about her, which is what made her a diva. She managed to escape her ordinary life, bringing her experiences to a curious and eager readership. And the more the public learned about her life, the more her ordinariness marked her as extraordinary. Because "the self-concept of Japan as a homogenous and unique nation still appears to have a firm grip on the official and popular imagination" (Siddle 2011:150), Kanehara's personal narrative was especially resonant, and even threatening to myths of national cohesion. Can we blame her for wanting to speak so openly about growing up on the fringes, for demonstrating to readers that Japanese social life is multidimensional and varied?

DAUGHTER DIVA

One of the important themes in *Snakes and Earrings* is protagonist Lui's interest in physical pain, evident in her singular devotion to body modification, or *shintai kaizō*. Some critics, such as Kusano Mitsuyo, praised Kanehara for introducing them to what remains, at least in Japan, a subcultural and defiant practice (*Bungei Shunjū* 2004b:127; DiNitto 2011:462); others, such Hayasaka Shigezō, contextualized tattooing and tongue splitting (the pinnacle of Lui's body modification experience) within a broader rhetoric of gendered self-harm, including alcoholism and recreational sex (*Bungei Shunjū* 2004b:121). Kanehara has long been interested in thematizing self-harm. In middle school she wrote a short piece called "Vampire Love" (*Bungei Shunjū* 2004b:322), making her protagonist a wrist cutter because Kanehara, too, was cutting her own wrists at that time. When asked why she turned to self-harm, Kanehara commented that she was "tired" and her boyfriend was being abusive (*Bungei Shunjū* 2004b:322). Kanehara says she had no one to talk to about her problems, so wove them into her fiction (*Bungei Shunjū* 2004b:322). For her, the pain of living could be relieved through the writing process, and by identifying with characters who, like her, hurt themselves as their only recourse to survival.

Following *Snakes and Earrings,* she offered a litany of novellas and short stories whose female protagonists are alcoholics, drug addicts, bulimics, and schizophrenics. Her 2009 collection of short stories, aptly titled *Yūutsu-tachi* (The depressed, Kanehara 2009b), made clear her interest in hurt, self-harm, and self-destruction. Divided into seven narratives, the collection of short stories chronicle the efforts of protagonist Kanda Yū to cure herself of depression. At the beginning of each narrative, she is on her way to therapy, but she never quite makes it there, and is never quite able to rid herself of her emotional problems. "The idea that people enjoy their lives, or have it easy," Kanehara said in an interview following the text's publication, "just isn't possible anymore" (Hon no Hanashi 2009). In this sense, reading her works is not unlike listening to *The Downward Spiral,* each intensely self-reflexive narrative giving the impression that she is working through something, and taking you along for the ride. Indeed, Trent Reznor's vision of hurting himself "to see if I still feel" and belief in pain as "the only thing that's real" (*Hurt*, Nine Inch Nails, 1994) is reworked in *Snakes and Earrings* when Lui remarks: "There was nothing for me to believe and nothing for me to feel. In fact, the only feeling with the power to kick me back to life was . . . acute pain" (Kanehara 2006b:91–92).

Kanehara does not mention Nine Inch Nails as an inspiration or influence. She does, however, recall finding as an unruly teenager solace in Bjork. Who better to identify with than an influential and international cult performer who dropped out of classical music school as a teenager to join a punk rock band (Van Meter 1997:96)? Kanehara recalls ditching class to listen to Bjork's music all day in her room (Saitō and Ishizuka 2004:30). She liked studying (*Bungei Shunjū* 2004a:321); she just did not like school, and began to lose interest in academics as early as fourth grade, in spite of the efforts of her mother, Chieko, who would walk her to the school grounds (Saitō and Ishizuka 2004:30). "I didn't like being told what to do," she explains, and found school to be "annoying" (*Bungei Shunjū* 2004a:320). Acknowledging that she was "a brat" back then, Kanehara preferred to hang out with friends rather than attend classes (*Bungei Shunjū* 2004a:320). But it was not until her first year of high school that Kanehara quit school entirely (Hosogai 2004:94). Kanehara says graduating from middle school was an important life milestone (Hosogai 2004:94) but was also a dark time for her; that is when she began to experiment with cutting, thought of suicide, and spent time in therapy (Saitō and Ishizuka 2004:30; Hosogai 2004:94). Her parents, Chieko and Mizuhito, were concerned about the growing number of scars on their daughter's wrists and arms, and when Hitomi approached them about leaving school for good it was her father, a professor at Hosei University and accomplished translator of children's stories, who convinced Chieko that it was in their daughter's best interest to let her walk her own path (*Bungei Shunjū* 2004a:320).

Although there are no fathers in Kanehara's fiction, her own father has a significant role in her personal narrative and development as a writer. (Her mother, it seems, has no place in this particular version of the Kanehara story.) Kanehara began writing creatively in elementary school, but, somewhat ironically, was exposed to her first major literary influences while living outside of Japan, when her father's research required relocation to San Francisco for one year. As she explains, "One day he brought a bunch of books home from [the Japanese bookstore] and said I could read them if I wanted to. . . . If he had told me to read them, I probably wouldn't have. But he just kind of left them there for me, so I picked some up and started reading" (*Bungei Shunjū* 2004a:321). In San Francisco, where she attended an American elementary school during the week and

Japanese school on Saturdays, she discovered the works of Murakami Ryū and Yamada Eimi, two authors who caused a commotion as young writers in the 1970s and 1980s; Murakami for violent and hedonistic stories of Japanese men, Yamada for sensual, erotic narratives of Japanese women, mostly with African American men.

Kanehara's works seem to draw inspiration from both authors. The sex and violence at the center of *Snakes and Earrings,* for instance, reflects Murakami's imperative to "challenge . . . the normative, conservative mainstream of Japanese society in the form of insistent representation of extreme violence and sexuality" (DiNitto 2011:466). At the same time, through Lui's self-aware sexuality and disregard of "proper" feminine behavior, Kanehara captures Yamada's famed "erotic descriptions of women pursuing sexual fulfillment" that scandalized Japan's conservative literary establishment in the 1980s (Cornyetz 1996:428). In an interesting twist of fate, both Murakami and Yamada are on the Akutagawa Prize selection committee, and both had a hand in nominating Kanehara's text for the prize. Murakami, for example, praised Kanehara 's "genius" in bringing to light the issues facing Japan's youth and argued that if young people like Kanehara did not write, the older generations would remain oblivious (Saitō 2004:71; DiNitto 2011:459).

And write she must: "The things that I just have to get out—I write them. . . . It's therapeutic" (Hosogai 2004:93). Elsewhere: "Writing calms me down. Like smoking a cigarette" (Saitō Juri 2004:19). She recalls putting pen to paper to express herself, even at a young age, because it was easier and more efficient than talking (Hosogai 2004:93). Kanehara's fiction is exhilarating because she puts so much of herself in it, in a sense channeling the "I novelists" of the early twentieth century who found the best fiction to be that which was based on reality and experience. "My dad tells me not to [write autobiographically]," she says. "But I just don't think I'm good at third-person narration" (Enomoto 2015). Mizuhito did more than introduce his young daughter to the kinds of provocative and sensational works for which she would gain recognition. As her words here suggest, he was instrumental in her pursuit of the craft of fiction. Back in Japan after a year in San Francisco, Hitomi turned against education and family, choosing instead to spend her time at karaoke bars and pachinko parlors, and to move in with her boyfriends. Chieko fretted and worried, Mizuhito kept his distance and let her make mistakes (Hosogai 2004:93). But Mizuhito was there for her when she needed him. As Hitomi struggled to find her footing in uncertain times, he was never more than a phone call away, and father and daughter talked regularly (*Bungei Shunjū* 2004a:321). He invited her to a fiction workshop for college sophomores, where she wrote a ten-page short story called "Suisō no naka" (In the fish's tank), about a woman having a conversation with her boyfriend's pet fish (*Bungei Shunjū* 2004a:321–22). Mizuhito was not impressed, but he was encouraging, and checked her manuscript for errors (*Bungei Shunjū* 2004a:322). As for Hitomi, she was pleased that none of the other students ever found out she was in middle school, and enjoyed writing and sharing her work with them (Hosogai 2004:93).

Years later, Mizuhito again took up his editor's pen, this time scrutinizing her manuscript of *Snakes and Earrings* before she submitted it to the Akutagawa committee. Aware of his daughter's tendency to write autobiographically, Mizuhito has never tried to understand his daughter through her fiction, perhaps aware of the blurry lines between autobiography and entertainment (Saitō and Ishizuka 2004:31). The resounding success of *Snakes and Earrings* reveals a powerful and touching literary bond between father and daughter. In a very literal sense, then, for Hitomi fiction has represented a safe place, a refuge, a means to connect or reconnect with her father, and a way to interact with other like-minded souls. Through the writing process, she was able to grasp what her characters continually find elusive: a place to rest, a way to connect with others (Hosogai 2004:94). Anne Allison (2013:47) has demonstrated that contemporary Japanese are plagued by a sense of not belonging, *ibasho ga nai* in Japanese, especially the elderly and those of Kanehara's generation. Drawing on the work of activist Amamiya Karin, who like Kanehara wears "cool clothes" (Allison 2009:104) and spent her youth trapped in the cycle of part-time labor, self-harm, and suicidal thoughts (Allison 2013:168), Allison calls attention to *ikizurasa*, or "the pain of life," that afflicts those without financial or personal stability in recessionary Japan, which remains in the shadows of an affluent postwar society (Allison 2013:65). But she also emphasizes that all hope is not lost, as marginalized Japanese are made increasingly visible through governmental works projects, community activism, and the sharing of stories.

For those who are invested in the lives of Japan's underclasses—like Amamiya, like Kanehara—"survival" is at the "heart of [their] politics" (Allison 2009:104). Kanehara's early fiction, especially *Snakes and Earrings,* prefigures much of the recent interest in Japan's "precarious" citizens, and as Kanehara explains, she captures the *ikizurasa* and "placelessness" (*ikiba no nasa*) of the post-postwar generation (Hosogai 2004:94), bringing to light the lives of people with few friends and even fewer options. She is doing activist work without the activism. Driscoll comments that Kanehara disrupted the stigma surrounding people in part-time work: she "helped consolidate a comparatively 'positive' image for freeters [temp workers] and—given her much-publicized refusal to go to high school or pursue any vocational training—the NEET [individuals not in education, employment, or training]" (Driscoll 2007:173). She has done much more than that, however. She writes of the "anxiety" (*fuan*) of life and the chronic instability afflicting many Japanese (Saitō 2004:19). She makes it okay to talk publicly about potentially private struggles.

Thus her personal narrative is an important dimension of her literary production: she can offer an authentic picture of what it is like to be on the fringes, consumed with anxiety. Yet Kanehara is not pessimistic in her writing and injects hope into her novellas and short stories. While Allison (2013:79) points out that "the word hope (*kibō*) is much used today [to convey a state of] stagnated imaginaries—horizons of expectation that are ebbing or shutting down," Kanehara speaks to the persistence of forward progress in the face of adversity. At the end of *Snakes and Earrings,* a text dominated by shadows and desperation, Lui gets out of bed and "squints" into the "unrelenting brightness" of the morning sun, thoughts of marriage to Shiba on the fringes of her mind (Kanehara 2006b:120). Having previously devoted herself to an iconoclastic existence, the intrusion of monogamy and marriage is jarring and not entirely convincing. The point of tying up loose ends is not about believability, but rather participation in the burgeoning discourse of hope that is central to how we think, write, and read about Japan's disenfranchised youth.

WHERE HAS THE DIVA GONE?

Having cut her teeth on generational strife and anguish, Kanehara is no longer invested in rebelling against the dominant culture, but rather on how to survive within it. It should come as no surprise that for someone so dedicated to the pseudo-autobiographical, her subject matter reflects her life changes. She married her longtime editor at Shūeisha Publishing in 2005, had her first daughter in 2007, her second daughter in 2011, and has slowly turned her literary attention to the issues married women face. Her novel *Mazāzu* (Mothers, Kanehara 2011) is an attempt to grapple with the expectations and inevitable letdowns of motherhood. It has been called her first "family novel" (*kazoku shōsetsu*), something she claims to have wanted to write since her literary debut (Enomoto 2015). She wrote *Mothers* from France, having decided to raise her children there over concerns of radiation in the wake of the Fukushima disaster. That disaster is the backdrop to her latest novella *Motazaru mono* (Without, Kanehara 2015), which appeared in *Subaru* magazine. This novella follows several individuals whose lives are adversely affected by the March 2011 disaster. A touching scene is when protagonist Chizu loses her baby to an unexpected illness. A similar scene appears in *Mothers,* when one of the characters loses her five-month-old daughter in a bicycle accident. Kanehara's own daughter was about that age when Kanehara was writing the novel. The aim of her fiction has always been about survival—whether in the form of facing the prospects of a hopeless future or dealing with the death of one's child—and overcoming what Berlant calls "impasse": the moment when life bottoms out, the sense of "dithering, tottering, bargaining, testing, or otherwise being worn out" by the world's broken promises (Berlant 2011: 8).

In the years since her debut, Kanehara has not been able to reproduce her initial success or fanfare, and her diva passport appears to have expired. If divas are in the spotlight and under scrutiny, "commodified and objectified" (see Laura Miller's Chapter 3 in this volume), Kanehara has slipped into a comfortable anonymity. She has made it clear that she is neither Japan's lost daughter (*Bungei Shunjū* 2004a:324) nor, despite media pleas to the contrary, the voice of young Japanese today: "I'm not speaking for my generation. I'm just writing what I feel" (Neustatter 2005). As her novels and stories pursue themes related to marriage, maternity, and maturity, the media seems to have lost interest. And some fans have been left in the dark. For example, popular blogsite Cyzowoman.com (2014) asks: "Where is Kanehara Hitomi?" In response, an editor at *Bungeishi* magazine says simply: "She doesn't seem like she is in the mood to write" and cites her "difficult nature" (*atsukainikui seikaku*) as a reason for her absence from the spotlight (Cyzowoman.com 2014). This same editor goes on to remark that Kanehara does not need to write: "Her husband probably has enough money. And her father, Kanehara Mizuhito, is a professor in the sociology department at Hosei University and a big name in translating. Between the two of them, Kanehara herself will be fine even if she doesn't write" (Cyzowoman.com 2014). Kanehara does not write for money; that has been clear all along. Even so, the question and its derisive answer are both puzzling because the reality is that Kanehara has been writing consistently since her literary debut. And she has been winning awards in the process: the Kawabata Yasunari Prize in

2010 for her short story *Natsu tabi* (Summer vacation), the Oda Sakuno-suke Prize that same year for *Trip Trap* (which includes *Natsu tabi*), and the Bunkamura Les Deux Magots Literature Award in 2012 for *Mazāzu* (Mothers). (Uchida Shungiku also won this award in 1993. See Amanda Seaman's Chapter 8 in this volume.) Readers may not realize that her stories often appear in literary magazines before being collected for anthologies. Or they may be used to the Kanehara of old, treated like a celebrity for her (extra)ordinary upbringing and sense of style. Indeed, one interview in 2004 closes with this observation: "She's wearing a miniskirt today, too" (Hosogai 2004:95).

Interestingly, when Kanehara first rose to fame, author and Akutagawa Prize recipient Maruyama Kenji, who was twenty-three when he won, offered her this warning: "Don't let them turn you into a celebrity writer just to toss you aside" (Hosogai 2004:94). At the time, Kanehara did not care about how the media treated her, commenting on just being "happy" that her fiction was being read (Hosogai 2004:94). In the years since, Murayama's words proved prophetic, for once the media stopped addressing her clothes and her childhood—in this regard, nearly all of the interviews that appeared in 2004 say more or less the same thing—the media lost interest. Kanehara has done nothing to redirect attention to herself. We would not expect her to.

Kanehara is not the only famous Japanese woman who comes with a compelling personal narrative. While other women may covet the spotlight and the diva appellation, using their personal narratives to "encourage all women to find their inner diva" (quoted from Jan Bardsley's Chapter 7 in this volume), for example, Kanehara does not. She just wants to write (*Bungei Shunjū* 2004a:324). In this light, her so-called disappearance speaks to a desire for anonymity and distance, a desire for a chance to write in peace and to be taken seriously as a writer, not as a diva. But to resist is to be a diva. To transgress expectation is to be a diva. To reconfigure the world around her by living according to nobody's expectation but her own is to be a diva. This is the diva's prerogative. And if we expect Kanehara to write for us, to perform her bad girl persona for us, that is our problem, not hers. This is not to say that Kanehara has disappeared from literary circles and critical commentary all together. Rather, when her fiction is addressed, her themes take center stage. And that suits Kanehara just fine.

CHAPTER 10

Ice Princess

Asada Mao the Demure Diva

MASAFUMI MONDEN

As a representative of the Japanese nation on such a big stage
as Olympic Games, perhaps I was not able to bring [to
Japan] a medal with me. But I believe I achieved the free
program performance that I aimed for, and really, thinking
about the overall result it was probably not as good as it
should have been, but, I believe I could repay for all the
support I have received, in my own way.

—Asada's interview in Sochi (Nippon Hōsō Kyōkai 2014)

A girl of fifteen waltzes on the ice. She wears a sheer, pale pink mini-dress
with a puff-sleeved white top resembling the corseted bodice of a ballerina's costume. Accompanied by a fairy tale Tchaikovsky melody, she
performs triple jumps one after another with the effortless lightness of a
ballet dancer. Her radiant smile blooms every time she takes flight, bely-
ing the excruciating difficulty and physical exertion required to perform
each jump. A final fist pump signals an innocent exultation. Fast forward
eight years. The skater, now a young woman of twenty-three, is still on
the ice. Her sparkling innocence has been replaced by an amalgam of
wistful grace and fierceness. She wears a beautiful bird-like blue outfit
with black tulle underskirt. Thousands of Swarovski crystals sewn onto
her dress glitter as she glides over the ice to the notes of dramatic Rach-
maninov music. This is Asada Mao, Olympic silver medalist, three-time
world champion, and Guinness world record holder. Asada's life is a narrative of struggle and triumph, from her meteoric rise to figure skating
stardom at the age of fifteen; followed by an agonizing period of fierce

public scrutiny, and then her sublime performance at 2014 Olympics that touched many around the world. To many Japanese, Asada represents the epitome of a wholesome, good girl who embodies Japanese ideals of both athlete and femininity. She is a popular athlete, a celebrity, a national icon, an ideal daughter figure, and a role model for girls. Her entire life has been enmeshed with popular culture.

This chapter attempts to reconsider Asada's public persona as a hardworking, diligent young athlete, the good-girl-next-door who speaks politely and almost always with a smile. Unlike many of the other divas in this volume, Asada seems to embody an ideal, normative mode of Japanese girlhood and young femininity. I argue in this chapter that behind this innocent persona is a diva with a fierce commitment to her professional performance and her audience and a skillful way of concealing her personal life from the public eye despite massive media attention. I believe the way Asada exercises her power allows her to act in accordance with her own desires while generally avoiding criticism, unlike some other powerful women. She is a diva who captures the heart of people with her extraordinary looks, artistry, and athletic talents; a diva whose spectacular performances and risk-taking behaviors always excite audiences, and whose good girl persona may be her greatest performance of all.

This chapter begins with a brief biography of Asada and her early achievements, from her girlhood to achieving her place as a national icon. Next, I examine her personality, looking behind the good girl image and into her diva narratives, from her conduct off the ice and with colleagues, and her high-stakes attachment to her signature triple axel jump that disrupts the boundary between "appropriate" male and female behaviors in sports. Finally, I explore how Asada's performances can be seen as representing both the concept of "the nobility of failure" and an original sense of diva as divine, superhuman. Through these explorations I question whether Asada is symbolic of a new, and perhaps "Japanese," way of diva-hood that utilizes her idealized girlish femininity to allow her to exercise authority and power without subjecting herself to the usual derogatory labels applied to powerful women: self-centered, aggressive, and manipulative.

MIRACLE MAO: ASADA'S EARLY ACHIEVEMENTS

Affectionately known by many Japanese people as Mao-chan, she was born in 1990 in Nagoya Prefecture. At the age of three she joined her older sister, Mai, in classical ballet classes (Utsunomiya 2006:55–56;

Yoshida 2011:15). While classical ballet has been included in after-school activities in Japan since the end of the Pacific War, ballet has been a less common activity than, for example, learning how to play musical instruments (Umino, Takahashi, and Koyama 2012:54). Asada's mother was determined that her daughters would train to be ballet dancers. A myth has developed over Asada's supposedly affluent upbringing (Smart FLASH 2017). After Asada's mother, Kyoko, learned that her favorite ballerina, Georgian Nina Ananishivili, first had a career (albeit brief) as a figure skater, Kyoko thought figure skating would benefit her daughters' ballet training (Yoshida 2011:21). Japanese figure skaters who were trained in ballet from their early ages have been rare (*Chūnichi Shinbun* 2013:18). Asada started skating at the age of five. In her first competition in February 1997, Asada placed fifth after Mai, who was fourth. Asada was so captivated by this first skating competition that she quit all other after-school activities and focused on skating and ballet.

Shortly after Yamada Machiko (who also trained the legendary Ito Midori) began coaching her in 2001, Asada started practicing the triple axel (Yoshida 2011:42), the most difficult triple jump, which I explore in detail below. Asada first landed this jump in a regional competition in October 2002 and began to attract media attention as a "girl prodigy" (*tensai shōjo*) (Yoshida 2011:54), an appellation which was solidified by her win at the Junior World Championships in 2005 (Yoshida 2011:65–68).

Asada's debut in senior competition followed in the 2005–6 season (Yoshida 2011:74). She electrified the senior competitions with her triple axel and triple-triple jumps. This "meteoric rise" of the apparently fearless, unbeatable fifteen-year-old girl lead to a groundswell of demands among the public to allow her to compete in the 2006 Winter Olympic Games in Turin, even though she was technically eighty-seven days too young (Yoshida 2011:85–86; Utsunomiya 2006:79). Even Koizumi Jun'ichirō, then Japanese Prime Minister, commented, "I wonder why she [Asada] can't compete in the Olympics . . . It will add to the excitement of the Olympics if more and more talented people compete" (*Asahi Shinbun* 2005:4; *Mainichi Shinbun* 2005). In the end, no exception was made, and Asada made her Olympic debut in Vancouver (2010), where she earned the silver medal. In addition, she became six-time National Champion (from 2006 to 2009, and again in 2011 and 2012) and three-time World Champion (2008, 2010, 2014), joining East German Katarina Witt and American Michelle Kwan as the only women to win at least three World Championships in the last forty-five years (Zaccardi 2014).

ASADA AS AN ICON

Asada's popularity in Japan is massive; she was voted as the most popular sports person by teen and preteen girls and boys (Bandai Co. Ltd. 2015:3), and claimed the top slot in the ranking of the most successful female athletes in 2015 (Hakuhodo DY Media Partners 2015:1). Media coverage of the women's free program for Audi Cap of China 2015 recorded a 23.2 percent rating average, peaking at 36 percent the moment Asada finished skating and her victory became certain (Yamane 2015). This is a staggering number for a minor sport like figure skating. Asada has also been voted the most popular female TV personality in Japan multiple times (Video Research Ltd. 2014–2015), the only athlete in the ranking usually dominated by popular actresses such as Ayase Haruka and Amami Yūki. Asada is therefore not only an athlete but also a celebrity.

Asada is frequently described as a national icon (e.g., in *Sports Graphics Number Web* 2015). According to Valerie Steele (2011:5): "An icon was originally an image of a sacred person worshipped by his or her followers. There is undeniably an element of enthusiasm bordering on worship in the popular response to celebrities." Sport stars are particularly well suited to become icons in this sense because they "are part of the pantheon of celebrities who are constituted as models for emulation, displacing the traditional role of sovereign royalty as symbols of higher conduct. They form a labor aristocracy" (Miller 2013:18). The world of sports is still considered a masculine domain designed to reaffirm conventionally "masculine" qualities of activeness, assertiveness, competition, challenge, and strength (Imamura 1993:46; Clasen 2001:36). This prejudice has often worked against female athletes. The Japanese women's national soccer team Nadeshiko Japan, for example, "confident, thickly muscled, often short-haired, and undeniably aggressive" (Edwards 2013:150), offers an image untypical of Japanese femininity. Yet, they have to bear the iconic feminine name of *Nadeshiko*. Figure skating, however, combines many of the aesthetic and athletic qualities of ballet with the aspect of competition that ennobles the activity as a sport.

Asada's doll-like good looks with long limbs, beautiful outfits and makeup as well as the artistry associated with figure skating and classical ballet, which offer the "universal sign of an appropriate style of femininity—couth and graceful, yet disciplined and regulated" (Peers 2008:73), allow her to reaffirm her femininity.[1] Simultaneously, her sports-star status and her dedication to sport, sportsmanship, and character have made her a role model among young women in Japan (e.g.,

Calpis Co. Ltd. 2012:7). In this sense, Asada is an icon of familiarity for many Japanese people. She embodies the concept of the celebrity sport figure described Toby Miller (2013:18): "The major sporting star is a stranger who is paradoxically part of daily life." This, like Japan's national pop music diva Misora Hibari (see Christine Yano's Chapter 5 in this volume), signals her as a binary figure—an "ordinary" girl-next-door who nevertheless achieves something extraordinary and whose "girlhood" has become the public property of the Japanese nation. To achieve her level of success, however, Asada has to be anything but ordinary. We might, then, question whether or not there is something behind her ingénue, ascetic image. Is she really ordinary, or is the girl-next-door persona a performance, a mask, that conceals a more complex personality?

ASADA AS A DIVA OFF THE ICE

Asada and her "good girl" persona might not, at first glance, fit the stereotypical diva image. "Derived from opera, the word *diva* means goddess," writes Angela Dalle Vacche (2000:45). In everyday use, it has come to encompass popular female performers and celebrities who have "a thoroughly captivating and commanding stage presence" (Bollinger and O'Neill 2008:147). Yet, the diva also connotes certain dark behaviors that some female stars are believed to display, a kind of conduct that "goes with the territory of opera stardom: tantrums, cancellations, stormings off, general hysteria" (White 2013). "By definition, a diva is a rampaging female ego redeemed only in part by a lovely voice [or a talent]" (Tyrangiel 2002:2). The diva, in this sense, shows flaws. Asada, on the other hand, always maintains her well-mannered image; she cherishes her fans, declaring that the cheers of Japanese audiences are very encouraging and supportive whenever she skates overseas (TBS Radio 2015). Outside Japan, Asada's good manners are remarked upon. In Barcelona, skating coach Tom Zakrajsek posted on his Instagram account:

> One of the most impressive moments was watching Mao Asada sign autographs for and take pictures with everyone of her hundreds of fans who followed her from the arena, across the street and into the hotel lobby. She did this with a genuine smile on her face and sincerity in the tone of her voice. She could have simply stopped after 15 minutes but she waited until every fan who showed up to see her was content. Mao, you rock! (Zakrajsek 2015).

Asada is vigilant in maintaining her *yūtōsei* (good and respectable girl) image, often in contrast to some of her contemporaries. Asada's chief competitor, Ando Miki (b. 1987), for example, is marked by her refusal to be framed within stereotypical (code: submissive) Japanese femininity, and her honest and candid attitude is closer to what we would normally expect from a diva. We need to remember that "Japanese femininity," embodied in the concept of *yamato nadeshiko* (literally, Japanese dianthus), is itself a socially motivated invention in modern Japan (Endo 2012:300), just as is the performative nature of gender (Butler 1990; De Lauretis 1987:3). Ando refused to perform appropriate femininity, and as a result her transgressive lifestyle and highly publicized romantic associations with men, followed by a widely reported single-motherhood, earned her fierce criticism.

It is interesting to compare Ando to Asada. First appearing as a girl prodigy just like Asada, Ando increasingly became the target of both media and public criticism when she did not perform well, especially in the season before the Turin Olympics. After making a comeback and becoming world champion in 2007 Ando, never afraid of showing her emotions, grew grumpy with the media, displaying a lack of trust in them. With the advice of her Russian coach, Ando also reinvented her image from a candid, perky teenaged girl to a mature, alluring woman, partly to appeal to the judges. Ando's refusal to be labelled as a good girl also fuelled public approval of Asada's ingénue image. Asada's image is powerful; her own sister has revealed that she herself adopted a "wild party girl" lifestyle before settling into a career as a sport journalist and a media celebrity, partly in rebellion against her "good and nationally-loved" sister (Oricon Style 2015).

Asada's upright public image might make some think she is bland, maybe even a victim of patriarchal society that demands a young woman be a good and respectable daughter of the nation. However, Asada is no victim; she is a remarkably strong person. Her control of her public image is impeccable and her ability to perform "angelic" is remarkable. She sometimes reveals fragility or personal pains but rarely in a spontaneous way, making her personality familiar yet enigmatic to many of us. The good girl persona allows her to navigate public situations that could otherwise become complex or nasty, and to turn them to her favor.

As Laura Miller and Rebecca Copeland point out (in the introduction to this volume), a diva is born of pain. Hers is a position that is found outside the status quo, a position that is vulnerable to scrutiny and trauma. Her talents invite her celebrity but also her suffering. When Ando stepped into the limelight with her naïve honesty, she was met with cruel censure by both the media and public, making her both a rebel and victim. In contrast, Asada, while concealing the extraordinary pain she endured for her success, has not been afraid to reveal her flaws. When she presents herself as honest and forthright about her emotions, she has earned the trust and respect of her public. For example, during a press conference in 2007, a German journalist asked Asada a political question: as a Japanese training in the United States, had she ever experienced people telling her that her country did very bad things and that her prime minister (Abe Shinzō) was not honest? Sixteen-year-old Asada answered with a smile "everyone [in LA where she was training] is friendly and talks to me" (Figyua Sukēto Yūchūbu Dōga Blog 2007). Her deft answer turned this political question into a positive affirmation, neutralizing the political tone of the original question. It was a non-answer worthy of any politician.

Asada's good girl image also protects her from being subjected to sensationalized gossip and the curious eyes of the media, from which Ando suffered greatly. Asada is not entirely immune from gossip, but her strategy is not to say anything she does not want the public to know, a strategy that she maintains whenever her father's shadowy background becomes the subject of speculation in the tabloids (e.g., *Daily Shinchō* 2015). She is personally shielded by her halo of the "good, upright and ascetic" image, through her media appearances and her on and off the ice activities (e.g., her engagement in philanthropy causes). The nature of her public image is also indicated by slight yet significant shifts, from perky "it girl" to a thoughtful young woman who tacitly yet diligently trains to compete for her nation.[2] In intimate settings Asada still refers to herself in the first person as "Mao," a very childlike way of addressing oneself, while in more official settings she uses "I (*watashi*)." This creates a balance of a soft, girlish image and the more respectful, serious, and official persona.[3] In this sense, Asada's extended girlhood is surrounded by mystique and carefully controlled; she is a producer of her own image. Having a "good girl," hardworking-athlete image does not, however, mean that Asada is not a diva. It means that we need to look much more carefully for evidence of Tyrangiel's (2002) "rampaging female ego."

One incident that gives some insight into Asada's ego was her decision not to return to train with her (then) coach Rafael Arutunian in the United States just two months prior to the world championships in March 2008. It was reported that the reason for her decision to train in Japan was due to the inability to get the kind of food she needed elsewhere, and also due to the fact that while earlier in the States she had to flee her training camp due to wildfires (*Nihon Keizai Shinbun* 2008:41). Asada has not spoken about what happened between her and her coach. But Arutunian revealed

192 | Masafumi Monden

in a later interview that Asada had phoned him and asked that he go to Japan, counter to their earlier arrangements. Because of other commitments he declined and an assistant coach went in his place. Although she asked again, he refused. Arutunian later found out that Asada wanted to stay in Japan because her mother was quite ill, but she never hinted at this. She just demanded that he come to Japan for her sake, which made him think that she was playing with him (Golden Skate 2016). This ended their professional relationship. Asada went on to skate in the championships and won the title without a formal coach. Asada publicly maintained that the relationship with Arutunian ended due to practical concerns involved in training overseas. Eventually, she replaced him with the renowned Tatiana Tarasova. What is revealing is not Asada's behavior, which taken at face value is that of a dedicated if private young athlete, but Arutunian's interpretation of it. Her coach, someone who knew her well, was quite prepared to believe she was toying with him, yet equally unsure of his own ability to resist her force of will in person.

In contrast to her image of passivity and docility, Asada is not afraid to exercise her power. In another example, she managed to force a major publisher to cancel the scheduled release of what would have been Asada's first autobiography. Slated to be released on February 8, 2012, over 100,000 copies had been pre-ordered by December of the previous year, indicating high expectations by book shops across Japan (*Nihon Keizai Shinbun* 2012:4). The cancellation of *Daijōbu, kitto ashita wa dekiru* (It's all right, tomorrow I'll be able to do it) came as a result of the way the publishing company had promoted the book. According to officials of Poplar Publishing, the disagreement was over a promotional poster of the book that read "Mom, thank you so much" (*Nihon Keizai Shinbun* 2012:4; *Yomiuri Shinbun* 2012:34). Asada's mother, Kyoko, had passed away in December 2011, and while the quotation would seem to be innocuous enough, Asada apparently did not approve. Her cancellation of a book that was already in print over a publicity blurb shows that Asada held sway over the creation of her public image and was able to get her own way.

These two incidents also reveal Asada's strongly protective attitude to her personal and family life. As David Holloway in Chapter 9 in this volume writes of literary diva Kanehara Hitomi, "divas are captivating for the ways in which their personal lives—in contrast to their public lives—are incongruous with conceptions of femininity." Asada denies both public and media access to the private sphere of her personal life. Perhaps this signals Asada's refusal to be framed within a conventional diva narrative.

What makes Asada distinct from some of the other divas discussed in this volume, and from our common perceptions of a modern-day diva, is that her diva qualities—the ego, desire for spectacle and adoration, power, temperament—are masked by a sweet and demure exterior. Instead of reacting with emotion and attacking the publisher, Asada simply and politely wrote in her blog that "the way the book was advertised was different from what I had in mind. Therefore, I had requested cancellation of the release of this book. My sincerest apologizes but I would greatly appreciate your understanding" (Mao-Blog 2012). Whether or not Asada consciously constructs her good girl persona to conceal her diva strength, is a point about which we cannot be certain. And Asada isn't saying. What we know is that the good girl persona has worked for her in terms of avoiding public and media criticism for exercising power. While Ando is labeled as a "bad girl," a scandalous diva, Asada has been able to make her public sympathetic to her, whatever she has done. As a result, Asada has been rewarded in the most valuable currency of the diva world, what goddesses desire most: applause, adoration, worship.

The good-girl-next-door image also masks Asada's extraordinariness. Asada is far from the ordinary girl that her character projection often makes us believe, both physically and athletically. An amalgam of her glamorous appearance on the ice and her extraordinary talent as an athlete, combined with her obstinate attachment to her skating ideals against all odds, makes her more than merely a hard-working athlete—she is a diva on the ice.

DIVA AS PERFORMANCE AND VIRTUE: THE BODY, OUTFITS, AND TALENT

Asada deconstructs the "ordinary" and the "extraordinary." In TV coverage of Asada practicing on the ice, a regular sight during the skating season, she wears plain practice clothing, no makeup, and a disheveled ponytail. But appearing in advertisements or in a competition, Asada is transformed into an immaculately crafted beauty with delicate makeup, perfectly coiffed hair, and dresses made of silk and chiffon adorned by Swarovski crystals. In contemporary mainstream culture, divas are characterized by their "*over-emphasized* femininity," such as "'ultra-feminine' outfits, accessories and gestures" (Padva 2006:27–28). They consciously play "the part of the 'ultimate' femmes, the admired superwoman that reveal the powerful theatricality of gender representations, manifestations, and manipulations in contemporary popular media" (Padva 2006:28).

The fact that Asada is a hard-training athlete, is often overshadowed by the popular image of women's figure skating, which, like ballet, is predominantly associated with mini-dresses and sequins (e.g., Ito 1993). Honda Masuko (1992) has argued that such sartorial items as frilly dresses, ribbons, and lace visually connote a highly idealized image of *shōjo* (literally, "girls" but the term also points to a cultural imagination of ideal girlish identity). Asada's lithe, ballerina or fashion model-like figure epitomizes a girlish image such as the one promoted by illustrator and designer Nakahara Jun'ichi, whose work is still considered an embodiment of *shōjo* (Dollase 2013:80; Monden 2015:81). The visual image of *shōjo*, as Honda (1992:179) has argued, allows one to emphasize a girlish femininity while its decorativeness, hiding adult sexuality, could be understood as an "active and dynamic way that Japanese women can control their sexuality" (Nakamura and Matsuo 2002:69). Asada performs the image of *shōjo* both through her physique and her costumes (Figure 24). The gap, the duplicity that we glimpse through the two images of Asada on the ice, signals the performative nature of her feminine beauty, which she crafts for judges, audiences, and her fans, making it a spectacle.

Asada's choice of changing outfits over the years is notable: black lace conveys the pathos of a lady poisoned by a jealous husband (2008–9); a frilly cerise dress sparks the excitement of a debutante at her first ball (2009–10); a lapis blue top and pantaloons glitter in her Scheherazade mode (2011–12); simple, white kimono-inspired outfits with gentle shades of sky-blue make her a Buddhist celestial maiden (2011–12); while a white feather dress metamorphoses her into the swan maiden (2012–13). Asada even cross-dresses with a top hat, tuxedo, and bowtie (2014–15). These are carefully crafted performances she makes with her coaches and costume designers. Asada maintains that she listens to the opinions of coaches and designers when deciding a program and outfits (e.g., TBS Radio 2015), but she nonetheless is the person who has the final say. In the 2009–10 season, some thought her free program of heavy Russian music did not fit for her and suggested a change, but Asada refused as she was determined to perfect the program (Tamura 2010). In mid-2014, Asada's exhibition "Smile" was held at several Takashimaya department stores across the country, showcasing her collection of costumes, photographs, and medals. It drew record crowds, reaching more than 600,000 visitors in total (*Asahi Shinbun* 2014:37). The event indicates Asada's awareness that not only her routines on the

24. Asada Mao at the 2012 World Figure Skating
Championships. Photo by Luu CC.

ice, but her outfits and pictures of her wearing them are equally important factors that appeal to audiences, to reassert her iconic status.

The configuration of a diva can be a complex process. While a diva can
be a persona, a performance, Dalle Vacche (2000:45) argues that a diva is
also a state of being "that requires no effort, no work, and that can defy
all forms of social order and explanation." A diva is an amalgam of representational and organic body. Wayne Koestenbaum (1993:139) reveals
this mechanism through operatic diva Maria Callas's loss of weight and of
voice: "Her body was a liability she had the power to revise; her voice was
a virtue she lacked the power to retain." Callas's body, which transformed
her from an overweight singer to a slender, glamorous diva, was a representation that she was able to control, but her voice was a virtue, a gift

over which she had minimal command. In other words, a diva can be representational, an image, but that image should be based on her virtue, which sets her apart, making her unique and extraordinary. Likewise, Asada is not merely a young woman who works hard to be a star, her status as "one of the best skaters in the world" (Christine Brennan, in *The Skating Lesson* 2016) is also based on her natively given physicality and talent. Asada's performance of hyper-girlishness/femininity is made credible by her lithe, elegant figure and pretty looks.

According to Robin Kietlinski (2011:130), "The public image of female athletes in Japan (as in the West) has revolved primarily around three main factors: the sport they play, their physical appearance and the success of the athlete." For Asada, the first two factors are interrelated. This is because figure skating is an "aesthetic sport" in which beauty and feminine grace factor largely into whether an athlete is successful (Kietlinski 2011:134). Figure skating is frequently seen as analogous to ballet, perhaps because both have origins in aristocratic activities aiming to display the qualities of (albeit initially male) beauty and grace (Adams 2007:875–76). The subjectivity associated with figure skating has been controversial, and this controversy is often embodied in the debate on artistry versus athleticism. "What is always close to the surface, but rarely acknowledged," writes Abigail M. Feder (1994:69) in her analysis of femininity in figure skating coverage, is that "for the women, artistry is indistinguishable from physical beauty." It is often alleged that "the more athletic (code: masculine, aberrant) skaters are also not as elegant, and because artistry continues to carry more weight in the judging process," media coverage often uses "elegance and artistry as a narrative ploy to judge a skater's moral character" (Fabos 2001:198). Asada, who is blessed with the "ideal" body shape of a female skater coupled with ballet-trained artistry, does not choose to conform to and restate this stereotyped binary but instead disrupts the boundary between the two with her dedication toward her skating ideals; to skate the athletically hardest possible program with a triple axel jump—her signature move.

What makes Asada special is, indeed, her deconstruction that subtly reconsiders the boundaries of gender politics in sports. Asada places herself in the complex position of being an "ultra-feminine" young woman competing in the male-dominated world of sports, albeit an aesthetic one that requires artistry and grace. It is her ability to delicately combine such "traditional" artistry and feminine beauty ideals with dynamic athleticism, or more precisely, technical difficulties, and her fierce challenging spirit against odds that makes her a unique icon of binaries.

THE QUEEN OF TRIPLE AXEL: RISK-TAKING
DIVA AS SPECTACLE

Asada is well known for skating a program as difficult as a man's would be (Sasaki 2015). Unlike gymnastics, there is relatively little difference between the skills exhibited by women and men in figure skating; they both perform the same kinds of jumps, with similar footwork and spins (Feder 1994:62; Adams 2011:203). Jumps like the quadruple, which has increasingly become a "must" for top senior males, still remain a rarity in women's events. Yet, there are exceptions. World Champion and Olympic Silver Medalist Ito Midori (b. 1969) has a reputation of jumping like or better than "men"; Olympian and Ito's contemporary Brian Orser has reportedly said that male skaters were glad that Ito did not compete in men's titles (Noguchi 2012:53–54). And Asada is surely one of the few women skaters whose technical proficiency rivals that of the men. It is the triple axel jump that makes her a woman skater who is closest to men in terms of technical difficulty. Her ability to constantly execute this "man's" jump makes her "extraordinary," a "superhuman" who pushes beyond human limits and thus marks her divahood.

The triple axel is the hardest among triple jumps. Its forward take-off requires three and a half revolutions. Only a handful of female figure skaters have successfully landed the jump in competition since Ito did so in 1988. Only Ito Midori, Nakano Yukari (b. 1985) and Asada have executed this jump over several seasons. Asada holds the two triple axel records, as the first junior female skater (at fourteen, 2004) and as the oldest woman skater (at twenty-five, Grand Prix Final 2015), ratified by the ISU (International Skating Union). Because of its extreme difficulty, no skater, male or female, has been able to land the triple axel consistently. Not only that, scoring often varies significantly from judge to judge (Ito 1993: 62), which makes it difficult for skaters to know whether or not their jumps, including a triple axel, would be ratified. Sasha Cohen (Clash 2016), in her 2016 *Forbes* interview explains: "skating is very hard to judge because everything is so subjective. It's not timed like swimming or running . . . Even skaters are going, 'I don't know—is that a good score?'" Despite her considerable aesthetic advantages, Asada nevertheless focuses on challenging her own athleticism, and the limits of women's figure skating, breaking the tradition in sport where obvious ambition and competitiveness are regarded as a properly male attitude (Clasen 2001:36). Steadiness and consistency, on the other hand, characterize a female attitude in sports (Feder 1994:71) and thus "for a woman, strong-willed behavior is obviously wrong, and punishment is the 'not surprising' outcome" (Feder 1994:74).

Criticism Asada has received over her insistence on including the risky triple axel in her programs (e.g., Gallagher 2014) proves this to be true. Male skaters like Asada's compatriots Takahashi Daisuke and Ha'nyū Yuzuru are rarely if ever subjected to such criticism for attempting difficult jumps, whether or not they succeed. Asada's devotion to the triple axel is a risk to delivering a consistent, predictable performance, and I believe this is the mark of a true diva. As I said earlier, the diva is spectacle; she needs audiences and in order to attract and hold them, she needs to excite, astonish or surprise; the diva takes a risk. A consistent performance of a clean, good, safe routine could win competitions. But it is the way of the diligent, persistent plodder. It would not excite audiences, and it does not make one a diva. As the former world champion Jeffrey Buttle says, Asada fulfills the cravings of audiences to be thrilled by difficult jumps and moved by artistically beautiful performances (*Nihon Keizai Shinbun* 2015), which have long been believed to be incompatible in women's skating (Ito 1993:78).

Asada's triple axel is her defining feature. Merely winning does not seem to be enough—she must eclipse other performers, both men and women, enthralling her audience even at the risk of failure. If winning were her one and only goal, Asada would have discarded the triple axel and focused instead on performing a consistent, clean, and technically less demanding program. Indeed, when she is asked if she would ever think about eliminating the difficult jump and instead aim for the gold with a predictable program like many other women skaters, Asada answered:

> . . . this [the triple axel] is something that I've always wanted to continue to do, to always be able to challenge myself and try the triple axel . . . I guess in some way I can say that the triple axel is the best possible thing that I can offer audiences, it's my showpiece, and it's not something that I willingly abandon (Foreign Correspondents' Club of Japan 2014).

While it is necessary for advancing women's figure skating (Bergman 2015), the triple axel jump for Asada is very important for her self-development; it keeps her motivation and competitiveness high (Yoshida 2013). Behind her diligent, ascetic persona, Asada acts in accordance with her own desires, perpetually taking risks for herself and for her audiences. This risk brings both failure and triumph, lending a strong operatic, and by extension melodramatic, aspect to Asada's life.

THE DIVA OF FAILURE AND TRIUMPH

Asada's public life is a media narrative of drama, criticism, suffering, and triumph. For Japanese people, her story began as a teenage prodigy who, despite putatively being "the best in the world," was not allowed to compete in the Olympics because she was too young, a familiar beginning to the trope of the "young heroine." As soon as she became the world champion in 2008, technical regulations were tightened so her jumps were placed under harsh scrutiny (Yoshida 2011:174). Around the same time, Asada's new coach (from 2008 to 2010), Tatiana Tarasova began choreographing her programs into much more artistically and technically demanding levels. Japanese media largely ignored her increased artistry and difficulty. Instead, they sensationalized her rivalry with her foreign competitors, which has rarely happened to other Japanese skaters, past or present, and started criticizing Asada for not being able to win all the time, as she once did (e.g., Narinari.com, 2008; Shirota 2012). The effect of both subjective scoring and inconsistent deployment of the jump-downgrade rules in figure skating are often absent in such criticism.

People also witnessed Asada's personal struggles. Her post-Vancouver Olympics decision to rebuild her skating, including jumps, under new coaching experts led to her jumps inevitably becoming inconsistent in the 2010–11 season (Yoshida 2013:26). Many were shocked to see her failing in five out of seven jumps at the NHK Trophy (Nippon Hōsō Kyōkai) free program in 2010, almost a completely different person from the skater of the past. Her mother, who had been unwell for years, passed away in December 2011, on the eve of the Grand Prix final competition in Canada, causing Asada to withdraw and fly back to Nagoya (Yoshida 2013:128).

Masked behind her demure persona is a strong sense of will and determination. To many people's astonishment, Asada competed in the Japan Championships only fifteen days later. Remembering what her mother used to tell her, "to carry through whatever you have decided to do," Asada went back to the rink four days after her return to Nagoya (Yoshida 2013:132–33), and claimed her fifth national title, determined not to show her personal grief to the audience. Instead of making excuses for bad performances like other skaters, Asada chose to train harder and deliver better results the next time. "I have never seen a skater who is both as talented and diligent in training as she is," says Tarasova (Sasaki 2015). Asada herself has said that "the more you practice, the more confident you get" (Utsunomiya 2009:88). Referring to Asada's status as a national icon, diligence fits the "longstanding Japanese ideas about self-development and discipline" (Miller 2008b:397). Her display of diligence perhaps appeals to Japanese people's fantasy that if you try hard (*ganbare-ba*), your dream will come true. In this sense, she carries people's hope. Her diligence is closely woven with narratives of heroism.

As an athlete, she almost never shuns the public. After winning all international competitions in the 2013–14 season, Asada was certainly a gold medal hopeful at the Sochi Olympics (2014). For her final preparation before the women's event, Asada trained on an ice rink in Armenia, where the ice was covered by sand, damaging her ice blades (*Nihon Keizai Shinbun* 2014b:38). Skating last in the women's short program, her disastrous performance left Asada in sixteenth place. She appeared in an interview straight after the performance, looking perplexed, and said "I don't know what happened" (*Nihon Keizai Shinbun* 2014a:11). In the free program, she nonetheless refused to look defeated. There was a weight of expectation on Asada not present for other Japanese skaters. Entering the rink, Asada looked serene, wearing an almost solemn air, and addressed the audience like a great diva. As the music commenced, she flew on the ice like a blue bird, landing jump after jump, enchanting the audience with her intricate footwork. Fighting back from her devastation and disappointment, Asada produced a soaring performance. For the first time in the history of women's figure skating, she landed eight triple jumps of six different kinds, including a triple axel and a very difficult combination, in one program (International Skating Union 2014). The previous maximum degree of difficulty for most female skaters was seven triple jumps of five different types in one free program, Ito's achievement in 1988 (Ito 1993:129). With her free program, Asada ascended to sixth overall, but what made her achievements truly extraordinary to Japanese people was her heroic *ganbare-ba* spirit—never to give up and always to believe in herself. When asked about what she learned from her disappointing short program at Sochi, Asada answered:

> I learnt this by myself that if one retains a strong will, if one does not give up, then one can overcome great difficulties. This is something that I knew but I was able to confirm, and I think the fact that I felt this so strongly is going to serve me for the rest of my life (Foreign Correspondents' Club of Japan 2014).

Asada represents Japan and presents an image of Japanese femininity. Her status as an international athlete who has competed in major international events such as the Olympics also means that her Japanese girl/womanhood has gained traction with a global audience. Asada was the athlete mentioned most in tweets throughout the Sochi games (Bauder

2014). One of them, Michelle Kwan (2014), tweeted after the program: "Mao Asada—made me cry. . . . a performance that we will all remember forever!" a tweet that was subsequently retweeted more than 13,500 times. One can argue that Asada's Sochi performance conforms to what Ivan Morris (1975) termed the "nobility of failure." What Morris argues is that in contrast to the success-worshipping culture of the West, the complex Japanese tradition has appreciated a type of hero "who waged their forlorn struggle against overwhelming odds; and the fact that all their efforts are crowned with failure lends them a pathos which characterizes the general vanity of human endeavor and makes them the most loved and evocative of heroes" (Morris 1975:xxii). This "very antithesis of an ethos of accomplishment" (Morris 1975:xxi) has bestowed dignity on worldly defeat and evocative appeal in the Japanese tradition.

What appears to be Asada's single-minded dedication to her skating ideals and her continuing retooling often did not allow her to "make the manoeuvres and compromises that are so often needed for mundane success" (Morris 1975:xxi). If we regard an Olympic gold as that success, her struggle has been useless and largely counterproductive. However, Japanese values and sensibility recognize the nobility of those who display uncalculated sincerity during their struggle, even if failing to achieve their concrete objectives. What Morris attempted in his book was to show that this nobility of failure also appeals to non-Japanese individuals, and as Kwan's tweet and the massive number of its retweets indicate, Asada's heroism did indeed capture the hearts of people both in and outside Japan.

What really defines Asada's divahood, then, is her "heroic" and "superhuman" attributes and determination to perfect her art. For Dalle Vacche (2000:45), the diva also "eludes such common attributes as 'superhuman' or 'heroic,'" a female icon that exudes divinity. It can also allude to a person who refuses to compromise, an ego who demands to have her own way for the sake of her art and perfection. Known as "the last of the divas," Romanian prima donna Angela Gheorghiu explains that a diva-esque conduct is necessary for her to pursue her role as an artist, as one who "makes people dream, or makes them cry, who moves thousands of people" by transcending reality through glamour and beauty (Classic FM n.d.). Asada's seemingly self-defeating struggle, her refusal to compromise on her skating ideals, and her almost "superhuman" comeback to execute a program that pushed the boundaries of her sport, reducing her audiences to tears, make her both a hero in the Japanese tradition and a diva in an original sense.

On April 10, 2017, Asada announced without warning that she was retiring (Mao-Blog, 2017). It was a quintessentially diva move that shocked the nation, and almost all TV stations reported the news as their lead story for the next few days. Asada conducted a press conference on April 12 in front of 430 reporters, in one of the nation's largest domestic press conferences (*Nikkan Sports* 2017). This undoubtedly indicates how her status transcends that of a mere athlete into that of a national icon. Her own staging of the farewell, where she maintained a radiant smile and a lack of regret marks her as strong-willed leading lady in true diva fashion, despite the politeness. Unlike "noble" heroes, Asada concluded her conference with a polite yet confident girl persona, by saying "I want to find new dreams and goals and progress further with a smile on my face" (*Nikkan Sports* 2017). Asada's embodiment of the nobility of failure, then, might just be another mask that she has worn, one that gives her the ability to act in accordance with her own desires without sacrificing the adoration of the public.

Asada embodies a mode of extended girlhood that is marked by binaries: upright/mystic, diligent/risk-taking, athletically powerful/artistically elegant, and familiar/extraordinary. Unlike others who may have been too honest, too moody, too lazy, and too vocal in protest about objectification, Asada devoted herself to skating without any complaints in public, and continued to be accessible to her audiences irrespective of her performance conditions. Instead of being a typical diva with a temper, Asada consciously or otherwise uses her demure, good girl persona to allow the exercise of the ego and power of a diva without attracting criticism, in a subtle, effective, and notably Japanese fashion. In this sense, Asada is an icon who demonstrates the potential of a new kind of divahood, as a young diva who gets her own way and refuses to give in, but in a polite, upright and amicable way that wins people's hearts.

NOTES

I am very grateful to D.J. Ellis for his careful reading and editing of this chapter. I also thank Rebecca Copeland and Laura Miller for their graceful guidance and constructive suggestions.

1. The analogy between Asada and a doll is often made. For example, to commemorate the fiftieth anniversary of the birth of the Licca-chan doll, the toymaker produced a new ice-skating doll with Asada's input in 2017 (*Japan Post* 2017).

2. This change is, for example, recognizable in the reasons people in Japan gave for why they like Mao, in the Annual Favorite Athlete Ranking (Oricon Inc. 2007–2014).

3. For example, TBS Radio (2015).

Diva tte nan desu ka?
(What Is a Diva?)

The Afterword for *Diva Nation* takes the form of a manga created by
Rokudenashiko ("Good For Nothing Girl"). Rokudenashiko attracted
world fame after making 3-D scans of genitals to use as templates for
objects that are incorporated or transformed into things such as row-
boats and dioramas. She was arrested by the Tokyo Metropolitan Police
for distribution of obscene material through the Internet. The court
found her guilty and fined her a few thousand dollars. Rokudenashiko
also created adorable anthropomorphized plastic vulvar models that
became mascots. She has produced comics that feature the problems
encountered by the cute mascot named Manko-chan (Miss Pussy). Her
motivation for the art is to destigmatize the vagina, to normalize references to the vagina in everyday life and to make it less of a taboo object.
Her Manko-chan character does this brilliantly, bringing the female genitals front and center while making statements about contemporary gender politics. In this two-page comic (panels on each page are to be read
right to left, from the top right), Manko-chan and the figure of the artist
(here shortened to Nashiko-chan) talk about what it means to be a diva
(Figure 25). Pipo-kun, the yellow mascot for the Tokyo Metropolitan
Police Department, Wonder Woman, a schoolgirl idol, and Céline Dion
join the mix of popular culture references and subtle associations. (*Laura
Miller*)

Page 2: *Manko-chan:* Nashiko-chan, you are scaring me . . .
Céline Dion: My heart will go on and on . . . teeheehee . . . For my beautiful hair
[Pipo-kun dances around and around.]
Nashiko-chan: Ah, come to think of it, there are also divas in Japan.

25. *Diva tte nan desu ka?* (What Is a Diva?), by Rokudenashiko, translated by Kazue Harada, page 1 (right) and page 2 (left).

Page 1: *Nashiko-chan* and *Manko-chan:* Hmm. Serious face. Girlish giggle. Clumsy. Shy. Non-assertive. Obedient. Not too smart. Naturally airheaded. Baby-faced. Big boobs. The most important thing is . . . BEING YOUNG!! A DIVA is required to have little-girl-like youth and adult-like broad-mindedness.
Media Dudes: We only employ women that fit our taste.

Bibliography

Abe, Hideko. 2010. *Queer Japanese: Gender and Sexual Identities Through Linguistic Practices*. New York: Palgrave Macmillan.

Abe, Shinzō. 2014. "Opening speech by Prime Minister Shinzō Abe at the Open Forum, World Assembly for Women in Tokyo: WAW! Tokyo 2014." Prime Minister of Japan and His Cabinet, Cabinet Public Relations Office, 12 September. Online at http://japan.kantei.go.jp/96_abe/statement/201409 /waw140912.html [accessed 11 February 2016].

Abowitz, Kathleen Knight, and Kate Rousmaniere. 2004. "Diva citizenship: A case study of Margaret Haley as feminist citizen-leader." *The Initiative Anthology: An Electronic Publication About Leadership, Culture & Schooling*, 2 March. Online at http://www.units.miamioh.edu/eduleadership /anthology/OA/OA04001.pdf. [accessed 16 August 2015].

Adams, Mary Louise. 2007. "The manly history of a 'girls' sport: Gender, class and the development of nineteenth-century figure skating." *The International Journal of the History of Sport* 24 (7): 872–93.

———. 2011. *Artistic Impressions: Figure Skating, Masculinity, and the Limits of Sport*. Toronto: University of Toronto Press.

Ahmed, Sara. 2010. *The Promise of Happiness*. Durham: Duke University Press.

Ahn, Patty Jeehyun. 2009. "Harisu: South Korean cosmetic media and the paradox of transgendered neoliberal embodiment." *Discourse* 31 (3): 248–72.

Allison, Anne. 1994. *Nightwork: Sexuality, Pleasure and Corporate Masculinity in a Tokyo Hostess Club*. Chicago: University of Chicago Press.

———. 2009. "The cool brand, affective activism and Japanese youth." *Theory, Culture & Society* 26 (2–3): 89–111.

———. 2013. *Precarious Japan*. Durham: Duke University Press.

Andassova, Maral. 2013. "Kojiki jindai (kamiyo) ni okeru Takamagahara no 'henbō'" (The transformation of the High Plains of Heaven in Kojiki age of *kami*). In *Nihon shinwa o hiraku: Kojiki hensan 1300-nen ni yosete* (Unfolding the Japanese mythology: For the 1300th anniversary of the compilation of the *Kojiki*), 131–50. Yokohama: Ferris University.

Aoyagi, Hiroshi. 2005. *Islands of Eight Million Smiles; Idol Performance and Symbolic Production in Contemporary Japan*. Cambridge, MA: Harvard University Asia Center, Harvard University Press.

Aoyama, Tomoko. 2012. "The aging Ame no Uzume: Gender and humor in Sano Yōko's writing." In *The Poetics of Ageing: Confronting, Resisting, and Transcending Mortality in the Japanese Narrative Arts*, edited by Hosea Hirata, Charles Inouye, Susan Napier, and Karen Thornber, 210–24. *Proceedings of the Association for Japanese Literary Studies* 13.

Ara, Konomi. 2010. "Josephine Baker: A chanteuse and a fighter." *Journal of Transnational American Studies* 2 (1): 1–17.

Arai, Andrea G. 2006. "The 'wild child' of 1990s Japan." In *Japan After Japan: Social and Cultural Life from the Recessionary 1990s to the Present*, edited by Tomiko Yoda and H. D. Harootunian, 216–38. Durham: Duke University Press.

Ariyoshi Sawako. 1969. *Izumo no Okuni* (Izumi no Okuni). Tokyo: Chūō Kōronsha.

———. 1975. *Fukugō osen* (Compound pollution). Tokyo: Shichōsha.

———. 1994. *Kabuki Dancer*. Translated by James R. Brandon. Tokyo, London and New York: Kodansha International.

Artists Against Fracking. 2013. "In new TV ad, Yoko Ono speaks to Gov. Cuomo about fracking." Artists Against Fracking group website. Online at http://artistsagainstfracking.com/tv-ad/ [accessed 2 March 2015].

Asahi Shinbun. 2005. "Asada senshu 'Naze gorin derarenu' shushō?'" (Prime Minister says 'Why can't Asada go to the Olympics?'), *Asahi Shinbun*, 4 December: 20.

———. 2014. "Asada Mao ten 60 man-nin toppa" (Asada Mao exhibition reached 600,000 visitors). *Asahi Shinbun*, 9 August: 37.

Azad, Nafiza. 2013. "The Goddess Chronicle—Natsuo Kirini [sic] (review)." Blog site Bibliographic Monologues, 4 February. Online at http://thebookwurrm.wordpress.com/2013/02/04/the-goddess-chronicle-natsuo-kirini review/ [accessed 27 February 2013].

Bakhtin, Mikhail. 1984a. *Problems of Dostoevsky's Poetics*. Edited and translated by Caryl Emerson. Minneapolis: University of Minnesota Press.

———. 1984b. *Rabelais and His World*. Translated by Hélène Iswolsky. Bloomington: Indiana University Press.

Bandai Co. Ltd. 2007. Misora Hibari, jazu o utau (Misora Hibari sings jazz). Little Jammer Pro, a robot. Tokyo: Bandai Co. Ltd.

———. 2015. Bandai kodomo ankēto repōto vol 224: Shōchūgakusei no supōtsu ni kansuru ishikichōsa kekka (Bandai children's survey report vol. 224: Primary and junior high school students' views on sports survey results). Press release, 6 October.

Bardsley, Jan. 2011. "The maiko boom: The revival of Kyoto's novice geisha." *Japanese Studies Review* 15: 35–60.

———. 2013. "Miss Japan on the global stage: The journey of Itō Kinuko." In *Modern Girls on the Go: Gender, Mobility, and Labor in Japan*, edited by Alisa Freedman, Laura Miller, and Christine Yano, 169–92. Stanford: Stanford University Press.

Barske, Valerie. 2013. "Visualizing priestesses or performing prostitutes? Ifa Fuyū's depiction of Okinawan women, 1913–1943." *Studies on Asia Series IV* 3 (1): 76.

Bauder, David. 2014. "Olympic viewing: Putin's seatmate, most tweeted." Associated Press. Online at http://wintergames.ap.org/article/olympic-viewing-putins-seatmate-most-tweeted [accessed 4 February 2015].

The Beatles, artists. 1995. *Anthology*. Documentary series and three double album CD set. London: EMI Records/Apple Corps.

Bergman, Justin. 2015. "'Did I really just do the triple axel at the world championships?' Tuktamysheva takes huge lead at figure-skating worlds." *Toronto Star*, 26 March. Online at https://www.thestar.com/sports/skating/2015/03/26/did-i-really-just-do-the-triple-axel-at-the-world-championships-tuktamysheva-takes-huge-lead-at-figure-skating-worlds.html [accessed 24 December 2015].

Berlant, Lauren. 1997. *The Queen of America Goes to Washington City: Essays on Sex and Citizenship*. Durham: Duke University Press.

———. 2008. *The Female Complaint; The Unfinished Business of Sentimentality in American Culture*. Durham: Duke University Press.

———. 2011. *Cruel Optimism*. Durham: Duke University Press.

Bernstein, Gail Lee, ed. 1991. *Recreating Japanese Women, 1600–1945*. Berkeley: University of California Press.

Bernstein, Jacob. 2012. "The world catches up to Yoko Ono." *New York Times*, 29 November.

Bollinger, Lee, and Carole O'Neill. 2008. *Women in Media Careers: Success Despite the Odds*. Lanham, MD: University Press of America.

Borgen, Robert, and Marian Ury. 1990. "Readable Japanese mythology: Selections from *Nihon shoki* and *Kojiki*." *Journal of the Association of Teachers of Japanese* 24 (1): 61–97.

Bourdaghs, Michael K. 2012. *Sayonara Amerika, Sayonara Nippon*. New York: Columbia University Press.

Brandon, James R. 1994. "Translator's note" to *Kabuki Dancer*, by Ariyoshi Sawako, 5–7. Translated by James R. Brandon. Tokyo, London and New York: Kodansha International.

Bungei Shunjū. 2004a. "Jushōsha intabyū: Futōkō to pachisuro no hibi ni chichi wa" (Interview with the prize winner: Kanehara Hitomi's father on his daughter dropping out of school and playing pachinko). *Bungei Shunjū*, March: 320–24.

———. 2004b. "Nihyakugojūman-nin ga yonda Akutagawa-shō nisakuhin no shōgeki" (Two Akutagawa Prize recipients shockingly command a readership of 250,000). *Bungei Shunjū*, April: 116–33.

Burns, Lori, and Melisse Lafrance. 2002. *Disruptive Divas; Feminism, Identity and Popular Music*. New York: Routledge.

Butler, Judith. 1990. *Gender Trouble: Feminism and the Subversion of Identity.* New York: Routledge.

Calpis Co. Ltd. 2012. "Hinamatsuri ni kansuru ishiki to jittai chōsa" (Consciousness and reality research about *hinamatsuri* doll festival). News release no. C1205, 24 January.

Carmichael, Hoagy, artist/composer. 1927. *Stardust.* Lyrics added in 1929 by Mitchell Parish. Richmond, IN: Gennett Records.

Carver, Lisa. 2012. *Reaching Out With No Hands: Reconsidering Yoko Ono.* Milwaukee: Backbeat Books.

The Chosun Ilbo. 2009. "Japanese cross-dressing star relishes new Korea role." *The Chosun Ilbo,* 3 March. Online at http://english.chosun.com/site/data/html_dir/2009/03/03/2009030361002.html [accessed 11 February 2016].

Christy, Desmond. 1999. "Widows and daughters." *The Guardian,* 6 December. Online at http://www.theguardian.com/media/1999/dec/06/tvandradio.television2 [accessed 26 February 2015].

Chūnichi Shinbun. 2013. "Tanoshiku mau, ima o ikiru" (Enjoying dancing, living the moment). *Chūnichi Shinbun,* 28 November: 18.

Clasen, Patricia R. W. 2001. "The female athlete: Dualisms and paradox in practice." *Women and Language* 24 (2): 36–41.

Clash, Jim. 2016. "Interview: Sasha Cohen to be inducted into U.S. Figure Skating Hall of Fame." *Forbes,* 5 January. Online at http://www.forbes.com/sites/jimclash/2016/01/05/interview-sasha-cohen-to-be-inducted-into-u-s-figure-skating-hall-of-fame/2/#54ac8d5470c7 [accessed 21 January 2016].

Classic FM. n.d. "Angela Gheorghiu: The diva who wants it all." Online at http://www.classicfm.com/artists/angela-gheorghiu/guides/angela-gheorghiu-diva-who-wants-it-all/#sFlMk5kkD7uMcKuf.97 [accessed 26 July 2016].

Clayson, Alan. 2004. *Woman: The Incredible Life of Yoko Ono.* With Barb Jungr and Robb Johnson. Surrey, UK: Chrome Dreams.

Coates, Jennifer. 2014. "The shape-shifting diva: Yamaguchi Yoshiko and the national body." *Journal of Japanese and Korean Cinema* 6 (1): 23–38.

Collins, David, and David Metzler, producers. 2003–2007. *Queer Eye for the Straight Guy.* Serialized television program. New York: Bravo Cable Network.

Conor, Liz. 2004. *The Spectacular Modern Woman: Feminine Visibility in the 1920s.* Bloomington: Indiana University Press.

Contemporary Museum of Modern Art. 2013. "Yoko Ono: War is over, if you want it." Interview with Yoko Ono and museum curator Rachel Hunt, 17 December. Online at http://edutv.informit.com.au.ezproxy.lib.monash.edu.au/watch-screen.php?videoID = 674442.

Cornyetz, Nina. 1996. "Power and gender in the narratives of Yamada Eimi." In *The Woman's Hand: Gender and Theory in Japanese Women's Writing,* edited by Paul Gordon Schalow and Janet A. Walker, 425–60. Stanford: Stanford University Press.

Cosgrove, Hollie, ed. 1997. Funk & Wagnalls New International Dictionary of the English Language. Chicago: World Publishers.

Culture Club, artists. 1983. *Karma Chameleon.* New York: Virgin Records.

Cwiertka, Katarzyna. 2006. *Modern Japanese Cuisine: Food, Power and National Identity*. London: Reaktion Books.

Cyzowoman.com. 2014. "Kanehara Hitomi ga 'kiekakete iru'!? Akutagawa-shō no ninki sakka ga botsuraku shita riyū" (Kanehara Hitomi has disappeared?! Behind the fall of the popular Akutagawa Prize-winning author). Blog site, 4 May. Online at http://www.cyzowoman.com/2014/05/post_12141.html [accessed 14 December 2015].

Daily Shinchō. 2015. "'Dokusen sukūpu': Asada Mao no chichioya bōkō yōgi de taiho sarete ita'"("Exclusive story": The father of Asada Mao has been arrested for domestic offences). *Daily Shinchō*, 6 August. Online at http://www.dailyshincho.jp/article/2015/07311200/ [accessed 7 August 2016].

Dalle Vacche, Angela. 2000. "Goddess of modernity." *Film Comment* 36 (5): 44–48.

Davies, Gloria, M.E. Davies, and Young-A Cho. 2010. "*Hallyu* ballyhoo and Harisu: Marketing and representing the transgendered in South Korea." In *Complicated Currents: Media Flows, Soft Power and East Asia*, edited by Daniel Black, Stephen Epstein, and Alison Tokita, 09.1–09.12. Melbourne: Monash University ePress.

Davis, Madison J. 2010. "Unimaginable things: The feminist noir of Natsuo Kirino." *Literature Today* 84 (1): 9–11.

De Lauretis, Teresa. 1987. *Technologies of Gender: Essays on Theory, Film, and Fiction*. Bloomington: Indiana University Press.

Dillon, Patrick. 2013. "Diva by definition." *Opera News* 77 (5): 18–19.

DiNitto, Rachel. 2011. "Between literature and subculture: Kanehara Hitomi, media commodification and the desire for agency in post-bubble Japan." *Japan Forum* 23 (4): 453–70.

Doane, Mary Ann. 1991. *Femmes Fatales: Feminism, Film Theory, Psychoanalysis*. London: Routledge.

Dollase, Hiromi Tsuchiya. 2013. "Kawabata's wartime message in beautiful voyage (Utsukushii tabi)." In *Negotiating Censorship in Modern Japan*, edited by Rachael Hutchinson, 74–92. Abingdon and New York: Routledge.

Dower, John. 2000. *Embracing Defeat: Japan in the Wake of World War II*. New York: W.W. Norton.

Driscoll, Mark. 2007. "Debt and denunciation in post-bubble Japan: On the two freeters." *Cultural Critique* 65: 164–87.

Dyer, Richard. 1986. *Heavenly Bodies; Film Stars and Society*. London: British Film Institute.

———. 1998. *Stars*. London: British Film Institute.

Edwards, Elise. 2013. "The promises and possibilities of the pitch: 1990s Ladies League soccer players as fin de siècle modern girls." In *Modern Girls on the Go: Gender, Mobility, and Labor in Japan*, edited by Alisa Freedman, Laura Miller and Christine R. Yano, 149–65. Stanford: Stanford University Press.

Endo, Masako. 2012. "The making of Japanese femininity: Women, civilization, and war, from 1868 to 1945." *History Research* 2 (4): 284–303.

Enomoto Masaki. 2015. "Shinsaigo no jikan o ikiru kojin to sono kazoku no unmei o egaita saishinsaku 'Motazaru mono' Kanehara Hitomi intabyū" (Interview with Kanehara Hitomi: Survival, family, and fate in the wake of disaster in her new work "Without"). *Da Binchi Nyūsu,* 7 May. Online at http://ddnavi.com/news/237166/a/2/ [accessed 5 August 2016].

Epstein, Robert. 2013. "IoS book review: *The Goddess Chronicle,* by Natsuo Kirino (translated by Rebecca Copeland)." *The Independent,* Sunday, 13 (January). Online at http://www.independent.co.uk/arts-entertainment/books /reviews/ios-book-review-the-goddess-chronicle-by-natsuo-kirino-trs-rebecca-copeland-8449198.html [accessed 21 February 2013].

Ettinger, Bracha L. 2006. "The matrixial gaze." In *The Matrixial Borderspace,* edited by Bracha L. Ettinger and Brain Massumi, 41–92. Minneapolis: University of Minnesota Press.

Fabos, Bettina. 2001. "Forcing the fairytale: Narrative strategies in figure skating competition coverage." *Culture, Sport, Society* 4(2): 185–212.

Feder, Abigail. M. 1994. "'A radiant smile from the lovely lady': Overdetermined femininity in 'ladies' figure skating." *The Drama Review* 38 (1): 62–78.

Figyua Sukēto Yūchūbu Dōga Blog (Figure skating YouTube video blog). 2007. "Asada Mao, gaikoku tokuha'in kyōkai deno kisha kaiken (6 April 2007)" (Asada Mao's press conference at the Foreign Correspondents' Club of Japan, 6 April 2007). Online at http://www.fgsk8.com/archives/50687742.html [accessed 3 June 2017].

Fleming, Victor, director. 1939. *The Wizard of Oz.* Los Angeles: Metro-Goldwyn-Mayer Pictures.

Foreign Correspondents' Club of Japan. 2014. Press Conference: Mao Asada, 25 February.

French, Howard. 2003. "A Tokyo novelist mixes felonies with feminism." *New York Times,* 17 November. Online at http://www.nytimes.com/2003/11/17 /books/a-tokyo-novelist-mixes-felonies-with-feminism.html [accessed 18 May 2006].

Fumiko and Noguchi Kōshun. 2011. *Akujo uranai* (Poison woman divination). Tokyo: Futami Shobō.

Furukawa Noriko. 2011. "Shishigami to Izanami 'Mono no ke hime'—gyoku no kogatana no chikai" (Forest sprites and Izanami, Princess Mononoke—The oath of the jeweled knife). In *Ajia megami taizen* (Collective study of Asian goddesses), edited by Yoshida Atsuhiko and Matsumura Kazuo, 54–56. Tokyo: Seidosha.

Gallagher, Jack. 2014. "Mao's Inflexibility Hurt Medal Chances." *Japan Times,* 23 February.

Geiger, Annette. 2014. "Column with a slit." In *Fashionable Queens: Body-Power-Gender,* edited by Eva Flicker and Monika Seidl, 161–75. New York: Peter Lang.

Gepphart, Lisette. 2010. *Nach Einbruch der Dunkelheit: Zeitgen "ossische japanische Literatur im Zeichen des Prek" aren* (After dark: Contemporary Japanese literature under the sign of precarity). Berlin: EB-Verlag.

Golden Skate. 2016. "Rafael Arutyunyan on coaching champions." Golden Skate, 8 April. YouTube video. Online at https://www.youtube.com/watch?v = nAdv_Gc5wr8 [accessed 2 June 2017].

Goldman, Albert. 1988. *The Lives of John Lennon.* New York: Bantam Books.

Gotō Sōichi. 2010. *Yamataikoku Ōmi setsu: Makimuku iseki "Hashihaka =*

Himiko no haka" setsu e no gimon (The country of Yamatai Ōmi theory: Some doubts about "Hashihaka = Himiko's Grave" in Makimuku ruins). Hikone-shi: Sanraizu Shuppan.

Graham, Whitney Rose. 2015. "Yoko Ono at MoMA: An exhibition 50 years in the making." *Inside/Out.* 9 June. Online at https://www.moma.org/explore/inside_out/2015/06/09/yoko-ono-at-moma-an-exhibition-50-years-in-the-making/ [accessed 5 December 2016].

Grapard, Allan G. 1991. "Visions of excess and excesses of vision—Women and transgression in Japanese myth." *Japanese Journal of Religious Studies* 18 (1): 3–23.

Gregus, Adam. 2014. "I Live to Love My Friends, Live to Love the Soil, Live for The People: The (Anti-)utopia of Kirino Natsuo's *Poritikon.*" Unpublished M.A. thesis (in English), University of Vienna.

Hakuhodo DY Media Partners. 2015. "Asurīto imēji hyōka chōsa 2015 nen sōkatsu tokubetsu-hen" (The special summary edition of 2015 athletes' image evaluation research). Hakuhodo DY Holdings news release, 21 December.

Hara Rokurō, artist. 1952. *Omatsuri manbo* (Festival Mambo). Lyrics by Hara Rokurō. Tokyo: Nippon Columbia.

Hara Takeshi. 2008. "Kaisetsu" (Critique). In *Joshinki* (The Goddess Chronicle), 261–62. Tokyo: Kadokawa Bunko.

Hartley, Barbara. 2017. "Women in love and hate in 1960s Japan: Re-reading Ariyoshi Sawako's *The Doctor's Wife.*" *Intersections: Gender and Sexuality in Asia and the Pacific,* 40 (January). Online at http://intersections.anu.edu.au/issue40/hartley.html [accessed 1 February].

Hashimoto Osamu and Okamura Kazue, eds. 2003. *Kawada Haruhisa to Misora Hibari: Amerika kōen* (Kawada Haruhisa and Hibari Misora: American garden). Tokyo: Chūō Kōron Shinsha.

Haugen, Jason D. 2003. "'Unladylike divas': Language, gender and female gangsta rappers." *Popular Music and Society* 26 (4): 429–43.

Hayashi Kumiko. 2012. "Izanami no nayami Kojiki to Joshinki ni miru" (Izanami's complaint: A look at the Kojiki and The Goddess Chronicle). *Chronos* 34:2–6.

Hein, Laura, and Rebecca Jennison, eds. 2017. *Imagination without Borders.* Online at http://imaginationwithoutborders.northwestern.edu/collections/hiruko/rev. ed. [accessed 25 June 2017].

Heldt, Gustav. 2014. *The Kojiki: An Account of Ancient Matters.* New York: Columbia University Press.

Hirono Takashi. 2012. *Himiko wa nani o tabete ita ka* (What did Himiko eat?). Tokyo: Shinchōsha.

Hon no Hanashi Web. 2009. "Yūutsu no kōtei kara hajimaru monogatari" (A story of acceptance in depression). Hon no Hanashi Web, 20 Sept. Online at https://hon.bunshun.jp/articles/-/232?page = 2 [accessed 5 August 2016].

Honda Masuko. 1992. *Ibunka to shite no kodomo* (Children as another culture). Tokyo: Chikuma Gakugei Bunko. First published in 1980.

Hopkins, Jerry. 1987. *Yoko Ono.* London: Sidgwick and Jackson.

Hosogai Sayaka. 2004. "Intabyū Kanehara Hitomi: Ikizurasa o katachi ni" (Interview with Kanehara Hitomi: Giving shape to the pain). *Subaru,* March: 92–95.

Idemitsu Museum of Arts, ed. 2015. *Kosugi Hōan: "Tōyō" e no ai*. Tokyo: Idemitsu Bijutsukan.

Ieki Miyoji, director. 1949 *Kanashiki kuchibue* (Lonesome Whistle). Tokyo: Shōchiku.

IKKO. 2007. *Onna no hōsoku* (Law of Woman). Tokyo: Sekai Bunkasha.

————. 2008. *IKKO: Kirei o migaku* in *Kankoku* (IKKO's Beautiful Days in Korea). Tokyo: Bungei Shunjū.

IKKO and Okada Mio. 2013. *Dondake no hōsoku* (Law of Dondake). First produced in 2007. Music video. Retrieved from https://www.youtube.com /watch?v = 6iXrsDAMRHY [accessed 11 February 2016].

Iles, Chrissie. 2000. "Erotic conceptualism: The films of Yoko Ono." In *Yes Yoko Ono*, edited by Alexandra Munroe and Jon Hendricks, 201–7. New York: Japan Society and Harry N. Abrams.

Illouz, Eva. 2003. *Oprah Winfrey and the Glamour of Misery: An Essay on Popular Culture*. New York: Columbia University Press.

Imamura Hiroaki. 1993. "Supōtsu shakaigaku no kanōsei" (The possibility of sports sociology). *Supōtsu shakaigaku kenkyū* 1: 41–48.

Inoue Mitsusada. 1964. *Nihon no rekishi 1: Shinwa kara rekishi e* (The history of Japan 1: From myth to history). Tokyo: Chūōkōronsha.

International Skating Union. 2014. Olympic Winter Games Sochi 2014 Figure Skating Ladies Free Skating Judges Details per Skater. Online at http://www. isuresults.com/results/owg2014/ [accessed 10 January 2016].

Itō Midori. 1993. *Taimu passēji* (Time passage). Tokyo: Kinokuniya Shoten.

Ito, Shingo. 2015. "Japan's cuddly yet costly mascots face extermination." *Japan Times*, April 8. Online at http://www.japantimes.co.jp/news/2015/04 /08/national/japans-cuddly-yet-costly-mascots-face-extermination/# .VpEUS1K1ClY [accessed 21 May 2016].

Itoh, Makino. 2013. "Demand booming for artisanal rice." *Japan Times*, 13 November. Online at http://www.japantimes.co.jp/life/2013/11/21/food /demand-booming-for-artisanal-rice/#.VzZfIuS1Bk8 [accessed 21 May 2016].

Iwata-Weickgenannt, Kristina. 2012. "Precarity discourses in Kirino Natsuo's Metabola: The Okinawan stage, fractured selves and the ambiguity of contemporary existence." *Japan Forum* 24 (2): 141–61.

Izbicki, Joanne. 2008. "Singing the orphan blues: Misora Hibari and the rehabilitation of post-surrender Japan." *Intersections* 16. Online at http:// intersections.anu.edu.au/ [accessed 22 December 2015].

Japan Post. 2017. "Asada Mao, Rika-chan ningyō setto" (Asada Mao and Licca-chan doll set). *Japan Post*. Online shopping site. Online at http://www.shop .post.japanpost.jp/shop/pages/licca_mao_asada.aspx [accessed 30 June 2017].

JOJO Kikaku. 2015. "*Shimai tachi yo: Onna no koyomi 2015*" (Sisters! The First Feminists in Japan 2015). Online at http://www014.upp.so-net.ne.jp /jojokikaku/products/koyomi/2015koyomi_chumon.pdf [accessed 29 January 2015].

Jung, Jeffrey. 1999. "The Diva at the Fin-de-siècle." Unpublished doctoral dissertation (UMI No. 9947019), University of California, Los Angeles.

Kamachi, Mitsuru. 2004. "East meets West: Japanese theater in the time of Shakespeare." *Shakespeare Studies* 32: 23–35.

Kanaseki Hiroshi. 1999. *Himiko no shokutaku* (Himiko's dining table). Tokyo: Yoshikawa Kōbunkan.

Kanda Hideo, Tsuboi Kiyotari, and Mayuzumi Hiromichi. 1978. *Nihon no koten 1: Kojiki* (Classical Japanese literature I: *Kojiki*). Tokyo: Shūeisha.

Kaneda Yukihiro, Itoi Seiichi, and Matsubara Noriko, producers. 2006–2009. *OnēMANS* (Older Sister Men). TV Program. Tokyo: Nippon TV.

Kanehara Hitomi. 2004a. *Hebi ni piasu* (Snakes and Earrings). Tokyo: Shūeisha.

———. 2004b. *Asshubeibii* (Ashbaby). Tokyo: Shūeisha.

———. 2005. *AMEBIC*. Tokyo: Shūeisha.

———. 2006a. *Ōtofikushon* (Autofiction). Tokyo: Shūeisha.

———. 2006b. *Snakes and Earrings*. Translated by David James Karashima. New York: Plume.

———. 2008. *Autofiction*. Translated by David James Karashima. New York: Vintage.

———. 2009a. *Trip Trap*. Tokyo: Kakukawa Shoten.

———. 2009b. *Yūutsu-tachi* (The Depressed). Tokyo: Bungei Shunjū.

———. 2011. *Mazāzu* (Mothers). Tokyo: Shinchōsha.

———. 2015. "Motazaru mono" (Without). *Subaru*, January: 82–232.

Kawamura Kunimitsu. 2005. *Himiko no keifu to saishi: Nihon shāmanizumu no kodai* (The genealogy of Himiko and religious rites: Ancient times through Japanese Shamanism). Tokyo: Gakuseisha.

Kaze Kaoru. 1974. "Himiko yo. Himiko." (It's Himiko. Himiko). *Bessatsu shōjō furendo* (Bessatsu friend), December: 9–68. Kodansha.

Kelly, William W. 1986. "Rationalization and nostalgia: Cultural dynamics of new middle-class Japan." *American Ethnologist* 13: 603–18.

Kennicott, Phillip. 2014. "Defining diva." *Opera News* 79 (5): 28–31.

Kidder, Edward J. 2007. *Himiko and Japan's Elusive Chiefdom of Yamatai: Archaeology, History, and Mythology*. Honolulu: University of Hawai'i Press.

Kietlinski, Robin. 2011. *Japanese Women and Sport: Beyond Baseball and Sumo*. London and New York: Bloomsbury Academic.

Kirino Natsuo. 1997. *AUTO* (OUT). Tokyo: Kōdansha.

———. 2003a. *OUT*. Translated by Stephen Snyder. New York: Kodansha International.

———. 2003b. *Gurotesuku* (Grotesque). Tokyo: Bungei Shunjū.

———. 2008. *Joshinki* (The Goddess Chronicle). Tokyo: Kadokawa Shoten.

———. 2012. *The Goddess Chronicle*. Translated by Rebecca Copeland. Edinburgh: Canongate Books.

Knight, Christine. 2011. "'Most people are simply not designed to eat pasta': Evolutionary explanations for obesity in the low-carbohydrate diet movement." *Public Understanding of Science* 20 (5): 706–19.

Koestenbaum, Wayne. 1993. *The Queen's Throat: Opera, Homosexuality and the Mystery of Desire*. New York: Poseidon Press.

Koga Masao, composer. 1964. *Yawara* (Judo). Lyrics by Sekizawa Shin'ichi. Tokyo: Nippon Columbia.

———. 1966. *Kanashii sake* (Mournful Sake). Lyrics by Ishimoto Miyuki. Tokyo: Nippon Columbia.

Komabayashi Shōichi, composer. 1962a. *Hibari no tsuisuto* (Hibari's Twist). Lyrics by Mizushima Tetsu. Tokyo: Nippon Columbia.

———. 1962b. *Buruu tsuisuto* (Blue Twist). Lyrics by Mizushima Tetsu. Tokyo: Nippon Columbia.

Kōno Fumiyo. 2012. *Bōrupen Kojiki* (A Ballpoint Pen *Kojiki*). Volume 1. Tokyo: Heibonsha.

———. 2013. *Bōrupen Kojiki* (A Ballpoint Pen *Kojiki*). Volume 3. Tokyo: Heibonsha.

Kōno Nobuko. 1995. "Megami no jikū e: Gensō no shokisei" (Towards the time/space of goddesses: The incipiency of fantasy). In *Onna to otoko no jikū: Nihon joseishi saikō* (The time/space of women and men: Rethinking the history of Japanese women), edited by Kōno Nobuko, 105–40. Tokyo: Fujiwara Shoten.

Kulwicki, Cara. 2011. "What a bastard the world is: The feminist politics of Yoko Ono's personal song." *The Curvature*, 6 July. Online at http://thecurvature.com/2011/07/06/what-a-bastard-the-world-is-the-feminist-politics-of-yoko-onos-personal-song/ [accessed 26 February 2015].

Kyodo News. 2014. "Himiko no kagami wa makyō" (Himiko's mirror is a magic mirror). *Kyodo News*, 29 January. YouTube video. Online at https://www.youtube.com/watch?v = _jQkRKwQlZ8 [accessed 21 May 2016].

Kwan, Michelle. 2014. Twitter post, 20 February. Online at https://twitter.com/michellewkwan/status/436542940719370240 [accessed 27 November 2016].

Langer, Susanne K. 1957. *Problems of Art: Ten Philosophical Lectures*. London: Kegan Paul.

Lee Byung-Hoon, director. 2003–2004. *Dae jang geum* (Jewel in the palace). Television series. Seoul: Munhwa Broadcasting.

Lee, Hyangjin. 2010. "Buying youth: Japanese fandom of the Korean Wave." In *Complicated Currents: Media Flows, Soft Power and East Asia,* edited by Daniel Black, Stephen Epstein, and Alison Tokita, 07.1–07.16. Melbourne: Monash University ePress.

Lennon, John (with Yoko Ono), artists/composers. 1970. *Instant Karma!* Single backed with *Who Has Seen the Wind*. Apple Corps. A live performance of this song can be seen at https://www.youtube.com/watch?v = zekIGdWdOpo [accessed 5 December 2016].

———. 1971a. *Power To The People*. Single backed with *Open Your Box* (UK release) and "Touch Me" (US release). Apple Corps. Online at https://www.youtube.com/watch?v = Wos-dDxpJlQ [accessed 5 December 2016].

———. 1971b. *Imagine*. Single backed with *It's So Hard* (US release) and *Working Class Hero* (UK release). Apple Corps. The music video of this song can be seen at https://www.youtube.com/watch?v = yRhq-yO1KN8 [accessed 5 December 2016].

———. 1972a. *Sometime in New York City*. Studio album, produced by John Lennon and Phil Spector. Apple Corps.

———. 1972b. *Woman Is the Nigger of the World*. Single backed with *Sisters, O Sisters*. Apple Corps. A live performance of this song can be seen at https://www.youtube.com/watch?v = CtY5bv-oxLE [accessed 5 December 2016].

―――. 1974. *Whatever Gets You thru the Night*. Single backed with *Beef Jerky* (US release). Apple Corps.

Lennon, John, and Yoko Ono. 1980. *Double Fantasy*. Studio album, produced by John Lennon, Yoko Ono, and Jack Douglas. Geffen Records.

Leung, On Yuk. 1993. "Ariyoshi Sawako *Izumo no Okuni* ron" (Ariyoshi Sawako: Discussion of *Izumo no Okuni*). *Jōchi Daigaku kokubungaku ronshū* (Sophia University Japanese literature essay collection) 26: 175–90.

Lindsey, William. 2005. "Religion and the good life: Motivation, myth, and metaphor in a Tokugawa female lifestyle guide." *Japanese Journal of Religious Studies* 32 (1): 35–52.

Mackie, Vera. 2003. *Feminism in Modern Japan: Citizenship, Embodiment and Sexuality*. Cambridge: Cambridge University Press.

―――. 2008. "How to be a girl: Mainstream media portrayals of transgendered lives in Japan." *Asian Studies Review* 32: 411–23.

―――. 2012. "Instructing, constructing, deconstruction: The embodied and disembodied performances of Yoko Ono." In *Rethinking Japanese Modernism*, edited by Roy Starrs, 490–501. Leiden: Global Oriental.

Macnaughton, Helen. 2015. "Womenomics for Japan: Is the Abe policy for gendered employment viable in an era of precarity?" *The Asia-Pacific Journal/ Japan Focus* 13 (12): 11–11. Online at http://apjjf.org/2015/13/12/Helen-Macnaughtan/4302.html [accessed 11 February 2016].

Mainichi Shinbun. 2005. "Figyua: Asada gorin fushutsujō de koizumi shushō 'fushigi da yo na'" (Figure skating: Prime Minister Koizumi says "how weird" upon Asada not competing at the Olympics). *Mainichi Shinbun*, 19 December.

Mao-Blog. 2012. Blog Post, 12 January. Blog post entry. Online at http://mao-asada.jp/mao/ [accessed 11 April 2017].

―――. 2017. Blog Post, 10 April. Blog post entry. Online at http://mao-asada.jp/mao/ [accessed 11 April 2017].

Maree, Claire. 2013. "Writing *onē*: Deviant orthography and heteronormativity in contemporary Japanese lifestyle culture." *Media International Australia, Incorporating Culture and Policy* 147: 98–110.

Marikofun. 2014a. *Marikofun no kofun bukku* (Marikofun's tomb book). Tokyo: Yamato Keikokusha.

―――. 2014b. *Kofun no aruki kata* (How to walk around tombs). Tokyo: Fusōsha.

―――. 2014c. *Kofun de kōfun* (Excited about tombs). Music CD. Saitama: Uruka Music.

―――. 2015. *Nara no kofun* (Tombs of Nara). Kyoto: Tankōsha.

Matsugi Takehiko. 2013. "Supūn, fōku, koppu Yayoi-jin no shokutaku wa ōbeifū!?" (Spoon, fork, cup: Did the Yayoi people dine Western style?). In *Shūkan shinhakken! Nihon no rekishi: Kofun jidai 1* (Weekly new discoveries! Japanese history: Kofun Era 1), edited by Matsugi Takehiko, 23. Tokyo: Asahi Shinbun Shuppan.

Matsuura Hisaki. 2007. *Kuronikuru* (Chronicle). Tokyo: Daigaku Shuppankai.

McCurry, Justin. 2015. "Japanese artist goes on trial over 'vagina selfies.'" *The Guardian*, April 15.

McLelland, Mark J. 2003. "Western intersections, Eastern approximations: Living more 'like oneself': Transgender identities and sexualities in Japan." In *Bisexuality and Transgenderism: InterSEXtions of the Others*, edited by Jonathan Alexander and Karen Yescavage, 205–30. New York: Harrington Park Press.

Merish, Lori. 1996. "Cuteness and commodity aesthetics: Tom Thumb and Shirley Temple." In *Freakery; Cultural Spectacles of the Extraordinary Body*, edited by Rosemarie Garland Thomson, 185–203. New York: New York University Press.

Mezur, Katherine. 2005. *Beautiful Boys/Outlaw Bodies; Devising Kabuki Female-Likeness*. London: Palgrave Macmillan.

Miller, Laura. 2006. *Beauty Up: Exploring Contemporary Japanese Body Aesthetics*. Berkeley: University of California Press.

———. 2008a. "Korean TV dramas and the Japan-style Korean Wave." *Post Script: Essays in Films and the Humanities* 27 (3): 17–24.

———. 2008b. "Japan's Cinderella motif: Beauty industry and mass culture interpretations of a popular icon." *Asian Studies Review* 32 (3): 393–409.

———. 2008c. "Extreme makeover for a Heian-Era wizard." In *Mechademia: An Annual Forum for Anime, Manga and the Fan Arts. Issue #3: Limits of the Human*, edited by Frenchy Lunning, 30–45. Minneapolis: University of Minnesota Press.

———. 2011. "Tantalizing tarot and cute cartomancy in Japan." *Japanese Studies*. 31 (1): 73–91.

———. 2014a. "Rebranding Himiko, the shaman queen of ancient history." In *Mechademia, An Annual Forum for Anime, Manga and the Fan Arts: Issue #9: Origins*, edited by Frenchy Lunning, 179–98. Minneapolis: University of Minnesota Press.

———. 2014b. "The divination arts in girl culture." In *Capturing Contemporary Japan: Differentiation and Uncertainty*, edited by Satsuki Kawano, Glenda S. Roberts, and Susan Long, 334–58. Honolulu: University of Hawai'i Press.

———. 2017. "Japanese tarot cards." *ASIA Network Exchange: A Journal for Asian Studies in the Liberal Art* 24 (1): 1–28.

Miller, Laura, and Jan Bardsley. 2005. *Bad Girls of Japan*. New York: Palgrave Macmillan.

Miller, Toby. 2013. "Exposing celebrity sports." In *Fallen Heroes, Media, and Celebrity Culture*, edited by Lawrence A. Wenner, 17–24. New York: P. Lang.

Mitaki Akira, composer. 1989. *Kawa no nagare no yō ni* (Like the River Flows). Lyrics by Akimoto Yasushi. Tokyo: Nippon Columbia.

Miura Sukeyuki. 1993. "Kodai bungaku ni miru warai: 'Emu' to 'warau' o megutte" (Laugh in the literature of Japanese antiquity: 'Emu' [to smile] and 'warau' [to laugh]). *Nihon no bigaku* 20: 4–23.

———. 2002. *Kōgo yaku Kojiki* (*Kojiki* in spoken Japanese). Tokyo: Bungei Shunjū.

Miyadai Shinji and Suzuki Takayuki. 1988. "Shōhi sareru jiko" (Consuming the self). In *Hayari no bunka* (Trends in culture), edited by Suzuki Takayuki, 12–28. Kyoto: Seigensha.

Miyauchi Atusko, ed. 1995. *Ariyoshi Sawako: Shinchōsha sakka arubamu 71* (Ariyoshi Sawako: Shinchosha writers' album, 71). Tokyo: Shinchōsha.

Monden, Masafumi. 2015. *Japanese Fashion Cultures: Dress and Gender in Contemporary Japan.* New York and London: Bloomsbury Academic.

Morris, Ivan. 1975. *The Nobility of Failure: Tragic Heroes in the History of Japan.* New York: Noonday Press.

Moyer, Edward. 2017. "Google Doodle celebrates Josephine Baker." C/Net technology news website. Online at https://www.cnet.com/news/google-doodle-celebrates-josephine-baker/ [accessed 8 June 2017].

Mulhern, Chieko Irie, ed. 1991. *Heroic with Grace: Legendary Women of Japan.* Armonk, NY: M.E. Sharpe.

Muñoz, José Esteban. 1999. *Disidentification: Queers of Color and the Performance of Politics.* Minneapolis: University of Minnesota Press.

———. 2009. *Cruising Utopia: The Then and There of Queer Futurity.* New York: New York University Press.

Munroe, Alexandra. 2000. "Spirit of YES: The art and life of Yoko Ono." In *Yes Yoko Ono,* edited by Alexandra Munroe and Jon Hendricks, 11–37. New York: Japan Society and Harry N. Abrams.

Munroe, Alexandra, and Jon Hendricks, eds. 2000. *Yes Yoko Ono.* New York: Japan Society and Harry N. Abrams.

Murai, Shusuke. 2015. "Schools in Japan to let transgender students use whichever locker room they prefer." *Japan Times,* 15 April. Online at http://www.japantimes.co.jp/news/2015/04/30/national/social-issues/schools-japan-let-transgender-students-use-whichever-locker-room-prefer/#.VrycH_IrKhe [accessed 8 February 2016].

Myers, Eric. 2011. "Women on the edge." *Opera News* 76 (4): 26–29.

Mynavi News. 2015. "Josei wa mina, Asada Mao ni naritai? Taikei ni akogareru josei figyua senshu rankingu" (All women want to be Asada Mao? The ranking of women figure skaters whose physique women aspire to have). *Mynavi News,* 27 August. Online at http://news.mynavi.jp/news/2015/08/27/115/ [accessed 31 December 2015].

Nagafuji Yasushi. 2004. "Ame no Uzume no 'sei' to butō" (The 'sexuality' and dance of Ame no Uzume). *Kokubungaku kaishaku to kanshō* 69 (12): 21–28.

Nagayama Hisao. 1997. *Himiko no furōshoku* (Himiko's food for perennial youth). Tokyo: Gogatsu Shobō.

———. 2010. *Tabemono bunkashi. The Cultural History of Japanese Food* (bilingual). Tokyo: Yasashii Shokutaku.

Nakaki Shigeo, director. 1952. *Futari no hitomi* (The pupil/eyes of two people; English title for foreign release, *Girls Hand in Hand*). Tokyo: Shōchiku.

Nakamichi, Hitomi. 2010. "The development of alternative production activities related to food safety and security and associated gender issues." In *From Community to Consumption: New and Classical Themes in Rural Sociological Research,* edited by Alessandro Bonanno, Hans Bakker, Raymond Jussaume, Yoshio Kawamura, and Mark Shucksmith, 31–44. Bingley, UK: Emerald Group Publishing.

Nakamura, Karen, and Hisako Matsuo. 2002. "Female masculinity and fantasy spaces: Transcending genders in the Takarazuka and Japanese popular culture."

In *Men and Masculinities in Modern Japan: Dislocating the Salaryman Doxa*, edited by J. E. Roberson and N. Suzuki, 59–75. New York: Routledge.

Nakanishi Susumu. 2013. *Nihon shinwa no sekai* (The world of Japanese mythology). Tokyo: Chikuma Shobō.

Nakano Yukari. 2013. *Toppu sukētā no ryūgi: Nakano Yukari ga kiku 9 nin no riaru sutōrī* (The styles of top skaters: The real stories of mine skaters interviewed by Nakano Yukari). Tokyo: Futabasha.

Nakayama Chinatsu. 1994. *Himetachi no densetsu: Kojiki ni hiraita onnagokoro* (Legends of princesses: The *Kojiki* and the flowering of the female heart). Tokyo: Chikuma Shobō.

Namura Jōhaku. 1989. "*Onna chōhōki 1692*" (A lady's treasury 1692). In *Tōyoko Gakuen joshi tanki daigaku josei bunka kenkyūjo sōsho: Daisanshū* (Tōyoko Gakuen Women's Junior College, Research Institute of Women's Culture Monograph: Third issue), edited by Arima Sumiko, Wakasugi Tetsuo, and Nishigaki Yoshiko, 1–141. Tokyo: Josei Bunka Kenkyūjo.

Narinari.com. 2008. "Asada Mao to Kimu Yona no hikaku hōdō ni ayamari, 'tokudane!' ga shazai" (There were errors in the story of Asada Mao/Kim Yu-na comparison: Tokudane! apologized), Narinari.com news site, 18 December. Online at http://www.narinari.com/Nd/20081210772.html [accessed 3 January 2016].

Neustatter, Angela. 2005. "With a rebel yell." *The Guardian*, 30 May.

Nihon Keizai Shinbun. 2004. "Akutagawashō o 20-sai de jushō Kanehara Hitomi-san" (Kanehara Hitomi wins the Akutagawa Prize at twenty). *Nihon Keizai Shinbun*, 19 January.

———. 2008. "Asada Mao, shitei kankei o kaishō, renshū kyoten, Nihon ni utsusu" (Asada Mao, separating from her coach, moving back to Japan). *Nihon Keizai Shinbun*, 27 February: 41.

———. 2012. "Asada senshu no hon, hatsubai o chūshi, 'omoi to kotonaru senden'" (The book of Asada, cancelled for publication, 'inacurate publicity'). *Nihon Keizai Shinbun*, 3 January: 14.

———. 2014a. "Mao masaka zen janpu shippai" (Oh no, Mao failed in all jumps). *Nihon Keizai Shinbun*, 20 February: 11.

———. 2014b. "Mao 3-kaiten han no daishō" (Mao: The price of 3 and a half revolution), *Nihon Keizai Shinbun*, 21 February: 38.

———. 2015. "Asada Mao wa kokoro yusaburu 'tokubetsu na senshu'" (Mao Asada is a special skater who moves our heart). *Nihon Keizai Shinbun*, 23 September. Online at http://www.nikkei.com/article/DGXLASDH11HoX_R10C15A9PE8000/ [accessed 25 September 2015].

Nikkan Sports. 2017. "*Asada Mao no intai kaiken konseiki saidaikyū 430-nin hōdōjin*" (The record number of 430 media presses gathered for Asada Mao's press conference for her retirement). *Nikkan Sports*, 12 April. Online at https://www.nikkansports.com/sports/news/1806668.html [accessed 19 May 2017].

Ninagawa Yukio, director. 2008. *Hebi ni piasu* (Snakes and Earrings). Feature film. Tokyo: ARK Entertainment.

Nine Inch Nails, artists. 1994. *Hurt*. Santa Monica, CA: Interscope Records.

Nippon Hōsō Kyōkai (NHK). 2014. *Sochi Olympics Figure Skating Women's Free Program*. February 21.

Nishiyama Matsunosuke. 1983. *Kabuki o miru: Migakareta gei no atarashisa* (Viewing Kabuki: The newness of a polished art). Tokyo: Iwanami Shoten.

Nishizawa Sō, composer. 1968. *Ai no bosa noba* (Bossa Nova of Love). Lyrics by Saeki Makoto. Tokyo: Nippon Columbia.

Noguchi Yoshie. 2012. *Itō Midori: Toripuru akuseru no saki e* (Itō Midori: Across the triple axel). Tokyo: Shufu no Tomo-sha.

Norman, Philip. 2009. *John Lennon: The Life.* London: Harper.

Ō no Yasumaro. 2014. *The Kojiki: An Account of Ancient Matters.* Translated by Gustav Heldt. New York: Columbia University Press.

Occhi, Debra J. 2014. "Yuru kyara, humanity and the uncanny instability of borders in the construction of Japanese identities and aesthetics." *Japan Studies: The Frontier,* 7–17.

O'Connor, Jane. 2008. *The Cultural Significance of the Child Star.* New York: Routledge.

Ogasawara Kyōko. 1978. "Kojiki no geinō to kayō" (The performing arts and ballads). In *Nihon no koten 1: Kojiki* (Classical Japanese literature 1: *Kojiki*), edited by Kanda Hideo, Kiyotari Tsuboi, and Hiromichi Mayuzumi, 92–108. Tokyo: Shūeisha.

Ohinata, Masami. 1995. "The mystique of motherhood: A key to understanding social change and family problems in Japan." In *Japanese Women: New Feminist Perspectives on the Past, Present, and Future,* edited by Kumiko Fujimura-Fanselow and Atsuko Kameda, 199–212. New York: Feminist Press at CUNY.

Ohnuki-Tierney, Emiko. 1994. *Rice as Self: Japanese Identities Through Time.* Princeton: Princeton University Press.

Oikawa Masamichi (illustrator) and Terayama Shūji (author). 1997. *Ōasa Danchi* (Marijuana apartments). Manga reprinted in *1970-nen Daihyakka* (The 1970s encyclopedia), 156–77. Tokyo: Takarajimasha.

Ōishi Manabu and Himekawa Akira. 2012. *Gakken manga NEW Nihon no rekishi 1: Kuni no naritachi* (Gakken comic new Japanese history vol. 1: How the country came about), 81. Tokyo. Gakken Kyōiku Shuppan.

Ōmura Tōru. 2016. *Bītoruzu to Nihon: Nekkyō no kiroku* (The Beatles and Japan: A record of [Beatle]mania). Tokyo: Shinko Music Entertainment.

Onishi, Norimitsu. 2004. "Just 20, she captures altered Japan in a debut novel." *New York Times,* 27 March. Online at http://www.nytimes.com/2004/03/27/world/the-saturday-profile-just-20-she-captures-altered-japan-in-a-debut-novel.html?_r = 0 [accessed 5 August 2016].

Ono, Yoko. 1966. *Yoko at Indica. Realization and Production by Tony Cox.* Original pamphlet from the Indica Gallery, 6 Mason's Yard, Duke Street, St James, London SW1 (courtesy Rare Books Collection, Monash University). Contains photographs and listings of pieces, and the essay "To The Wesleyan People."

———. 1969. *Rape.* 77-minute film. Online at https://www.youtube.com/watch?v = ax9so9F3i-4 [accessed 29 January 2015].

———, artist/composer. 1971. *Sisters, O Sisters.* B-side to *Woman Is the Nigger of the World* single. Apple Corps. This song can be heard at https://www.youtube.com/watch?v = W1XSt_HqAmA [accessed 5 December 2016].

————. 1974. "*Waga ai, waga tōsō*" (My Love, My Struggle). *Bungei Shunjū* 52 (10): 236–60.

————, artist/composer. 1981a. *Walking on Thin Ice*. Single backed with *It Happened*. Geffen Records. A re-edit of the 1981 version of song can be heard at https://www.youtube.com/watch?v = VS5p345HBIM [accessed 5 December 2016].

————. 1981b. *Season of Glass*. Studio album, produced by Yoko Ono and Phil Spector. Geffen Records.

————. 2012. "The final days." In *Rolling Stone John Lennon: The Ultimate Guide to his Life, Music & Legend*, edited by J. Wenner, 88–95. New York: Rolling Stone/Wenner Media LLC.

————. 2014. "#HeForShe, The Feminization of Society & O Sisters O Sisters by Yoko Ono." Blog post by Ono with reprint of the 1972 article "The Feminization of Society." Imagine Peace website. Online at http://imaginepeace .com/archives/2565 [accessed 29 January 2015].

————. 2015. @yokoonoofficial (Instagram). 13 February post. Online at http://instagram.com/p/zAeIgqjzuH/ [accessed 16 February 2015].

Ōno Yuriko. 2008. *Nihon no Kamisama kādo: Gods and Goddesses of Japan* (bilingual title). Oracle card deck. Tokyo: Visionary Company.

Orbaugh, Sharalyn. 2007. *Japanese Fiction of the Allied Occupation: Vision, Embodiment, Identity*. Boston: Brill.

Oricon Inc. 2007–2014. "The annual favorite athlete ranking." Online at http:// www.oricon.co.jp/special/766/ [accessed: 26 December 2015].

Oricon Style. 2015. "*Asada Mao, 'idai na imōto' e no rettōkan hanenoke kakuritsu shita pojishon*" (Asada Mao, the position she achieved by letting go her inferior complex over her 'great sister'). Oricon Style, 23 May. Online at http://www.oricon.co.jp/special/47977/ [accessed 30 June 2017].

Orikuchi Shinobu. 1966. *Orikuchi Shinobu zenshū* (The collected works of Orikuchi Shinobu). Volume 12. Tokyo: Chūōkōronsha.

Orwell, George. 1949. "Reflections on Gandhi." *Partisan Review* 16 (1): 85–92.

Ōtsuka Hikari. 2011. *Ai to maguwai no Kojiki* (Love and sex in *Kojiki*). Tokyo: Chikuma Shobō.

Padva, Gilad. 2006. "Unruly womanliness, gender dysphoria, and Anita Faleli's iconography." *Feminist Media Studies* 6, 1: 25–45.

Paglia, Camille. 1992. "Endangered rock." *New York Times*, 16 April. Online at http://www.nytimes.com/1992/04/16/opinion/endangered-rock.html [accessed 26 February 2015].

Peers, Juliette. 2008. "Ballet and Girl Culture." In *Girl Culture: An Encyclopedia Vol. 1*, edited by Claudia M. Mitchell and Jacqueline Reid-Walsh, 73–84. Westport, CN: Greenwood.

Philippi, Donald L. 1968. *Kojiki*. Princeton University Press and University of Tokyo Press.

Piaf, Edith, artist. 1947. *La Vie en Rose* (Life in Rosy Hues). Originally written in 1945. New York: Columbia Records.

Rahn, Kim. 2009. "Japanese transgender celeb becomes Korea tourism Amb." *Korea Times*, 1 March. Online at http://www.koreatimes.co.kr/www/news /special/2009/03/178_40486.html [accessed 11 February 2016].

Rath, Eric. 2015. "The invention of local food." In *The Globalization of Asian Cuisines*, edited by James Farrer, 145–64. New York: Palgrave Macmillan.

Reader, Ian. 2005. *Making Pilgrimages: Meaning and Practice in Shikoku*. Honolulu: University of Hawai'i Press.

Rekidama Henshūbu. 2013. *Bijuaru Nihon no hiroin* (Visual Japanese heroines). Tokyo: Asukiii Media Wākusu (ASCII Media Works).

Rekishi no Shinsō Kenkyūkai. 2012. *Gakkō de oshiete kurenai: Hontō no Nihonshi* (You aren't taught this in school: The real history of Japan). Tokyo: Asahi Shinbunsha.

Riley, Tim. 2011. *Lennon: The Man, The Myth, The Music*. New York: Hyperion.

Robertson, Jennifer. 1988. "Furusato Japan: The culture and politics of nostalgia." *International Journal of Politics, Culture, and Society* 1 (4): 494–518.

———. 1991. *Native and Newcomer: Making and Remaking a Japanese City*. Berkeley: University of California Press.

———. 1998. *Takarazuka: Sexual Politics and Popular Culture in Modern Japan*. Berkeley: University of California Press.

Rojek, Chris. 2001. *Celebrity*. London: Reaktion Books.

Rokudenashiko. 2015. *Waisetsu tte nan desu ka? Jishō geijutsuka to yobareta watashi* (What is obscenity? I'm called a self-proclaimed artist). Tokyo: Kin'yōbi.

Rosenbaum, Roman. 2015. "Japan's literature of precarity." In *Visions of Precarity in Japanese Popular Culture and Literature*, edited by Kristina Iwata-Weickgenannt and Roman Rosenbaum, 1–23. New York: Routledge.

Ross, David. 2000. "Not here." In *Yes Yoko Ono*, edited by Alexandra Munroe and Jon Hendricks, 55–57. New York: Japan Society and Harry N. Abrams.

Saitō Hideki. 2006. *Yomikaerareta Nihon shinwa* (Reinterpretations of Japanese mythology). Tokyo: Kōdansha Gendai Shinsho.

———. 2010. *Kojiki: Seichō suru kamigami* (*Kojiki*: Deities continue to grow). Tokyo: BNP (Biingu Netto Puresu).

Saitō Juri. 2004. "Akutagawa-shō wa wakai josei no jidai" (Young women rule the Akutagawa Prize). *AERA*, 26 January: 71.

Saitō Juri and Ishizuka Tomoko. 2004. "Ikuji tensai kosodate no shuraba: Akutagawa-shō Kanehara Hitomi, dokugaku puroguramā, chūgakusei gorufā ra" (Difficulties in raising prodigies: Akutagwa Prize winner Kanehara Hitomi, a self-taught programer, and a middle school golfer). *AERA*, 9 February: 30–34.

Saitō Torajirō, director. 1950. *Tōkyō kiddo* (Tokyo Kid*)*. Tokyo: Shōchiku.

Sakaki, Atsuko. 1999. *Recontextualizing Texts: Narrative Performance in Modern Japanese Fiction*. Cambridge, MA: Harvard University Press.

Sarkeesian, Anita. 2013. "Damsel in distress: Part 1—Tropes vs women in video games." YouTube video. 7 March. Online at https://www.youtube.com/watch?v = X6p5AZp7r_Q [accessed 16 June 2013].

Sasaki Masaaki. 2015. "Roshia kara ai o komete: Gen'eki fukki no Asada Mao ni moto kōchi Tachiana Tarasowa san ga atsui ēru 'kanojo wa saikō no sukētā'" (From Russia with love: Former coach Tatiana Tarasova sends Asada Mao who makes a comeback, a passionate cheer "she is the best skater"). *Sankei Shinbun*, 5 December. Online at http://www.sankei.com

/premium/print/151205/prm151205/prm151205014-c.html [accessed 6 December 2015].

Sawai Ryūsuke. 2010. *Yamataikoku Ōmi setsu: Kodai Ōmi no ten to sen* (The Yamatai country Ōmi theory: Points and lines to ancient Ōmi). Tokyo: Gentōsha Renaissance.

Sayle, Murray. 2000. "The making of Yoko Ono, prophet of the 1960s." In *Yes Yoko Ono,* edited by Alexandra Munroe and Jon Hendricks, 51–54. New York: Japan Society and Harry N. Abrams.

Sellers, Susan. 2001. *Myth and Fairy Tale in Contemporary Women's Fiction.* New York: Palgrave.

Shamoon, Deborah. 1999. "Narrative and Genre in the Works of Uchida Shungiku." M.A. thesis, University of Washington.

———. 2009. "Misora Hibari and the girl star in postwar Japanese cinema." *Signs: Journal of Women in Culture and Society* 35 (1): 131–55.

Shaver, Ruth M. 1966. *Kabuki Costume.* Rutland, VT and Tokyo: Charles E. Tuttle.

Shigematsu, Setsu. 2005. "Feminism and the media in the late twentieth century: Reading the limits of a politics of transgression." In *Gendering Modern Japanese History,* edited by Barbara Molony and Kathleen Uno, 555–89. Cambridge, MA: Harvard University Asia Center, Harvard University Press.

Shils, Edward A. 1965. "Charisma, order, and status." *American Sociological Review* 30: 199–213.

Shimanaka, Kazutaka. 2016. "Wily woman works out a way to walk with Tenga sex aid." *Tokyo Reporter* news site. Online at http://twisted438.rssing.com /browser.php?indx = 24913495&item = 1 [accessed 17 May 2016].

Shimazu Taku. 2004. *Ōsutoraria no nihongo kyōiku to Nihon no tai-Ōsutoraria Nihongo fukyū: Sono "seisaku" no senkanki ni okeru dōkō* (Japanese language education in Australia and Japan's policy for dissemination of Japanese language in Australia: Changes in policies in the interwar period). Tokyo: Hitsuji Shobō.

———. 2012. "Tsurumi Yūsuke to 1930-nendai no Ōsutoraria ni okeru Nihongo kyōiku: 'Nihongo netsu' no hakken to sono senchū sengo e no eikyō" (Yūsuke Tsurumi and Japanese language education in Australia in the 1930s: The discovery of 'Japanese language learning boom' and its influence during and after World War II). *Ōsutoraria kenkyū* (Australian studies) 25: 17–28.

Shindō Ken. 1994. *Boku wa akunin* (I am a wicked person). Osaka: Tōhō Shuppan.

Shintō no Kokoro o Tsutaeru. 2016. Izanami kaisetsu (Commentary on Izanami). YouTube video. Online at https://www.youtube.com/watch?v = jgw4 AIU8uYo [accessed 1 December 2016].

Shirota Noriko. 2012. "Shirota Noriko no me: Janpu no seido o ageru shika nai" (Shirota Noriko's eyes: For her, polishing her jumps is the only way for winning). *Sports Hōchi,* 12 December.

Siddle, Richard. 2011. "Race, ethnicity, and minorities in modern Japan." In *Routledge Handbook of Japanese Culture and Society,* edited by Victoria Bestor, Theodore C. Bestor, and Akiko Yamagata, 150–62. New York: Routledge.

Sievers, Sharon. 1983. *Flowers in Salt: The Beginnings of Feminist Conscious-ness in Modern Japan*. Stanford: Stanford University Press.

The Skating Lesson. 2016. "TSL and Christine Brennan Preview the Ladies Event at the 2016 World Championships." YouTube video, 21 March. Online at https://www.youtube.com/watch?v = JiNMR_terZM [accessed 3 June 2017].

Slaymaker, Douglas. 2004. *The Body in Postwar Japanese Fiction*. New York: Routledge.

Smart FLASH. 2017. "Figyua no nenkan-keihi 300 man'en 'dai 2 no Asada Mao' no michi wa kewashii" (3 million yen required annually for learning figure skating: No easy path for being the second Mao Asada). Kōbunsha Publishing sports, entertainment, current events website, 14 April. Online at https://smart-flash.jp/sports/18422 [accessed 30 June 2017].

Sophie. 2016. Review of *The Goddess Chronicle*, Sophie's Reviews, on the Goodreads social cataloging network for readers, February 03. Online at http://www.goodreads.com/review/show/525361190 [accessed 12 July, 2016].

Sports Graphics Number. 2015. "Asada Mao sumairu agein" (Asada Mao smile again). Biweekly magazine cover. *Sports Graphics Number*, no. 890, 19 November.

Sports Graphics Number Web. 2015. "Miwa Akihiro ga kataru Asada Mao no miryoku. Kokumin-teki sutā no jōken towa" (Asada Mao's greatness dis-cussed by Miwa Akihiro. What are her requirments to be a national icon). *Sports Graphics Number Web*, 26 November. Online at http://number .bunshun.jp/articles/-/824600 [accessed 12 January 2016].

Springer, Kimberly. 2007. "Divas, evil black bitches, and bitter black women: African American women in postfeminist and post-civil-rights popular cul-ture." In *Interrogating Postfeminism: Gender and the Politics of Popular Culture*, edited by Yvonne Tasker and Diane Negra, 249–276. Durham: Duke University Press.

Standing, Guy. 2011. *The Precariat: The New Dangerous Class*. London: Bloomsbury Academic.

Standish, Isolde. 2005. *A New History of Japanese Cinema: A Century of Nar-rative Film*. New York: Continuum International Publishing Group.

Steele, Valerie. 2011. *Daphne Guinness*. New York and New Haven: Yale Univer-sity Press.

Stevenson, Angus, and Christine A. Lindberg, eds. 2005–2011. New Oxford American Dictionary. Apple Inc.'s Mac version 2.2.1. Oxford: Oxford Uni-versity Press.

Stovall, Tyler. 2008. "The New Woman and the New Empire: Josephine Baker and changing views of femininity in interwar France." *S&F Online*. Spring 6 (1–2). http://sfonline.barnard.edu/baker/stovall_01.htm [accessed 17 June 2017].

Strayhorn, Billy, composer. 1939. *Take the A Train*. Lyrics added in 1944 by Joya Sherrill. Recorded by Duke Ellington Orchestra in 1941. Chicago: Bluebird Records.

Sturmer, Andy, producer. 2003. *Nice*. Music album featuring PUFFY (Ōnuki Ami and Yoshimura Yumi). Los Angeles: Epic/Sony.

Sumita Minoru. 1996. *Maboroshi no joō Himiko no shokuseikatsu no himitsu* (Secrets of the eating habits of the elusive Queen Himiko). Kyoto: Higashi-yama Shobō.

Suzuki, Tomi. 1996. *Narrating the Self: Fictions of Japanese Modernity*. Stanford: Stanford University Press.

Takumi Promotion Company. 2016. *Yaoyorozu no kami kādo* (Eight million gods postcards). Postcards. Nagasaki: Takumi Promotion Company.

Takemoto Nobara. 2008. *Shimotsuma monogatari* (Shimotsuma story). Tokyo: Shōgakukan.

Takii Asayo. 2010. "Intabyū Kanehara Hitomi hinichijō de deau 'onna' to iu jibun" (Just an ordinary "girl": Interview with Kanehara Hitomi). *Hon no Tabibito* 16 (1): 22–29.

Tamura, Akiko. 2010. *Perfect Program*. Tokyo: Shinchō-sha.

Tamura Taijirō. 1978. "Nikutai no mon" (Gate of flesh). In *Tamura Taijirō, Kimu Darusu, Ōhara Tomie shū* (The Tamura Taijirō, Tal su Kim, and Ōhara Tomie collection). Chikuma gendai bungaku taikei 62 (Chikuma collection of modern literature 62), 33–54. Tokyo: Chikuma Shobō.

Tansman, Alan. 1996. "Mournful tears and sake: The postwar myth of Misora Hibari." In *Contemporary Japan and Popular Culture*, edited by John Whittier Treat, 103–33. Honolulu: University of Hawai'i Press.

Tasaka, Jack. 1985. *A Hundred Year History of Japanese Culture and Entertainment in Hawaii*. Honolulu: East-West Journal.

Tashiro Hideki, Masahiro Tokadama, Kaori Watanabe, and Takanobu Genta, producers. 2007. "Gakkō e IKKO! Dondake supesharu!" (IKKO goes to school! Dondake special!). TBS (Tokyo Broadcasting System) television program *Gakkō e ikkō* (Let's Go to School!). Aired 20 November.

TBS Radio. 2015. Asada Mao no Nippon Sumairu (Asada Mao's Nippon smile). TBS (Tokyo Broadcasting System) radio program, 20 April, 27 April, 8 June. Online at http://www.tbs.co.jp/radio/maosmile/ [accessed 3 June 2017].

Tokita, Alison. 2010. "*Winter Sonata* and the politics of memory." In *Complicated Currents: Media Flows, Soft Power and East Asia*, edited by Daniel Black, Stephen Epstein, and Alison Tokita, 03.1–03.12. Melbourne: Monash University ePress.

Tomiyama Taeko and Takahashi Yūji. 2009. *Kugutsu to Hiruko: Tabigeinin to monogatari. Hiruko and the Puppeteers: A Tale of Sea Wanderers*. Bilingual book and DVD. Tokyo: Gendaikikashitsu Publishers.

Torigoe Kenzaburō. 1975. *Ōinaru Yamataikoku*. (The great country of Yamatai). Tokyo: Kōdansha.

Tsurumi Shunsuke. 2001. *Tsurumi Shunsuke shū zoku*, vol. 5 (Collected works of Tsurumi Shunsuke, vol. 5). *Ame no Uzume den* (The life of Ame no Uzume). Tokyo: Chikuma Shobō.

———. 2015. *Manazashi* (Gaze). Tokyo: Fujiwara Shoten.

Tsurumi Shunsuke and Kurokawa Sō (interviewer). 2009. *Futei rōjin* (The recalcitrant old man). Tokyo: Kawade Shobō Shinsha.

Tyrangiel, Josh. 2002. "The new-diva disease." *Time*, 21 October.

Uchida Shungiku. 1994. *Watashitachi wa hanshoku shite iru iero* (We are breeding yellow). Tokyo: Kadokawa Bunko.

———. 1996a. *Fazā fakkā* (Father Fucker). Tokyo: Bungei Shunjū.

———. 1996b. *Watashitachi wa hanshoku shite iru pinku* (We are breeding pink). Tokyo: Kadokawa Bunko.

———. 1998. *Anata mo ninpu shashin o torō* (You too can take pregnancy pictures). Tokyo: Poplar Press.

———. 1999. *Watashitachi wa hanshoku shite iru burū* (We are breeding blue). Tokyo: Kadokawa Bunko.

———. 2002. *Inu no hō ga shitto bukai* (The dog's jealousy is deep). Tokyo: Bunkasha.

———. 2007. *S4G: Sex For Girls: Onna no ko no tame no sei no hanashi.* (S4G: Sex for girls: Talking about sex for girls). Tokyo: Asuka.

———. 2015. *Yūko no yume wa itsu hiraku* (When will Yuko's dream start?). Theatrical play. Performed 23–27 December. Tokyo: SPACE Zatsuyū Theater.

Umino, Bin, Ayumi Takahashi, and Kumi Koyama. 2012. "Comparative analysis of large-scale social surveys focusing on the number and the rate of ballet students in Japan." *Toyo Daigaku Shakaigakubu Kiyo* 50 (1): 51–65.

Unknown. 1956. *Day O: The Banana Boat Song.* Originally a Jamaican folk song. Lyrics added in 1955 by Lord Burgess and William Attaway. Recorded by Harry Belafonte in 1956. New York: RCA Victor.

Utsunomiya Naoko. 2006. *Asada Mao, 15 sai* (Asada Mao, she is fifteen years old). Tokyo: Bungei Shunjū.

———. 2009. *Asada Mao, 18 sai* (Asada Mao, brilliant eighteen). Tokyo: Bungei Shunjū.

Van Meter, Jonathan. 1997. "The outer limits." *Spin* 13 (9): 93–98.

Video Research Ltd. 2014,2015. "*Tarento imēji chōsa kekka*" (Celebrity image research results). Online at http://www.videor.co.jp/casestudies/products-release/talent_woman/index.htm [accessed 12 January 2016].

Village People, artists. 1978. *Macho Man.* Los Angeles: Casablanca Records.

Waelti-Walters, Jennifer. 1982. *Fairy Tales and the Female Imagination.* Montreal, Canada: Eden Press.

Watanabe, Nobuyuki. 2008. "Final resting place of Himiko discovered?" *Asahi Shinbun,* 30 May. Online at http://archive.today/lMpUH [accessed 21 May 2016].

Weber, Max. 1968. *On Charisma and Institution Building.* Edited and with introduction by S. N. Eisenstadt. Chicago: University of Chicago Press.

Wenner, Jann S. 2004. "The ballad of John and Yoko." In *Yes Yoko Ono,* edited by Alexandra Munroe and Jon Hendricks, 58–61. New York: Japan Society and Harry N. Abrams.

White, Michael. 2013. "Angela Gheorghiu: It's opera—everyone has to suffer for their art." *The Telegraph,* 6 July. Online at http://www.telegraph.co.uk/culture/music/opera/10163883/Angela-Gheorghiu-Its-opera-everyone-has-to-suffer-for-their-art.html [accessed 26 July 2016].

Yamaguchi Masao. 1990. *Warai to itsudatsu* (Laughter and deviation). Tokyo: Chikuma Shobō.

Yamane Satoshi. 2015. "11/2–8 Asada Mao yūshō-shunkan 36.0%" (2–8 November, 36 percent at the moment of Asada Mao's victory). *Sankei*

Shinbun, 11 November. Online at http://www.sankei.com/entertainments /news/151111/enti51111 0001-n1.html [accessed 26 December 2015].

Yano, Christine R. 2002. *Tears of Longing: Nostalgia and the Nation in Japanese Popular Song.* Cambridge, MA: Harvard University Asia Center, Harvard University Press.

————. 2006. *Crowning the Nice Girl; Gender, Ethnicity, and Culture in Hawai'i's Cherry Blossom Festival.* Honolulu: University of Hawai'i Press.

Yokochi Ikuei, producer. *Bara-iro no seisen* (Rose-colored crusade), episode 1. Serialized drama. Tokyo: TV Asahi.

Yomiuri Shinbun. 2012. "Asada senshu no essē hatsubai chūshi" (Asada's monograph cancelled for publication). *Yomiuri Shinbun,* 13 January: 34.

Yoneyama Masao, composer. 1956. *Hibari no cha cha cha* (Hibari's Cha Cha Cha). Lyrics by Yoneyama Masao. Tokyo: Nippon Columbia.

————. 1960a. *Rokabirii geisha* (Rockabilly Geisha). Lyrics by Saijō Yaso. Tokyo: Nippon Columbia.

————. 1960b. *Naki warai no mambo* (Crying Laughing Mambo). Lyrics by Misora Hibari. Tokyo: Nippon Columbia.

————. 1966. *Baibai bigin* (Bye-bye Beguine). Lyrics by Yoneyama Masao. Tokyo: Nippon Columbia.

Yoon Seok-Ho, director. 2002. *Gyeoul Yeonga* (Winter Sonata). Seoul: Korean Broadcasting.

Yoshida Atsuhiko. 1989. *Nihon shinwa no tokushoku* (The characteristics of Japanese mythology). Tokyo: Seidosha.

Yoshida Jun. 2011. *Asada Mao, saranaru takami e* (Asada Mao, stepping higher). Tokyo: Gakken Kyōiku Shuppan.

————. 2013. *Asada Mao, soshite, sono shun'kan e* (Asada Mao, and then to that moment). Tokyo: Gakken Kyōiku Shuppan.

Yoshida, Mitsukuni, Ikko Tanaka, and Sesoko Tsune, eds. 1987. *Asobi: The Sensibilities at Play.* Hiroshima: Mazda Motor Corp.

Yoshie Akiko. 2005. *Tsukurareta Himiko: "Onna" no sōshutsu to kokka* (The construction of Himiko: The creation of "Woman" and the state). Tokyo: Chikuma Shinso.

————. 2013. "Gendered interpretations of female rule: The case of Himiko, ruler of Yamatai." Adapted by Hitomi Tonomura and translated by Azumi Ann Takata. *U.S.–Japan Women's Journal* 44: 3–23.

Zaccardi, Nick. 2014. "Mao Asada wins World Championship; U.S. finishes with no medals." *NBC Sports,* 29 March. Online at http://olympics.nbcsports .com/2014/03/29/mao-asada-wins-world-figure-skating-championship /#comments [accessed 31 December 2015].

Zakrajsek, Tom. 2015. Instagram entry, 13 December. Online at https://www .instagram.com/p/_MyA2DjY6X/ [accessed 23 December 2015].

Zoladz, Lindsay. 2015. "Yoko Ono and the myth that deserves to die." *Vulture: Devouring Culture.* Blog site. Online at http://www.vulture.com/2015/05 /yoko-ono-one-woman-show.html [accessed 14 May 2015].

Zombiehero. 2013. "Review of The Goddess Chronicle by Natsuo Kirino." 29 January. Online at http://wordslikemagic.wordpress.com/2013/01/29/the-goddess-chronicle-by-natsuo-kirino/ [accessed 12 July, 2016].

Contributors

TOMOKO AOYAMA is Associate Professor of Japanese at the University of Queensland, Australia. Her research interests include parody and intertextuality in Japanese literature and girls' manga, and older women's humor in contemporary Japanese culture. She is the author of *Reading Food in Modern Japanese Literature* (University of Hawai'i Press 2008) and the co-editor of *Girl Reading Girl in Japan* (Routledge 2010) and *Configurations of Family in Contemporary Japan* (Routledge 2015). She has also translated Kanai Mieko's novels: *Indian Summer* (with Barbara Hartley, Cornell East Asia Series 2012) and *Oh, Tama!* (with Paul McCarthy, Kurodahan Press 2014).

JAN BARDSLEY, Professor of Asian Studies in the Department of Asian Studies at the University of North Carolina at Chapel Hill, specializes in Japanese Humanities and Women's Studies. She is the author of *Women and Democracy in Cold War Japan* (Bloomsbury Academic 2014) and *The Bluestockings of Japan: New Women Fiction and Essays from Seitō, 1911–1916* (University of Michigan, Center for Japanese Studies 2007), which was awarded the 2011 Hiratsuka Raichō Prize by Japan Women's University. With Laura Miller, she has co-edited two books, *Manners and Mischief: Gender, Power, and Etiquette in Japan* (University of California Press 2011) and *Bad Girls of Japan* (Palgrave Macmillan 2005).

REBECCA COPELAND is Professor of Japanese literature at Washington University in St. Louis, where she is Chair of the Department of East Asian Languages and Cultures. She is the author of *Lost Leaves: Women Writers of Meiji Japan* (University of Hawai'i Press 2000); and *The Sound of the Wind: The Life and Works of Uno Chiyo* (University of Hawai'i Press 1992). She edited or co-edited *The Modern Murasaki: Writing by Women of Meiji Japan* (with Melek Ortabasi, Columbia University Press 2006), *Woman Critiqued: Translated Essays on Japanese Women's Writing* (University of Hawai'i Press 2006), *The Father-Daughter Plot: Japanese Literary Women and the Law of the Father* (with Esperanza Ramirez-Christensen, University of Hawai'i Press 2001).

KAZUE HARADA is Assistant Professor of Japanese at Miami University, Oxford, Ohio, where she teaches courses on Japanese language and culture. Her research interests include Japanese science fiction, technology and environment in Japanese literature, and issues of race, ethnicity and gender. She has published articles on Ueda Sayuri, Ōhara Mariko, and Yoshiya Nobuko.

BARBARA HARTLEY is attached to the School of Humanities at the University of Tasmania. While completing her doctoral studies, she closely examined several Ariyoshi Sawako works. Although Hartley writes extensively on representations of women and girls, she also has a strong interest in representations of the discursive space of China in Japanese narrative and visual art. As an International Centre for Japanese Studies Overseas Researcher (2016–2017), she examined Shōwa era (1926–1989) narrative and visual representations of Asia, with emphasis on constructions of women and girls. She is currently working on translations of the work of poet Takarabe Toriko.

LAURA HEIN is Professor of modern Japanese history at Northwestern University. She works on a wide variety of topics that situate twentieth-century Japan in its international context. Her most recent book is *Post-Fascist Japan: Political Culture in Kamakura after World War II* (Bloomsbury Academic, due out in winter 2018).

DAVID HOLLOWAY is Assistant Professor of Japanese at the University of Rochester, where he teaches courses on Japanese literature, popular culture, and gender. Having completed graduate degrees at the University of Colorado at Boulder (2007) and Washington University in St. Louis (1999, 2014), his specialization is contemporary Japanese fiction with emphasis on gender and sexuality. Recent publications have appeared in *U.S.-Japan Women's Journal, Japanese Language and Literature, Electronic Journal of Contemporary Japanese Studies,* and *Sungkyun Journal of East Asian Studies.* His current book project is tentatively titled *The End of Transgression: Toward a New Nationalism in Contemporary Japanese Texts.*

LAURA MILLER is the Ei'ichi Shibusawa-Seigo Arai Endowed Professor of Japanese Studies at the University of Missouri-St. Louis. She has published more than 70 articles and book chapters on Japanese culture and language. She is the author of *Beauty Up: Exploring Contemporary Japanese Body Aesthetics* (University of California Press 2006), and co-editor of three other books, *Modern Girls on the Go: Gender, Mobility, and Labor in Japan* (with Asisa Freedman and Christine Yano, Stanford University Press 2013), *Manners and Mischief: Gender, Power, and Etiquette in Japan* (with Jan Bardsley, University of California Press 2011), and *Bad Girls of Japan* (with Jan Bardsley, Palgrave Macmillan 2005).

MASAFUMI MONDEN is a postdoctoral Research Fellow at the School of Design, University of Technology Sydney, specializing in Japanese fashion and culture. He lectures and publishes widely in the areas of men's and women's clothing, Japan, art, youth, and popular culture. His first book, *Japanese Fashion Cultures: Dress and Gender in Contemporary Japan* (Bloomsbury Academic 2015), details the relationship between fashion, culture, and gender within contemporary Japan, and its relevance to an increasingly transcultural world. He is currently conducting research on cultural imaginations of Japanese girlhood and boyhood, and the cultural history of male fashion models in Japan.

ROKUDENASHIKO (Igarashi Megumi) is a sculptor, manga artist, and writer known for her artwork featuring cute and sometimes anthropomorphized female genitalia. She is the author of *Waisetsu tte nandesu ka: Jisho geijutsuka to yobareta watakushi* (What is obscenity? I'm called a self-proclaimed artist, Kin'yobi 2015; also translated into English by Anne Ishii and published under a modified title by Koyama Press 2016), *Dekoman: Asoko seikei mangaka ga kimyo na ato o tsukutta riyu* (Decorated pussy: The reason a plaster art manga artist of the nether region made that unusual art, Bunkasha, 2012), and *Watashi no karada ga waisetsu?! Onna no sokodake naze tabū* (My body is obscene?! Why is it that only a woman's *Va-jay-jay* is taboo?, Chikuma Shobō 2015).

AMANDA C. SEAMAN teaches at the University of Massachusetts Amherst, where she is Professor of modern Japanese literature. A scholar of modern women's literature, genre fiction, and gender studies, she is the author of *Bodies of Evidence: Women, Society and Detective Fiction in 1990s Japan* (University of Hawai'i Press 2004) and *Writing Pregnancy in Low-Fertility Japan* (University of Hawai'i Press 2016). Her current research explores the representation of illness and the afflicted in postwar Japanese literature, film, and popular media.

CAROLYN S. STEVENS is Professor of Japanese Studies and Director of the Japanese Studies Centre at Monash University. Her recent major publications include *Japanese Popular Music: Culture, Authenticity and Power* (Routledge 2008) and *Disability in Japan* (Routledge 2013), as well as the co-edited volumes *Sound, Space and Sociality in Modern Japan* (with Joseph Hankins, Routledge 2014) and *Internationalising Japan* (with Jeremy Breaden and Stacey Steele, Routledge 2014). Her monograph, *The Beatles in Japan*, was published in early 2018. She also serves as the editor in chief of the interdisciplinary journal *Japanese Studies*.

CHRISTINE R. YANO, Professor of Anthropology at the University of Hawai'i, has conducted research on Japan and Japanese Americans with a focus on popular culture. Her sole-authored publications include *Tears of Longing: Nostalgia and the Nation in Japanese Popular Song* (Harvard University Press 2002), *Crowning the Nice Girl; Gender, Ethnicity, and Culture in Hawaii's Cherry Blossom Festival* (University of Hawai'i Press 2006), *Airborne Dreams: "Nisei" Stewardesses and Pan American World Airways* (Duke University Press 2011), and *Pink Globalization: Hello Kitty and its Trek Across the Pacific* (Duke University Press 2013).

Index

234 | Index

Lafrance, Melisse, 112
Langer, Susanne, 44
language, 24, 25
Lee, Hyangjin, 144
Lennon, John, 10, 49, 127–28, 131; FBI
    harassment of, 122; first meeting with
    Yoko Ono, 119; legacy of, 130;
    marriage to Yoko Ono, 121; murder of,
    116, 122; music composed/produced
    with Yoko Ono, 122, 123; relationship
    with Yoko Ono, 115, 120, 124, 129,
    132n1
Lennon, Taro Ono, 122
lesbians/lesbian fandom, 73, 108, 128
Leung On Yuk, 94
Lévi-Strauss, Claude, 38
Lonesome Whistle [Kanashiki kuchibue]
    (film, 1949, dir. Ieki), 9
Love, Courtney, 112

Maciunas, George, 119
magatama beads, 70, 76n22; cookies, 67,
    69, 75n19; divination and, 72; Itoigawa
    jade, 71
Mahoroba no Sato Himiko (shop in
    Sakurai), 57–58, 58
mai dance, 39, 85, 88
Mama Riina, 62, 73
manga, 10, 49, 55; Garo magazine, 151;
    Himiko in, 52, 52, 69, 73; Izumo no
    Okuni in, 84, 84; Ono (Yoko) in, 120;
    of Rokudenashiko, 48, 56, 203, 204–5.
    See also Uchida Shungiku, works of
manko (vagina), 48
Manko-chan (Miss Pussy) mascot, 203,
    204–5
Manto-kun mascot, 57
Maree, Claire, 137
Marikofun (blues singer), 70–71, 73, 75n21
Maruyama Kenji, 184
Masahito, Prince, 118–19
Masako, New Age shop at Hashihaka
    Kofun, 71–72, 73
masculinity, Japanese, 105
masochism, 174
masquerade, 8
matrixial borderspace, 27–29
Matsugi Takehiko, 64
Mazāu [Mothers] (Kanehara, 2011),
    182–83, 184
Meiji era (1868–1912), 63
menstruation, 162, 163–64
Merish, Lori, 108
Miller, Laura, xi, xiv, 2, 43, 190

Miller, Toby, 189
mimicry, 101, 103, 113
Mishima Yukio, 119
misogyny, 34
Misora Hibari, xiii, xiv, 95–96, 98, 171,
    189; asobi/camp and, 111–12; as
    bad-girl/good-girl diva, 112–14;
    charisma of, 99, 106; as child star,
    99–103, 113; cross-dressing of, 5–6,
    10, 104–6, 110–11; death of, 95, 107,
    114; Garland (Judy) compared with,
    107–10; Hawai'i's Hibari look-alike,
    101; Korean ancestry rumors, xiv,
    103–4; in Lonesome Whistle (film,
    1949), 9, 101, 106; morality tales and,
    96; as "Queen of Enka," 95, 107; song
    and dance genres performed by, 103;
    space for female play and, 8; as symbol
    of national perseverance, 6; Uchida
    Shungiku compared to, 153
Miura Sukeyuki, 35, 39, 41, 42
Miyadai Shinji, 174
moga (modern girl), xii
Monden, Masafumi xvi, 2
Moriyama, town of, 60, 62, 66–67; food
    culture and Himiko in, 67–69; Himiko
    map, 67, 68
Morris, Ivan, 201
Motazaru mono [Without] (Kanehara,
    2015), 183
mothers/motherhood, xvi, 149, 153, 157,
    182; cultural norms for, 158–59;
    education of daughters and, 162–65;
    importance in popular consciousness,
    172; in Kanehara's fiction, 182–83;
    maternal archetype, 172; Ono's views
    on, 118, 132n1; sexuality and, 158,
    166; single, 146, 190; stage mothers,
    102
Muñoz, José Esteban, 78, 86, 88, 89,
    91–92, 94
Munroe, Alexandra, 123
Murakami Haruki, 1
Murakami Ryū, 180
myths, national, 3, 5

Nadeshiko (Japan's national women's soccer
    team), 188
Nagafuji Yasushi, 38
Nagase Kiyoko, 46–47
Nagayama Hisao, 64, 65
Nagoya Sanzaburō (Sanzaemon), 83, 89
Nakahara Junichi, 194
Nakaki Shigeo, 102